THE GREAT ILLUSION

THE GREAT ILLUSION

J. BERNARD HUTTON

DAVID BRUCE & WATSON

LONDON

First published 1970 by
DAVID BRUCE & WATSON LTD

277–9 Gray's Inn Road
London WC1

SBN 85127 030 1

This book has been set in Bembo and printed in
Great Britain by Balding & Mansell Ltd, of London and Wisbech.

To the memory of Lyubov and Abel Yenukidze, as well as all my other Russian friends—dead and alive; and, in particular to Abram Abramovich without whose help I could not have survived.

Contents

List of illustrations

Publisher's Note

This is a book which could only have been written by a man who mixed in high circles in Russia, and from whose searching eyes little, if anything, was concealed. J. Bernard Hutton is such a man. What is more he is not Russian at all, but a Czech who, as a confirmed Communist, went to work in the Soviet Union.

The late SIR ROBERT BRUCE LOCKHART, K.C.M.G.—acknowledged to be the greatest expert on Russia and Communism; former Head of the Political Intelligence Department of the British Foreign Office; from 1941 to 1945, Deputy Under-Secretary of State at the Foreign Office; and Director General of the Political Warfare Executive—said the following about the author:

'His qualifications for writing such a book are very considerable. He is a Slav intellectual and was born in Czechoslovakia. From his early manhood he has earned his living as a writer and journalist. When he was twenty-two he was sent to Moscow where he was foreign editor of the Russian newspaper, *Vecherniaya Moskva*.

'During the four years (1934–1938) which he spent in Moscow he made friends with leading Soviet Communists including Yenukidze, Radek, Kalinin, Rosa Kaganovich (Stalin's third wife), Ordzhonikidze, Nadiezhda Krupskaya (Lenin's widow), and many other Soviet leaders and publicists.

'His Moscow sojourn was the period of Stalin's dreadful purges, and the chapters devoted to this gruesome subject are the best in the book mainly because Mr. Hutton was so close to the people who were near to Stalin and who therefore were most in fear of him.

'Stalin, who was haunted by suspicion, could not bear rivals, and

Yagoda and Yezhov, who did his dirty work for him, were even greater villains than their master. Stalin's main principle in life was that dead men tell no lies, and both Yagoda and Yezhov were removed in the usual way.

'It remains for me to state that in 1938 Mr. Hutton gave up dabbling in Communism and returned to Prague where he wrote for democratic newspapers. Before the war started, he came to England and worked under Jan Masaryk in the Department of Information of the Czechoslovak Ministry for Foreign Affairs in London. In 1948 Czechoslovakia went Communist, and Mr. Bernard Hutton left the Czechoslovak Government.'

Recent announcements by Soviet leaders and Russian radio and newspaper reports reveal the same conditions that Hutton knew during his stay in the 'Worker's Paradise'. Similar inadequate working conditions; equally stringent Party and Trade Union 'discipline'; the same degree of nationwide spy mania; the resurrection of Stalin and the dreaded Secret Police; the danger of being accused an enemy of the people or State, which is still a crucial charge in the U.S.S.R.

Much of what happened in the Soviet Union in the 'thirties is still happening today.

CHAPTER ONE

A Detained 'Guest'

ACROSS the track there was a gate with white letters on a red background, saying in many languages: WORKERS OF ALL COUNTRIES UNITE! As soon as the last carriage was through, the train stopped. We were on Soviet soil.

A detachment of grim-faced men searched the train inside and out. They were the G.P.U., ensuring that no one was trying to enter their country without permission. When they were satisfied that the three of us, who were the sole occupants of the eight express-train carriages, had proper entry visas, they took possession of our passports. Minutes later the train was allowed to make its way to the railway station at Niegoreloye.

At this time, travellers from Central European countries were able to buy tickets only as far as the Soviet frontier. The fare from there to Moscow had to be paid over at Niegoreloye. My visa and journey had been arranged by the Central Committee of the Czech Communist Party. I was on my way to Moscow (with official blessings) to work as a journalist and writer so that I could become acquainted with its Press and see at first hand life in the glorious Soviet Union. Sufficient roubles for my fare were to be available at the office of the Commandant of Niegoreloye station, so when we arrived there I asked to be shown to the Kommandatura. However, a young G.P.U. officer told me that I had to see my luggage through the Customs first. As the luggage was still on the train, and I would have to wait for it, I suggested to the officer that it would save time later if I could see the Commandant now. The officer refused to co-operate.

I

Some time later my luggage was brought into the hall and the same G.P.U. man took his place behind the examination counter. Before he had even looked at my suitcase he asked where I was travelling to. I told him I was going to Moscow. He then asked for my ticket. I reminded him that I could only purchase my ticket— once I had received my money from the Commandant.

'The rule is that you can only see the comrade Commandant when your luggage has been cleared,' he declared.

'Then clear my luggage,' I said.

'The rule is that the luggage can only be cleared when a valid railway ticket is produced.'

It all seemed so pointless, so stupid, and, because I was tired, I let my annoyance get the better of me and lost my temper and called him a bureaucratic idiot.

Another officer came across the hall and asked what the trouble was. He was an older, more senior man. I explained the position to him, and he heard me out, and then said he was Colonel Ilyin, the station Commandant. He asked me to accompany him to the Kommandatura, and when we got there told me that he had no money for me. I insisted that this could not be so, that it had all been arranged. Finally he said that perhaps the money had been mistaken-ly sent to the post office. The only thing was that the post office was now closed and would not re-open until the next day.

I had no intention of staying at Niegoreloye, especially when I found out that the *next* train for Moscow would not leave until the following evening. I suggested that I pay the fare with foreign currency. But the Commandant said that he could not allow me to spend foreign currency if I had been instructed by Communist headquarters that roubles were to be used for this purpose. He made it quite plain that I would *have* to stay in Niegoreloye overnight.

Shortly afterwards the train for Moscow left, with its now reduced complement of *two* passengers plus a considerable number of G.P.U. officers. I was shown to a room in the station hotel and my suitcases—which were never opened—were brought to me.

I had been bare minutes in the room when there was a knock at the door. A G.P.U. officer—a young fellow with a Mongolian face—told me that the comrade Commandant wanted to see me. He took me to a restaurant where Colonel Ilyin and some other officers were sitting at a table. To my surprise I was asked to join them and I partook of a meal the richness of which amazed me. It didn't tie up with what I had been told about food shortage in Russia.

After a while the pleasant conversation changed character. From being a series of amusing exchanges, it became an interrogation. They were the questioners, I the questioned.

'Why have you come to the Soviet Union, comrade?'

'The Central Committee has sent me.'

'Why were *you* specially chosen?'

'Why not ask them?' I answered. 'I have no idea.'

'I understand you lived for many years in Germany,' one of the aides said. 'Did you make any friends there?'

'Of course!'

'Were any of them in the Nazi party?'

I didn't like being cross-examined like this.

'None of my friends were Nazis when I knew them,' I answered.

The conversation changed to other and more trivial subjects but every now and then a question was slipped in which probed my past.

The Commandant himself saw me to my room later in the evening, and before going to bed, I put my shoes outside to be cleaned for the morning. A G.P.U. man was standing opposite my door. I was being watched. Once again annoyance flared up, and I asked hotly whether I was now some sort of prisoner. He said I was being guarded so that no enemy of the State could try to harm me. But—though, as a confirmed Communist, I was used to obeying orders—I couldn't believe what the G.P.U. man said. What enemy of the State could possibly want to harm me here in Russia? It was no use arguing with this youth who was only doing his duty. But it was clear that for some reason I was deliberately being held at Niegoreloye, and there was nothing I could do.

Next morning things started to change.

When I opened the bedroom door, there was no guard to be seen, nor did I meet anyone on my way downstairs. In the restaurant, a pretty waitress brought me lots of food and told me that the Commandant would like to see me when I had finished breakfast. But before I was halfway through, he walked in, grinning hugely, and told me that he had heard from Moscow that my money was at the post office across the road, and that I would be leaving on the evening train. He added that he would be only too pleased to consider me the guest of the Niegoreloye G.P.U. and that he would do his best to make it as pleasant a day for me as possible.

Shortly afterwards in the post office, the clerk, a woman with oily black hair, wearing an ill-fitting khaki uniform, paid out the money. When I signed the receipt I noticed that it bore the rubber date stamp of the previous day. To make sure I was not mistaken, I asked when the money had arrived, and the woman told me that it had been there on the morning of the previous day. She also told me, without being asked, that she had expected me to collect the money last night. When I explained that I had been told that the post office closed before the train from Poland arrived, she insisted that her office was always open until the train for Moscow left, and that I must have misunderstood the information received.

To make sure there would be no more delays, I went to the ticket office to pay my fare to Moscow. The G.P.U. officer in charge told me that I did not need a ticket as I was 'on the list' and would travel on an official pass. He added that the comrade Commandant would put me on the train himself so that I would get the best available accommodation.

From then on I was not left alone for a second. An officer came and told me that he had instructions from Colonel Ilyin to look after me and to show me round. First stop was the local saw mill—the pride of Niegoreloye as most of its timber was exported all over the world. Next I was shown a collective farm; and the entire day was filled with toings and froings as the officer pointed out places of interest. This was V.I.P. treatment with a vengeance.

We arrived back at the station a few minutes before the express train from Poland was due. Colonel Ilyin greeted me like an old friend and asked if I would dine with him. I said that I would rather wait in the hall, so as not to miss my train.

'You can't miss it if you are with me,' he explained. 'It cannot leave until the comrade Commissar of the train has my signed permission to proceed to Moscow.'

Just then the train hissed and roared into the station. Colonel Ilyin did not seem to be interested and showed me into the restaurant, where we settled down to another huge meal. 'Eat, comrade, you won't get another dinner like this one for a long time,' he said.

Trying to sound casual, I asked: 'Why didn't you tell me last night that my money had arrived?' For a moment he looked dangerous, then decided to be expansive, and smiled as he said: 'Now that I have confirmation from headquarters in Moscow that you are under *Comintern* orders, you might as well know the truth. Being the Commandant of one of the most important Soviet frontier posts, I have to be most careful what individuals I let into the U.S.S.R. You see, the capitalist world, and especially Nazi Germany, is trying to get its spies into our country. In your case, for instance, I could not be sure that you were genuine so I had to check with headquarters. Unfortunately their answer did not arrive until this morning, so . . . I had to hold you back.' He re-filled my glass. 'I am sure you understand and don't bear me any grudge.' The smile was all-embracing.

I did not know then that the G.P.U. was obsessed with the idea that every country was trying to send their spies to Russia.

Colonel Ilyin returned my passport, escorted me to the train, saw to it that my luggage was put on, and introduced me to the officer in charge.

When I opened the door of the sleeper compartment I saw a young girl sitting on the opposite bed. 'I think one of us must be in the wrong compartment,' I said.

'*You* must be mistaken,' she replied in English with an American accent, 'Here's my reservation.'

I went back to the officer in charge and found that the same compartment had been allocated to the girl and to myself. I could not understand why this had been done, especially as the adjoining compartments were not occupied. The officer told me that the other compartments would be filled up in Minsk, and that in the U.S.S.R. sleepers were allocated in strict rotation, regardless of sex.

My co-traveller's name was, I soon found out, Susan Goldberg, and she had come all the way from Chicago to join her father who was working in Russia. She was neither a member of the Communist Party nor was she interested in politics. I wondered how she would find life in a country so different from that which she had left.

I was not to know that her future would be clouded in strange and frightening ways.

CHAPTER TWO

Arrival in the Red Capital

The year was 1934, the day May Day, and according to the rail schedule, the train arrived in Moscow on time.

I was met at the station by Beatrice Georgovna, secretary of my *Comintern* Section. (She had been working at Communist head-quarters in Prague and knew me.) She was accompanied by a small broad-shouldered man who was introduced to me as comrade Saina. He was the secretary of the Trade Union Employment Office. They told me that they would take me by *Comintern* car direct to the Hotel Luks to leave my luggage, and from there we would go on to Red Square to attend the May Day parade.

The streets of Moscow were full of people carrying red flags, and huge posters were to be seen everywhere. However, the official car easily got through the crowds, and in Red Square I saw the awesome sight of the huge parade—Communism and Communists on show in one of the most exciting exhibitions I had ever seen.

*   *   *

The Hotel Luks in Gorky Street was the *Comintern* hotel. I was given a room on the third floor. It wasn't long before I realised that having a room to myself was a privilege—one that not many people in Moscow enjoyed.

When the Commandant of Luks—a Colonel of the O.G.P.U. —handed me the key, he also gave me a small red-bound book.

'This is a very important document, comrade,' he said. 'It is the pass which enables you to enter and to leave Luks at any time of the day or night. Nobody is allowed in here without permission, and you have to show your pass to the officer in charge whenever you come or go. If you want to see anyone in your room, other than those who are residents of Luks, you must apply in advance for a special pass. And think long and deeply, comrade, before inviting any visitors. I'm sure I don't have to amplify this! Anyone you do invite must leave by midnight at the latest.'

Once again I found traces of annoyance beginning to well up in me. It was the attitudinising, and the constant implied threats which I found increasingly distasteful. I passed some remark to Beatrice Georgovna about the place seeming more like a prison than a hotel. She clearly objected to my rebellious views.

'These precautions are absolutely necessary,' she said. 'Don't you realise that this is a *Comintern* hotel? The comrades who live here are the élite of Communist Parties from all over the world and every precaution *must* be taken to safeguard them.'

'But what possible danger can there be to any of us in Moscow?' I said.

'The enemies of the U.S.S.R. are always trying to get their spies and saboteurs into this country,' she said. 'Sometimes they manage to infiltrate . . .' She left the rest unsaid.

I found these 'precautions' preposterous, but I did not say this. I did not want to come under suspicion. I knew the dangers.

As though reading my thoughts, she advised me to be careful about what I said and even thought. She added that in fact she ought to report my remark to the security officer at the *Comintern*, but that she would not do so this time. I was grateful and frightened.

She then handed me a bundle of rouble notes in advance of my salary and told me that I was to report to the *Comintern* after the holidays. She also gave me coupons for breakfasts, lunches and dinners at the Luks or *Comintern* canteen.

Together we went to the Luks canteen which was full to capacity. Because of the holidays 'special' dinners were on the menu: soup, meat balls or steamed fish, boiled potatoes, *kysel,** and a slice of dark sour Russian bread.

'What is "special" about this food?' I enquired when I read the menu.

*A jelly-like strange-tasting pudding.

'There are meat balls *or* fish. Usually it is only one or the other,' she answered. 'And the meat balls today contain more meat than usual. You also get the slice of bread with your meal without surrendering a bread coupon for it as you have to do on any other day.'

'How different from the delicious food in Niegoreloye,' I commented when I had eaten the watery cabbage soup and the meat balls which consisted almost entirely of bread and potatoes.

'How can you compare the food in Niegoreloye with that at a Moscow canteen?' Beatrice answered, surprised. 'The station restaurant in Niegoreloye is run by Intourist.'

This remark did not mean anything to me then.

*   *   *

It was a rule in Soviet Russia that every official visitor to Moscow should be taken to Lenin's tomb in Red Square. Every day people queue there to pay a visit to the founder of the U.S.S.R. They usually begin to queue several hours before the red marble mausoleum is opened by the Kremlin guards.

My *Comintern* and Trade Union escorts took me to the mausoleum, on top of which Stalin, Voroshilov, Kalinin, and all the other Politburo dignitaries stood during the May Day parades. We did not have to queue up; the *Comintern* pass allowed us to go through. In semi darkness we descended the black stone steps into the vault where the 'Great Lenin' lay in an illuminated glass chamber. He was dressed in a simple khaki uniform, the lower half of the body being covered with a heavy red cloth. One had the impression that this small man who created the vast U.S.S.R. was just lying in peaceful sleep. Many a man and woman was not ashamed to shed tears, for to the Russians Lenin was a saint. Much later I found out from people all over the country, that they believed that Lenin had planned a different future for them and, had he been alive, matters would have been entirely different.

When we stepped out of the mausoleum into the blazing sunshine, Saina remarked: 'A great man—Vladimir Ilyich Lenin. Maybe one day Stalin will lie next to him—maybe he will never . . .' He did not finish his sentence.

At the time neither Beatrice nor I attached any significance to this remark.

★ ★ ★

When I first saw that all the shop windows were decorated with red flags and pictures of Lenin and Stalin, Marx and Engels, I thought that this was to celebrate May Day, because the streets and squares too were decorated with banners, flags, posters, and pictures. I soon discovered that this was not so. There was nothing to display, and in order not to have empty shop windows they were used as show-cases for the Communist leaders.

The food situation was very bad indeed. After a few days in Moscow I could no longer eat the food in the Luks canteen. It never varied. I had been issued with ration cards which entitled me, like anyone else, to a few slices of dark sour bread per day, and to the following allocation per month: half-a-pound of meat, a few leaves of tea, about three ounces of sugar, the same amount of butter (stale) and an ounce or so of boiled sweets. It was, however, almost impossible to get these rations. The queues were endless and by the time one reached the counter nothing was left. The only food one could buy in Moscow *without* coupons were cakes, which consisted of some yellow rubber-like dough, decorated with soapy tasting 'cream' in gay colours. I always threw the 'cream' away.

Walking along Revolution Square a few days after I arrived, I happened to meet Franz Guttmann, a colleague of mine, who had come to Moscow to attend some Trade Union affair. Somehow the conversation touched the food situation, and Guttmann was surprised that I did not know that at Torgsin one could get everything one wanted—for foreign currency. He offered to give me a few dollars and Swiss francs to help me to get some proper food but I declined as I still had some foreign currency of my own. But I asked him what and where Torgsin was. He soon showed me.

Torgsin had been set up in order to drain out of the people their last foreign coins, gold, silver, and any other valuables. The Soviet Union was desperately short of foreign currency and had created this system to squeeze out as much as possible. The

Torgsin establishments were real aladdin's caves. Practically anything was available there—meat, butter, white bread, ham, smoked salmon, caviar, cigarettes, chocolates, spirits. Prices were ridiculously low. Most things in Torgsin cost only a half or even a third of what one would have to pay in London or elsewhere. One had to exchange one's foreign money or valuables for Torgsin money and then pay for the goods with these coupons.

So I had my first good meal since leaving Niegoreloye, consisting of hors d'oeuvres, grilled sole, huge rump steaks with chips and green peas, peach melba, coffee and gateaux.

CHAPTER THREE

I Look for a Job

WHEN I reported at the *Comintern*, Emil Birne, who was my section leader, informed me that it had been decided that I was to go to work in a printing works to learn type-setting. This, in order to enable me to run an illegal newspaper at home in case the police suppressed the daily paper. I objected and told him that the Central Committee had sent me to the U.S.S.R. so that I should work there as a *journalist*. Birne remained firm and insisted that I was to do as he directed.

Back home, I had heard from many people who had already been sent to the U.S.S.R. that it always took a considerable time for the *Comintern* to find anyone a job, and so I decided whether I could meanwhile find a job on my own with a Russian newspaper.

I went to see the Editor of *Pravda*, the mouthpiece of the Russian Communist Party. He offered me a job immediately and took me to the Partorg, a young man in a khaki tunic and blue trousers. As soon as he heard that I was billeted at the Luks, he said that there should be no difficulty in my getting *Comintern* permission to work for *Pravda*. He asked me to get my section leader to give me a letter to that effect. But I already knew what Birne's reaction would be—a vociferous refusal.

My reception at *Pravda* showed me, however, that Soviet papers were short of staff, so I decided to try my luck at *Izvyestiya*, the Government paper and not under direct control of the Communist Party. I managed to see the Deputy Editor, Karl Radek, who wanted me to start as News Editor immediately. He told me that he would settle matters with the *Comintern* in no time, and that I needn't worry. Having nothing to lose, I told him what plans my section leader had for me. He remarked acidly that this was typical but that if matters were as I said, it would be useless for him to try to obtain *Comintern* consent. Wanting to help me, however, he advised me to see Abram Abramovich Kraskyn, Deputy Editor of *Vecherniaya Moskva*. He pointed out that this paper belonged to the Mossoviet and that consequently they did not have to observe all the strict rules. I was extremely grateful to Radek, and when he asked me to let him know how I was getting on and to keep in touch with him, I promised to do so.

Vecherniaya Moskva was quite a distance from *Izvyestiya* and the best way to get there was by tram. Up till then I had only used buses in Moscow and, although they were always filled to capacity, they were comfortable to ride in. Anyone who has not experienced a Moscow tram can hardly imagine what it was like. People often complain that the London Underground in the rush hours is hell, but I can assure them that compared with Moscow trams, the Underground is sheer luxury. Passengers usually hung on outside the trams like bunches of grapes and if one managed to be pushed inside it was impossible to move. The conductress stood at the back entrance and took the fares of 15 kopyeks; the front of the carriage was the exit. If one was not lucky enough to be shoved out at the requested stop by the compact mass of travellers, one had no alternative but to travel on until one *could* finally get on to the front platform.

On this particular occasion I was pushed out—although I fought against the stream with all my strength—long before I wanted to get off, and had to walk for about another mile. On top of this, I was short two buttons when I did get off!

The Deputy Editor of *Vecherniaya Moskva* was a very pleasant man whom I liked from the beginning. He told me he wanted short stories and articles and invited me to let him have my first contribution as soon as possible. I addressed him as Comrade Kraskyn but he told me to call him Abram Abramovich instead of the formal 'Comrade Kraskyn.' The 'Great October Revolution' had not managed to change the old Russian habit, and as soon as people became acquainted they dropped the formal 'comrade' and called each other by their own and their father's Christian names. This they considered to be less formal. My new friend's Christian name was Abram and so was that of his father. He was therefore Abram Abramovich, meaning 'Abram, son of Abram.' His secretary's name was Lydia Ossipovna, I, thus, was Bernard Frederickovich.

The next afternoon I gave Abram Abramovich my first story. He told me that he would have a look at it as soon as he found the time and that he would contact me in due course. When I returned to the Luks, the receptionist told me that somebody had telephoned and had wanted to speak to me very urgently. I asked who it was but received the usual reply: '*Nieznayu*'—I don't know.

*   *   *

There was a great shortage of newsprint in the U.S.S.R. at the time, and only a few lucky people got their papers regularly—and then only if they were fortunate enough to be accepted as subscribers. Others had to read the papers displayed in show-cases all over Moscow, or had to queue up long before the newsvendors received their supply. This was always much smaller than the demand. I passed a queue for the *Vecherniaya Moskva* the next day and when I saw it consisted only of some thirty people, I decided to join it. I was lucky. Twenty minutes or so later the newspaper van arrived with a bundle of papers. I bought my copy. Only a few of the people behind me, however, managed to get theirs. The rest of the long queue dispersed without grumbling.

I was pleased when I saw my story on the front page but thought that Abram Abramovich could have let me know. When I saw him shortly afterwards, he told me that he had telephoned the evening before and had left a message for me to ring him as soon as I came home. He was not surprised at my not having received the message and said this was nothing unusual in Moscow.

'I will tell them off at the Luks,' I said.

'That won't be any use,' he replied. 'It happens everywhere and all the time.' He started to fill in a printed form saying: 'You're just in time to get to the cashier's office and collect your fee. We always pay on the fourth day of every week.'

I saw the figure 10 on the voucher and asked whether this was all they were going to pay me. He confirmed that this was the amount the Editor had mentioned. I regarded it an insult to be offered ten roubles for a story, and objected.

'It isn't a bad fee,' Abram replied. 'I can assure you that we frequently pay only three quarters or even half of that.'

'If your paper can't pay more than that, I am quite prepared to write for you without any fee at all,' I said firmly.

'We don't want any present,' he replied. 'What would your idea of an appropriate fee be?'

'I think that fifty ought to be the figure,' I said, not wanting to be unreasonable. 'But, if you think that that is too much . . .'

'No, no, Bernard Frederickovich,' he interrupted me. 'It's not a question of our not having enough money or of our not being able to afford it. It is simply that we are not accustomed to paying such fees. You're asking for the very top fee and, honestly, I can't recall that such fee has ever been paid to anyone by our paper.'

'If that is so, I must say the fees in the U.S.S.R. are much lower than those in my country,' I explained.

'Please wait a minute,' Abram said and stood up. 'I'll see the Editor and see what he has got to say.' It did not take long before he was back, and, handing me a voucher, he said: 'He accepted the figure you're asking for and said he would like to see you when you cashed your voucher as he would like to speak to you about further work.'

Together we went to the cashier's office where I had to sign the voucher. The cashier started to count out the money and handed me a bundle of five hundred roubles. I returned it and said that he must have made a mistake, but he assured me that he was right and was paying me fifty *chervonci*—as stated on the voucher.

I suddenly felt very embarrassed. I knew, of course, that a *chervoniec* was the equivalent of ten roubles but it had never occurred to me that they were still used. I explained my mistake to Abram and suggested that I return the surplus money to the Editor and apologise to him for the misunderstanding.

'You can't do that, Bernard Frederickovich,' he advised me, saying that the Editor had been impressed and had immediately agreed that I ought to be paid this sum. He pointed out that this had put me into the top grade and added: 'If you explain now you might risk spoiling what you have achieved.'

Presently we saw Maksim Vasilyevich Sokolovsky, the Editor. He greeted me like an old friend and offered me a contract to write for his paper. When he added that the fees would be the same as for my first contribution, I felt awkward and had it on the tip of my tongue to tell him how it all came about. Abram was, however, watching me, so I decided to take his advice and to say nothing.

While we were waiting for the contract to be typed, Sokolovsky asked whether I would consider a job as Foreign News Editor. I had to tell him then what plans the *Comintern* had for me, mentioned my experiences at *Pravda* and *Izvyestiya*, and regretted that I could not consider his offer because the *Comintern* would never give the required consent.

'If this worries you then forget it,' he encouraged me. 'Our paper is not run by the Party but by Mossoviet. We don't need the *Comintern's* consent. All we are concerned with is that your permit to live in the U.S.S.R. states that you are allowed to work as a journalist and writer, and you have that. You will have to join the Trade Union section of our paper, but that is a mere formality.'

I accepted, and Sokolovsky was pleased as they were desperately short of staff. He pointed out, though, that as far as my salary for my editorial job was concerned, I would not be able to make my own terms but would have to be content with eight hundred roubles per month which was the rate and could not be changed. He added, however, that this salary would be in addition to my contract for writing at least one story a week for the newspaper. I accepted all his conditions.

In the meantime the contract had been typed out and we signed it then and there. As far as my editorial job was concerned I had to see the Party, Trade Union, and Establishment Organisers and my employment was sanctioned. I started work straight away.

CHAPTER FOUR

Life in Moscow

THE impressions I gained of Moscow in these first weeks were chastening and unsettling. Everywhere there seemed to be grey drabness, shortages, poverty, and a massive atmosphere of depression. Clothes were shabby and unimaginative. Food was scarce. There were queues everywhere. And people didn't mind queueing even though they had no idea what the queue was for—there was always the *chance* of getting something badly needed. You couldn't afford not to queue.

One day, in June 1934, I was walking along Arbat Square with Abram Abramovich and we came across a very long queue. A poster in the shop window said:

WALK IN, COMRADE!
WHITE BREAD, BUTTER, EGGS AND MEAT,
CLOTHES AND SHOES FOR YOU!
BEGIN LIVING!
WALK IN, COMRADE!

We looked at each other and decided to find out what there was in this aladdin's cave. By showing our Press passes we were allowed to walk ahead of the queue.

Instead of finding any of the articles mentioned in the shop window, we were confronted by large pictures of Lenin and Stalin on the walls, and by officials sitting at long tables selling savings certificates. I whispered to Abram that I considered the posters to be a poor form of cheating but he whispered back that I should be quiet and buy a savings certificate if I wanted to avoid trouble. I took his advice, but innocently asked the fellow who handed me

c

the Government voucher what all this had to do with the poster in the window. He looked at me in surprise and said that the savings of the people would eventually make it possible to achieve everything the poster said.

* * *

Due to my stories appearing regularly in *Vecherniaya Moskva*, other Russian papers approached me to write for them, and before long I was contributing to *Komsomolskaya Pravda*, *Rabochaya Moskva*, *Literaturnaya Gazeta*, and many other papers and periodicals all over the U.S.S.R.

In well over two months I had neither seen nor heard anything from Birne. Nor was I particularly anxious to contact him. I liked what I was doing, and didn't want to have a halt called.

Then one day I received a letter from him requesting me to appear without fail to receive my directions for starting work at the International Printing Works *Iskra Revolucii*. I showed this at once to Abram Abramovich, who suggested we should see the Editor.

'So they didn't forget you,' said the Editor when he read the letter. He promised that he would have a word with Mossoviet and would arrange *Comintern* release. 'Leave it to me, Bernard Frederickovich, and go and get your page ready . . .'

During the afternoon, my Editor (Sokolovsky), Abram Abramovich, and the Party, Trade Union, and Establishment Organisers went with me to the *Comintern* to see Birne. I was anticipating awkwardness and was most surprised when Birne consented immediately to my remaining with *Vecherniaya Moskva;* but we agreed I should make arrangements with *Iskra Revolucii* to work there part-time. The letter permitting me to stay with *Vecherniaya Moskva* was typed on the official *Comintern* letterheading and duly stamped and counter-signed by Manuilsky, the Russian delegate and head of all sections of the *Comintern*. By the time the letter was handed to Sokolovsky it looked a very impressive document, indeed.

CHAPTER FIVE

Freedom of the Press

BEFORE I came to the U.S.S.R. I had had some years of newspaper experience. This was, however, of little use, as the Soviet papers were run in a completely different way from that to which I had been accustomed in my own country.

Though *Vecherniaya Moskva* belonged to Mossoviet and was not regarded as a Party paper, the Press Department of the Russian Communist Party nevertheless had its say. They, and the Soviet News Agency TASS, supplied us with Soviet and foreign news which we were ordered to use. They also supplied ready-made articles in a wide choice, to enable us to make our selection, but some bore the words '*must be printed!*' *Headlines were provided and it was even stated what type of print was to be used.* This accounts for the fact that so many Soviet papers publish the same articles and regardless of which paper one reads, those articles and news items which the Press Department wants included are found in all of them.

In a small way, we had a free hand—that is to say, we had about one page for articles of our own choice. This space was used for material supplied by our own correspondents—stories, poems and cartoons. Every day a meeting of all the editorial staff took place in the Editor's office and there it was agreed what was to be in that day's edition. If too many articles and photographs had been supplied, marked '*must be printed!*' and no space was left for our own material, the Editor had to make use of his position to seek the consent of the head of the Press Department to leave out or cut one or another article. This was not always easy to get and it happened from time to time that the Press Department insisted on its demands being carried out. Then our own material had to be left over for the next day or, if it was too topical, it had to be junked.

On several occasions during the time I was there we received orders from the Press Department to change the material which they sent us for material which the despatch rider brought in at the last minute. It was no use objecting; these orders had to be complied with to the letter. The type-setters and printers had to work like mad to try to get the paper printed in time. Though it disorganised other papers and journals which were printed in our works, this did not make any difference.

On one occasion we received a telephone call from the Press Department telling us to wait for fresh material, at a time when about half the edition had already been printed. Consequently *Vecherniaya Moskva* appeared a few hours late. Our Editor was called to the Central Committee and was blamed for the delay and loss of paper. He was able to prove that it was not his fault but that the Press Department was to blame. This was a grave mistake on his part as he was immediately transferred from being the Editor of the Moscow evening paper, to a small periodical in Kazan. Shortly afterwards he was purged, accused of being an enemy of the State, a saboteur, and sentenced to hard labour. Many months later we heard that he had been sent to a slave-labour camp and was working on the White Sea Canal. Another Editor was immediately appointed, a youngster who was considered a most reliable and devoted *Bolshevik*. He had never been in a newspaper office before! But before he joined *Vecherniaya Moskva* he had been the Commandant of a Communist Party hostel.

Though I had been only a comparatively short time with *Vecherniaya Moskva* at the time of the 'removal' of our Editor, Sokolovsky, I had been quite fond of him as he was an intelligent, honest person and had been a newspaper man all his life. We considered him a real colleague.

I revolted against this unbelievable injustice and in our buffet I voiced the opinion that in my country even on a Communist paper we would not tolerate anything of that sort, and I suggested that we should protest to the Central Committee. I was in such a temper that I did not mind the fact that the Partorg was present. When I saw the flabbergasted faces of my colleagues, I realised that I should not have spoken this way. The Partorg, however, came to me later and said in a very severe tone of voice that he attributed my remark to my being an alien, and that I surely did not mean what I said. He stressed the fact that never in my life, was I to say or even think anything of that sort again, as otherwise, he would have to report me. I was lucky. Nobody ever reported my words to the Secret Police, the reason probably being that I had said what they all had been feeling.

One of the laws laid down by the Press Department demanded that all material which it stopped had to be returned to it in a sealed envelope, and if it had already been made up in type-setting and galley proofs had been done, the type-setting was to be destroyed at once and the proofs were to be added to the material and enclosed in the envelope. Every Editor all over the Soviet Union obviously complied strictly with all these rules, as it would have been suicide not to.

All this created a state of fear. Nobody would risk printing an article or story which criticised anything 'official.' If there was the slightest doubt as to whether a contribution from a correspondent would be to the liking of the Press Department, the Editor would send it to them for approval. If it was passed, it was returned with a big imprint in red lettering saying 'fit for publication;' if it was prohibited by the censor, they would want to know who had written it. Sometimes we could truthfully report back that we didn't know, as the article had been sent to us without the name or address of the writer and so we tried our best not to get the correspondent into trouble. Sometimes, however, the Press Department directed us to cancel any arrangement which we had with a particular contributor as he or she was not to be considered as *persona grata*.

Such is the 'Freedom of the Press' in the U.S.S.R. If there *is* a gleam of Press freedom, it exists only in their so-called 'free space.'

So far as hundreds of provincial papers in all the languages of the Soviet republics and autonomous districts are concerned, there is nothing for the editorial staff to do. The Press Department prepares

whole editions for them and all the editorial staff has to do is to
translate from Russian into their various national languages. It was
explained to me that there were not enough qualified people available who could run a newspaper on their own, and that this was
why the Press Department operated in such a seemingly beaurocratic
way.

Sometimes on my paper we had very little to do, for instance
whenever Stalin made a long speech, or when some Congress took
place. The speeches then had to be printed in full, and pictures
(which were also supplied by the Press Department) had to be
inserted—the official text forming the edition. However, the Editor
who was in charge of the paper when it went to print—we all had
to do that in rotation—had to read the proof of each page very
carefully before signing it, thus passing it for publication. If he overlooked any mistake or misprint, especially in Stalin's speech, or in a
speech by any other Politburo dignitary, he was almost certain to
end up in a slave-labour camp at the very least. There have been
cases where the penalty had been the bullet.

I found myself in trouble with the Secret Police because of
'having permitted a dangerous anti-Soviet headline to be printed
in *Vecherniaya Moskva.*' Fortunately for me, it happened in the
autumn of 1934—before the actual blood-purge had started with all
its fierce terror—and I not only survived but was even allowed to
continue my job as Foreign News Editor and Special Correspondent.
Had it occurred a few months later, my fate would have been a
bullet in the nape of the neck . . .

It happened like this—

Vecherniaya Moskva was ready to go to press, when we received
an urgent call from the Press Department, ordering us to scrap our
front and middle pages and publish instead the official reports and
photographs of the Red Army's autumn manoeuvres which we
would receive by despatch rider. We were in time to comply with
the order and, as soon as we received the official text and pictures
at once set to work.

That particular day it was my turn to be Duty Editor at the
printing works—responsible that *Vecherniaya Moskva* strictly con-

formed with the Press Department's orders. We were already well over two hours late and were holding up other publications due to be printed on our machines. Accordingly, I did not object to the badly printed page proofs and, although I could not read clearly every single letter, I took a chance that all was in order. I signed the proofs so that printing could start, and went home.

A short time later, there was lound banging on my door, and several uniformed Secret Police officers were waiting for me. They ordered me to accompany them to Lubyanka—Moscow's Secret Police Headquarters.

'You must be mistaken,' I said. 'Why would you want *me* to come to Lubyanka?'

'You'll find out from the Investigations Officer,' a youngster with the rank of a Captain replied curtly, and added: 'Are you coming along quietly with us or do we have to drag you out?'

There was nothing else I could do but accompany them to the waiting secret police car. I was ordered to sit on the back seat between two officers, and all they said to me during the short journey to Lubyanka was that they would shoot if I made any attempt at escape.

On our arrival at Lubyanka, my escorts handed me over to the Duty Officer. My particulars were taken down and then all my pockets were emptied. The Duty Officer was not prepared to divulge why I had been brought to Lubyanka—he adhered to the standard secret police phrase that I would find out from the In-vestigations Officer. Then he had me escorted by two armed sentries to the third floor.

The office they took me to was brightly lit and furnished with two chairs and a table on which there were two telephones and a number of files. Behind the table sat a middle-aged man in the uniform of a Secret Police Colonel. After having dismissed my escorts, he looked at me searchingly and said in a matter-of-fact tone:

'I would not have thought that you would be connected with such a serious crime.'

'What are you talking about?' I said surprised. 'Perhaps you'll explain why I have been brought here?'

Instead of replying, he took out from a folder a copy of *Vecherniaya Moskva* and, handing it to me, said:

'It is you who has the explaining to do, not I. Have a look at it and say what you have to say.'

I could not see anything wrong with the front page and told him so. He told me to examine carefully each single letter of the thick headline. Only then did I see that it contained a misspelling which I had overlooked in the great hurry on the badly printed proof copy. I told him with genuine surprise that I could not understand why I had been arrested and brought to Lubyanka because of a mere spelling mistake.

'A mere spelling mistake!' he exclaimed. 'I call it a very serious crime. The People's Judge will consider it so as well!'

'I don't understand,' I said. 'I agree that I am responsible for the spelling mistake which occurred because we were in such a hurry to get the paper out and because the proof copy of the page was hardly readable, but surely that's not a crime . . .'

'Not a crime!' he thundered. 'You consider that publishing a headline on the front page "The Autumn Manoeuvres of the Incapable Red Army" is not a most serious crime!'

'It doesn't say that,' I objected. 'The headline reads "The Autumn Manoeuvres of the Invincible Red Army" . . .'

'No it does not!' the Colonel shouted. 'Your spelling means incapable and not invincible!'

'You're joking . . .'

'Being an Editor you know full well that your deliberate headline means *incapable!* If you confess and tell me who is behind the anti-Soviet plot, you'll be shown mercy. But if you shield those who are behind it all, you'll be dealt with severely!'

I did my utmost to convince him that I had no idea that the meaning of the misspelling was 'incapable' until he had told me, and I again explained that the whole unfortunate thing had happened because of the great rush and the badly printed proof copy. A long cross examination followed, and the Colonel did his best to persuade me to sign a confession. But, neither the blinding search-light which was directed into my eyes, nor the threats that I could be shot if I didn't co-operate, induced me to confess to something I was innocent of. I admitted, however, that I was guilty of having permitted the misspelling to be printed.

The interrogation lasted for several hours. Other Secret Police investigators joined the Colonel and tried to break me down. Then, another officer entered and brought the proof copy of the front page which I had signed and which, fortunately for me, had not been destroyed. Having made still more attempts to try to make me sign a confession, the Colonel at last said:

'Taking into consideration that you are an alien and perhaps not entirely familiar with the full meanings of our rich and intricate Russian language, and that the proof copy indeed does not show at first glance that there is any misspelling, we'll believe you. But you are fully to blame for this terrible crime, because it is no excuse that the proof copy is not clearly printed. It was your duty to request a well printed proof copy so that you could make sure everything was in perfect order. But you did not do this. Let it be a warning to you. Don't ever neglect your duties as an Editor and Communist because, if you do, there won't be any leniency the next time.'

He then offered me a papiros and lit it for me.

'Fortunately, irreparable harm has been prevented because of the vigilance of our Control Officer,' the Colonel continued in a friendlier voice. 'Had he not spotted the disastrous headline in time, and stopped the machines, a most serious public crime would have been committed and I would not have been justified in permitting you to go.'

I was then requested to sign an undertaking that I would not divulge to anyone the nature of the interrogation and, when this was done, I was handed a note which certified that my arrest had been 'the result of wrong information,' so that no one could suspect me of being an Enemy of the People. My belongings were then returned to me, I was released, and taken by official secret police car home.

The head printer in our works whose duty it was to check the first printed copy before permitting the edition to be published, was decorated with the 'Order of the Red Flag.' He was the Secret

Police Control Officer who had spotted the treacherous headline, and who had rectified the misprint, and had indirectly saved me.

*   *   *

Conditions in the production of journals and magazines were much the same as in the daily papers.

As far as the publishing of books and pamphlets was concerned, every manuscript had to be studied by several readers—most of them were executives of the Press Department—and only when they recommended a script for publication could the Editor of the publishing establishment, accept it. Even then, the galley proofs had to be sent to the censor to be finally passed. This did not apply only to political books but also to fiction and even poetry. The censor, whose apparent level of intelligence frequently gave rise to despair among discerning writers, often ordered piecemeal deletions to be made. The deletions had to be done, and the galley proofs sent back to the censor for his final O.K. Sometimes, however, the censor who had ordered the changes had in the meantime been transferred to some other job or had been purged. The galley proofs then went to his successor, and he gave his own orders for deletion, changes or addition. It occasionally happened that the successor ordered the book to be restored to its original version, and then thought he was responsible for an enormous improvement!

I worked closely with the publishing establishments 'Dietizdat' and 'Molodaya Gvardiya' and became very friendly with some of the editors. This is how I learned that some books went seven or eight times to and from the censor and these particularly unlucky ones were delayed in this way for over a year.

*   *   *

The rulers of the U.S.S.R. considered radio to be the spoken Press. The news, articles, essays, and reviews were usually supplied by the Press Department or, at least, sanctioned by them. The Russian Party hierarchy lived in constant fear that some enemy of the State might try to speak some counter-revolutionary words into the microphone and, therefore, they had a Secret Police officer in every studio. His job was to follow from the script every word that was spoken into the microphone. He had his hand on a master switch and, should the speaker make an attempt to say something different from the typed and censored script, the programme would immediately cease to be broadcast.

Though Soviet factories turned out wireless receivers, it was impossible at that time to buy a set powerful enough to get foreign broadcasts. The Soviet-made receivers were just good enough to pick up the strongest local services. And to make sure that nobody who might have built himself an individual set would be able to listen to foreign programmes, the strong Soviet transmitters deliberately broadcast on the same wave-lengths as foreign stations. It was thus almost impossible for a Soviet citizen to receive any foreign broadcast. If anybody brought a powerful foreign radio set to the U.S.S.R. it was doctored to bring it down to the receiving level of those manufactured in Soviet factories. Apart from all this, nobody was allowed to have an outside aerial.

Loudspeakers were installed everywhere; in dwelling houses, hotels, hostels, offices, factories and even at regular intervals on lamp posts and trees in the streets, squares and boulevards. The programmes were strictly in line with the Press Department propaganda drives, and consisted of readings of the leaders from *Pravda*, *Izvyestiya*, *Komsomolskaya Pravda* and other papers. In between, revolutionary marches and songs were broadcast. Regardless of where one was, one was always near a loudspeaker and heard the propaganda.

During my visits to factories all over the U.S.S.R. I found that during the time the loudspeakers were blaring out propaganda, no one was allowed to speak. People were requested to listen. In the State Tobacco Factory No. 1—and in many other works too—I was surprised to find that the Partorg regularly called a meeting of factory workers, during which time the leading article of *Pravda*, a Stalin speech, or anything else which had been broadcast that same morning was fully discussed.

Whenever there was a speech by Stalin or another member of the *Politburo*, masses if people would flock to the exhibition cases

in the streets to read every word, or would stop near a loudspeaker
to listen to the announcer.

*   *   *

Reverting to the freedom of the Press in the U.S.S.R. I must
point out that only a small number of the editorial staff—and these
were the only ones who knew the exact ins-and-outs—were dis-
satisfied with the Press Department commanding the papers. Many
of them—in Moscow, Leningrad, Kiev, Minsk and elsewhere—
tried to convince me that the Soviet Press was the most free in the
world. Most of these were men and women of considerable intelligence. They were, of course, devoted members of the Party, and
their brains worked only in strict accordance with the Party line.
In their view, freedom of the Press meant that the Soviet rulers had
the opportunity to speak to the workers—they forgot to point out
that a speech or declaration of even a Peoples' Commissar had to be
approved by the *Politburo*. They also maintained that everything
that was published in the Soviet Press was not only in the interests
of the workers of the U.S.S.R., but also of those of the whole
world. If that was not freedom of the Press, then, they said, they
did not know what the term meant.

In *Vecherniaya Moskva* the situation was somewhat different.
Abram Abramovich was not the only one aware that there was no
freedom of the Press in the U.S.S.R.; most of the rest of the
editorial staff felt the same way. Not that any of us broadcast our
views. We wanted to stay alive.

CHAPTER SIX

Everything under Control

In Russia, everyone, apart from people you knew really intimately and trusted them a hundred per cent, was considered a stranger. This applied even to those who may have worked alongside you for years. And talk to a stranger was always extremely guarded. Or, put another way, lacking in freedom.

If one were indiscreet enough to mention the terrible shortage of food, the unavailability of clothes, shoes, and other consumer goods, the housing shortage, the usual reply was:

'It is only temporary, comrade. Of course, the Soviet Union is not yet perfect but it soon will be. The capitalist world is preparing a war against us. We must be ready for that, and must give all priority to building up a strong Red Army, Air Force and Navy. We must produce all sorts of weapons and make the Soviet Union the strongest fortress in the world. When we have achieved that, then everything will be plentiful and cheap, and much better than in any capitalist country.'

Although I had been a member of the Communist Party for some years before I came to the U.S.S.R. and, in my country, was considered a 'Good *Bolshevik*,' I was nevertheless accustomed to free thinking and more or less free speech. I could not accept entirely the conception that the capitalist world was the cause of *all* the trouble in the Soviet Union. There was little doubt in my mind that the U.S.S.R. had to hold its share of bureaucracy, inefficiency, and bad organisation.

* * *

All over the U.S.S.R. networks of nurseries were set up, to which

mothers took their children from the earliest age so as to be able
to go to work. These nurseries were run strictly on Soviet lines and
the *bolshevic* doctrine was hammered into the little brains right
from the cradle. Small children of pre-school age were politically
organised and were made members of *Oktiabriata*. When they went
to school, which in the U.S.S.R. was when the child reached eight
years of age, they became a *Pioneer* and finally ended up in the
Communist Youth League (*Komsomol*).

The next stage was membership of the Communist Party. Not
all, however, were eligible for the Soviet élite—the Party. Only the
best would be recommended by their Komsomol leaders for Party
membership. Many had to start as 'Sympathisers' which was the
lowest step on the ladder. The next step was 'Probationers.' If the
probationers were considered to be 'Good *Bolsheviks*' they were
nominated by some senior Party members and finally got their
'Full Member's' card. Though most citizens of the Soviet Union
had the same upbringing, only 'the best ones' were allowed to become members of the all-powerful Party for the élite had to remain
the top class of the minority. Everything in Russia has its basis in
control.

The Soviet rulers were always anxious to keep real conditions in
the U.S.S.R. a secret from the outside world, and they did everything possible to prevent foreign visitors from glimpsing the true
nature of things.

If Communist Party or Trade Union members of other countries
were sent to Russia as delegates, the Secret Police took every precaution to ensure that these foreign comrades saw only that which
the Soviet rulers wanted them to see, and only came in touch with
selected people who would tell them what they had been briefed
to say. The men in the Kremlin and in the *Comintern* knew only
too well that it would be disastrous for the revolutionary movement
all over the world if the truth came to light.

Foreign diplomats, trade and other bourgeois delegations, as well
as tourists, were permanently under the observation and direction
of the Secret Police, and could only go to places and meet people
as arranged. Every foreign visitor, official or tourist, was provided

with Soviet interpreters, who, in fact, were trusted officers of the Secret Police or *Comintern*. That is why visitors to the U.S.S.R. never ascertained the complete truth about what was going on and had to rely merely on the little they saw and on hearsay, to form their opinion.

One day, while I was at the printing works *Iskra Revolucii*, the Partorg and some G.P.U. officers asked everyone to stop work for a short meeting. When everybody was assembled in the hall, one of the officers addressed us:

'In about an hour's time a group of foreign tourists will be coming to visit these works. It has been decided to show them round so that they may see for themselves that the Soviet Union is a centre of international culture.

'You are, of course, aware of the fact that these tourists are capitalist spies who have come to our country to collect lies against our beloved Soviet Motherland, so as to be able to stage anti-Soviet campaigns in their countries when they return home. Yes, comrades, that is their only purpose. They have come to our country as tourists, pretending that they are friendly people who are interested in Soviet conditions. We are not so easily deceived, we see through these wolves in sheep's clothing.

'What despicable creatures these servants of the capitalist world are. Their sole intention is to organise a terrible and merciless war against the U.S.S.R. in an effort to destroy the cradle of the workers' rights.'

When he had finished his tirade he concluded:

'These capitalist spies will, of course, take this opportunity to speak to some of you, and to try to worm out of you all kinds of important secrets. They will probably also try to get confirmation that there is still a shortage of food and other things in our country, so that they can use this for anti-Soviet campaigns.

'We rely on you, comrades, to answer like good *bolsheviks*. Let these capitalists leave with the knowledge that all Soviet citizens love the wonderful, vast, and mighty U.S.S.R. and that the whole nation stands as one behind our great leader Stalin and is prepared to defend our great country and ideas against any aggression.

'You will no doubt be happy to hear that these animals will be accompanied by interpreters who will be present at the conversations. They will note which of you make the best replies, and these will be rewarded with a cash gratuity to show you how much a true act of devoted citizenship is appreciated in this country.'

Some time afterwards a group of about twenty tourists arrived, escorted by a strong group of 'interpreters.' These men and women who had come from France did not look to me like capitalist spies. There was little doubt that they had come to the Soviet Union as honest visitors who really wished to foster friendly relations between France and the U.S.S.R.

       ★   ★   ★

As long as a foreign visitor complied with the rules and regulations of the G.P.U. and did not try to explore the country on his own, the treatment he received lacked nothing. Everyone he came in touch with was extremely polite and helpful. The accommodation in the Hotel Metropol or at any other Intourist hotel all over the country was good, and the choice of food available to him was comparable with that of a first class restaurant in London. If, however, anybody dared to violate the fixed programme, it was asking for serious trouble. To illustrate this, let me recall an incident.

In January 1938 *Vecherniaya Moskva* sent me to the Ukraine to represent them at some Ukrainian Press conference in Kiev and Kharkov. My secretary, Tanya Fyodorovna and I, managed to get berths on the International Express to Kharkov. This connected Shepetovka, the Soviet-Ukrainian frontier station, with Baku. The compartment next to ours was occupied by two Dutch engineers who were travelling through the Soviet Union on their way to the oilfields of the Middle East. There were Soviet Secret Police officers on the train, some of them assigned to keep a special eye on the two Dutchmen. The train left Kiev in the evening and was due in Kharkov next morning.

The next morning, while we were eating breakfast, the train stopped at some small station although it was not scheduled to do so, as the next official stop was Kharkov. There was still another hour to go before we were due there.

No one noticed one of the Dutchmen leaving his table. After a few minutes the train started again and continued on its way as if nothing had happened. Almost immediately one of the Secret Police came into the dining compartment and went straight to the table where the second Dutchman was sitting alone.

'Where is your friend?' the policeman asked.

'He went to get some cigarettes.'

'From where?'

'From the station kiosk.'

Without losing a second, the officer pulled the communication cord. The train had pulled out of the station very slowly and the last carriage was still near the platform. Looking out of the window, I could see that the Dutchman had made every effort to catch up with the slow moving train, and when it suddenly stopped, he jumped onto it. A minute or so later he arrived breathless in the dining car, to be immediately questioned by the Russian:

'Where have you been?'

'To the tobacco kiosk at the station,' the Dutchman replied without hesitation. 'I had run out of cigarettes and wanted to get some.'

'I told you so,' his friend said.

'You be quiet,' the Secret Police officer said, and turned again to the offending engineer: 'Why didn't you buy the cigarettes here in the dining car?'

'They haven't any.'

'They have,' the interrogator flared up. 'They have got a whole selection.'

'I said I wanted *cigarettes*,' the Dutchman insisted. 'These are papirosy.'

'What is wrong with papirosy?'

'You ought to know. You smoke them. I don't want that rubbish.'

'They are *not* rubbish, they are excellent!' the Russian shouted. 'Of course for a capitalist spy everything Soviet is rubbish.'

The Dutchman pretended not to have heard this remark and tried to get past the Secret Police officer to return to his table.

'Stay where you are!' the officer shouted. 'You are under arrest!'

D

Two other Secret Police officers materialised and immediately stood on either side of the engineer.

'What am I arrested for?' the Dutchman wanted to know.

'For trying to enter the Soviet Union illegally,' the reply came without hesitation. 'That is a very grave charge in this country.'

'This is ridiculous!' the other Dutchman joined in. 'My friend and I are transit passengers through your country. We hold valid transit visas.'

'That is so,' one of the Secret Police men confirmed. 'It allows you to travel on this train from one end of the Soviet Union to the other. It does not allow you to leave the train, to try to get into our country and to spy on our oilfields.'

'Don't talk such rubbish, man,' the Dutchman under arrest shouted. 'Who wants to spy anyway?'

'You! That's why you are under arrest.'

'Can't you see how preposterous this accusation is?' said the Dutchman realising the seriousness of the position he was in and trying to reason with the officer. 'I can assure you, I am not a spy, I am not even interested in your country.'

The train was still standing where it had stopped. Station officials, Secret Police men and others were hustling about, shouting and gesticulating. Some uniformed Secret Police officers boarded the dining car, wanting to know what was going on. As soon as they heard the story of their colleagues on the train they immediately took hold of the Dutch engineer and pushed him out.

'I demand to be allowed to telephone our Consul,' the other Dutchman addressed the Secret Police officers. 'The whole thing is outrageous.'

'You are under arrest, too,' was the reply to his demand. 'Take him away!'

Tanya Fyodorovna looked at me with disgust in her eyes. She knew only too well that it would be suicide to try to help these two strangers who, we had no doubt, were innocent travellers. One felt so helpless, so despondent that all one could do was to be a silent observer.

What happened to the two Dutchmen I do not know. I tried to

get the incident made known to the Dutch Consul but whether he ever received my communication or whether he was able to help his countrymen I never ascertained. There were rumours that the two Dutch engineers were convicted by a Secret Police tribunal and sentenced to be shot as spies, but, whether that was so, or not, I could not say.

CHAPTER SEVEN
Children of the Cheka

ABRAM Abramovich Kraskyn struck me from the very outset as being the sort of man I should value as a friend, but in an atmosphere of tenseness and suspicion, there was no knowing if a man really was what he appeared to be. Our association started as an elaborate cat-and-mouse game. Each of us tried to discover what the other was thinking. For my part I was conscious of the possibility of his being a Secret Police agent. I was later to find out that he suspected me of the same thing, but in time we became real friends, and spoke freely to one another. This relaxation of tension was a great release valve.

The longer I knew Abram the fonder I became of him. He was a fine human being.

Abram had not always lived comfortably, and he knew only too well what it was to be hungry and nearly frozen to death. He was not a Russian but came from Georgia, Stalin's country. His father Abram Yakovovich was a little Jewish tailor who lived on the outskirts of Tiflis. In Tsarist times, he had to work in his shop from dawn till dusk to make ends meet. With a wife, two sons and three daughters it was a constant struggle.

When the 1914-18 war broke out the little tailor was called upon to fight for the Tsar, and life became even harder for the Kraskyns, especially as Rosa Isaakovna, Abram's mother, was a frail woman who—besides keeping house—now had to do her husband's work. Shortly after the revolution in 1917 father Kraskyn returned to his family to find tremendous poverty all round and he realised that as things were he would hardly be able to keep his family with his

36

tailor's shop. He became a victim of *bolshevik* propaganda which called upon the working population to join the Red Guards and fight for prosperity and a better life. Not long after he had left his family for a second time, he was killed.

A few months later Rosa Isaakovna fell ill with influenza, which was then sweeping most parts of the country. She was too under-nourished and run down to resist the illness and died shortly afterwards. Neighbours looked after the Kraskyn children as well as they could, but the poverty was crippling, and the orphaned Kraskyns looked like living skeletons.

When his mother died, Abram was only just seven years old. The eldest child was his sister Esfir who was then nearly thirteen; then came Salo, a year younger and Olga who was ten, and Esther, eight. All the Kraskyn children tried to earn a few kopyeks by doing odd jobs. When things became a little more established in the new Soviet Union, the District Revolutionary Committee thought it their duty to look after the children of a comrade who had been killed while fighting for the cause.

'I was very small when I went to the Children's Home, but I had already made up my mind that I would never join any *bolshevik* organisation,' Abram said, one day, as he told me the story of his life. 'It was the practice there to assemble twice a week and undergo "self criticism" as was usual in the Party.'

He looked at me and explained:

'In our home there were children ranging from three to sixteen years of age and everyone had to undergo "self criticism." I hated it like hell. It was an awful sight to see the children admitting whatever little "crimes" they had committed, and then to see them criticise themselves for their bad conduct, and finally promising that they would do their utmost to become good and useful members of the community.'

He went on to describe the incident which made him decide not to join any *bolshevik* organisation. When his turn came to undergo 'self criticism,' he admitted to the housefather:

'I did not wash my neck and ears yesterday or today.'

'What a dirty little skunk you are, Abram Abramovich,' his

housefather reprimanded him in front of everybody. 'You must wash your neck and ears every day. Dirt is dangerous because of germs. Germs are the enemy of health and can make you very ill and make you die like your mother did. Not that it matters whether *you* die, but your germs can make others ill and make *them* die. And that would be a very great pity. Do you understand, Abram Abramovich?'

'Yes . . .'

'What other misdemeanours have you committed?' the house-father continued.

'None, none, comrade housefather, I swear,' little Abram replied. 'Since I came here I have always been a good boy.'

'And before you came here?'

'I . . . I . . .,' the little boy stammered.

'Go on,' the housefather demanded, 'let's hear your crimes.'

'When I ran errands for the co-operative shop I once . . . I stole a loaf of bread . . .'

The housefather shouted: 'How could you do such a thing? You stole from a shop which belongs to the State! *We* are the State. You have, therefore, stolen from *us!* Why did you do that?'

'We were hungry. My sisters and my brother and I. We did not have enough money to buy a loaf. I stole because we were hungry.'

'You liar!' the housefather shouted and shook the boy. 'Nobody need steal a loaf of bread. Everyone can get food from the Revolutionary Committee. You stole because you are wicked!'

'No, no—because we were hungry.'

'Don't argue with me!' The housefather pushed him away. 'If you don't learn to do what you are told you will never become a good *bolshevik*. You will end up in jail as a thief.'

Abram, as he told me this, suddenly stood up, visibly moved by the memory. 'I can still hear the housefather saying these words. I will never forget them . . . It was then that I made up my mind to remain outside the *bolshevik* movement, and I have remained true to that decision.'

He admitted that, in fact, he was grateful to the housefather for that.

Esfir suggested that they run away from the home and try to find some relatives of their mother who lived in the Donbas. Salo was against this and thought it was the duty of a good citizen to stay where the Revolutionary Committee had put him. However, he was the only one who took this view, and since Esther and Olga agreed with their sister, he then decided to join them. Esfir immediately started preparations for their departure. Salo helped and finally the plan was ready to be put into operation. But before the young orphans could get away, death again struck at them. Esther and Olga contracted typhoid, and within days they were dead. Shattered by the tragedy, the three remaining youngsters were, for a time, emotionally adrift, but when a semblance of normality returned to their minds, they fled the home.

'Looking back at it now,' Abram said, 'I really cannot understand how we three managed to get out of Tiflis. The Civil War was on, all movement was restricted, and one had to pass check-points to get from zone to zone. We travelled on roofs of railway wagons and nearly froze to death, or were all but swept off when the trains travelled through tunnels. Peasants gave us lifts in their ox carts. We even travelled on Red Army trucks going our way.'

He showed me some faded photographs in which he, his brother and sister were to be seen—pitiful little creatures, all skin and bone and dressed in dirty rags. Though the prints were faded and not perfect, I could nevertheless see their hungry eyes, set deeply in their sockets. In another snapshot little Abram was clad in a uniform jacket which hung from his shoulders. On his head was stuck an army fur cap and he had no shoes or boots—his feet were wrapped in rags and held together with string.

'Then our luck changed,' he continued. 'One afternoon we arrived in Donetsk, a little god-forsaken place, and were held by the Cheka Command. They alleged that children were being used by the Whites and foreign Interventionists as couriers, to smuggle important documents through the Red lines, so we were searched and subjected to endless questioning. The Cheka Commandant, whose name was Vassiliy Feofilovich Movshin, had pity on us. He did not agree with his men that we were liars, who should be shot on the spot. For some reason Commandant Movshin believed our story. But he wanted to confirm it with the Tiflis housefather. Apparently, our fate depended on what he was told about us. Our luck held, however. It was impossible to get through to Tiflis and postal communication was non-existent at that time. What to do with us? There were no Children's Homes in the district, no place for us to go to. Esfir and I implored him to let us go to the Donbas. Salo wanted to stay with the regiment to fight the enemy. However, Movshin would not allow us to continue our journey as we would have to cross enemy territory. He decided that for the time being we should stay on with the regiment though "it might not always be like eating honey," to use a Russian saying.'

Commandant Movshin's unit was a mobile one and moved about the district. The Kraskyn children became part of it and were soon liked by all its members. Esfir was called 'mother of the regiment' and though only a child, the rough Cheka men regarded her as a full member of their community. When an enemy convoy was captured and looted, they picked out things they thought would please Esfir and gave them to her before sending the loot on to the Soviet Command. Salo, who saw a kind of father in Movshin, was growing into a real Chekist. He was armed like the others, had learned to handle the Maxim machine gun, and had acquired the art of horse riding—with or without a saddle—like Cossack boys who, from earliest childhood were at home on horseback.

Abram, because of his age, was regarded as the baby of the unit. All the rough fellows of the Movshin gang, tried their utmost to do little things for him to make him happy, and he in turn repaid them with all sorts of kindnesses. To get hold of a book or paper at those times, in districts which were in the midst of Civil War, was almost an impossibility. Commandant Movshin and his men managed, however, to get some and even secured school books for Abram. Those who could read and write gave him lessons whenever they could spare a moment. Movshin called the Kraskyns 'Children of the Cheka' and Abram liked to recall his days with the Movshin unit and often said that this was the first time in their lives since his parents' death that anybody had been kind to them and treated them like human beings. All three Kraskyns loved Movshin and called him Diadia* Vasiliy.

The 'Children of the Cheka' experienced the horrors of Civil War with Movshin's unit. They saw how enemies were shot in the back of the head by Cheka men, they saw the indescribable hunger in the land—the peasant population was dying in thousands from starvation, and corpses could be seen everywhere. They also saw members of the regiment, who had been their friends, dying in agony from their wounds. There was practically no medical aid available and many a man who could easily have been saved, died a horrible death.

One day the regiment came to a little Ukrainian village and Movshin sought out the mayor. He could not be found, and Movshin directed the whole population of the village into the square before the wooden church which had been burned down some months before by Soviet partisans.

'Where is the comrade mayor?' Movshin enquired in his clear voice.

Complete silence.

'I want to know where the comrade mayor is.' Movshin feared that the administrator of Soviet power had been murdered by enemies of the State. 'Quick! Where is he?'

The peasants became uneasy. 'He's dead,' one of them finally replied.

'How did he die?' Movshin shouted.

'He died.'

'Where did you bury him?'

'We didn't.'

'Where is his corpse then?'

There was a long uneasy silence, and then one of them half whispered it.

'We ate him.'

Movshin wanted to mow them all down there and then with machine guns. He was convinced that the mayor had been killed because he was a Soviet executive. It transpired that no political

*Uncle.

motive had been at stake but that they had simply killed and eaten
him because of desperate hunger. This was not an isolated instance.
Cannibalism had taken place in the Ukraine and elsewhere before.

'Why did you pick out the mayor?' Movshin asked.

'He had plenty of flesh on him,' came the explanation, 'and he
was old and would have died soon in any case.'

'How could you kill the mayor?' Movshin raged. 'He was the
State, he was the Law, he was the Soviet.'

'Nobody liked him,' said a peasant trying hard to defend their
action. 'He was too bossy, he was too conceited . . .'

The Cheka could not tolerate cannibalism, and they had received
strict orders to stamp it out. Commandant Movshin had no alternative but to search out those who had planned and carried out the
murder. He had them shot in front of the villagers. The bodies
were then burned to avoid any further cannibalism.

'Unfortunately for us our stay with Movshin's regiment was not
to be a long one,' Abram continued. 'One day orders were received
from Lenin that the unit was to make its way towards the Crimea
to help the Red Army and partisans in their fight against the forces
of the counter-revolution. Every man was required. Movshin took
us to the nearest point from which we could travel in comparative
safety to the Donbas. However, only Esfir and I went. Salo managed
to persuade Diadia Vasiliy to take him along and to allow him to
fight for the freedom of the Soviet Union.'

From then onwards life became very difficult again for the two
Kraskyn children. They managed, despite great difficulties to get to
the Donbas and reach the village where their mother's relatives
were supposed to live. When they arrived they found to their
dismay that the whole family had moved to Kharkov; nobody
knew their address. Kharkov was a town of considerable size and if
one did not have an exact address it would be extremely difficult
to find someone. But the Kraskyn children set out and reached
the then capital of the Ukraine. The letter which they had from
Movshin and which bore the big red Cheka seal, helped them and
they discovered from the Kommandatura that their mother's
relatives had gone to Moscow. First the head of the Kommandatura

wanted to take them to a Children's Home but Esfir persuaded him that her mother's relatives would not like that and would want them to stay with them in Moscow.

'That is how Esfir and I came to Moscow,' Abram ended his story. 'We never found my mother's relatives, and on going from Kommandatura to Kommandatura we somehow attracted attention and were taken to the Cheka headquarters at Lubyanka, probably because we had Diadia Vasiliy's letter. First they wanted to send us back to Tiflis where we originally came from; then they changed their minds and wanted to send us to Kharkov, probably because that was nearer; but in the end Esfir and I managed to get permission to stay in Moscow.'

He paused for a moment and then said:

'You'll find people of our age group all over the Soviet Union who had a very similar life. If I think of what others, less fortunate than we, went through then I must say that we had quite a good childhood. Things being as they were, Esfir managed to finish her education and got quite a good job at the Trade Union headquarters, and I went to the University when I finished school, studied literature and languages and became a newspaper man. How long this will last depends entirely on the G.P.U. You know, in our country instead of the old proverb, "the only certainty in life is that death will come for you," we now have the new Soviet version, "the only certainty in life is that the G.P.U. will come for you." All one can do is to be as careful as possible, to pretend even to close acquaintances that one is a devoted *bolshevik* even if one has not joined the Party. Anybody in this country who wishes to stay alive and out of prison has to deceive others and shout that he is an ardent Soviet citizen. The most depressing thing is that you never know to whom you are talking, enemy, or friend.'

Had I not been lucky enough to have met Abram and become friends with him, I honestly doubt whether I would have escaped from the clutches of the Soviet Secret Police.

CHAPTER EIGHT

Bolshevik Initiative

ONE method of pressing the workers to increase and to raise the quality of production was by means of the 'Wall Newspapers' which they called *Stiengazeta*. Workers wrote articles and reports, Partorgs supplied political propaganda, Proforgs production figures, and the editor of the *Stiengazeta* decided what he wanted to exhibit and had his selections typed. These were then pasted on to a large piece of paper or cardboard and affixed to a board in the entrance hall or the assembly room. The aim was to praise good workers and to discredit bad ones. It was believed that this method of publishing good and bad had a great effect and helped the common cause.

When I visited Elektrozavod, a factory where electric light bulbs were manufactured, the Partorg who was showing me around invited me to stop at the *Stiengazeta* which was neatly made up and bore headlines in various colours. Most articles praised various comrades who had managed to increase production and had thus made it possible for more people to avail themselves of electric light. There was, however, one article, framed in thick red and blue lines. This was the text:

For the second week in succession Anya Mikhailovna Orlova behaves like an enemy of the State. Till recently she was a good and reliable worker with a very good record. As soon as appreciation of her work was shown and her name was published in this *Stiengazeta*, she became a bad worker. Not only does she turn out much less than she used to do, and still less than the output of the average worker, but on some days she turns out up to 65% rejects.

This cannot go on! The raw materials are, as you all know, to a great extent imported from foreign countries and have to be paid for in gold. It is, therefore, the greatest crime Orlova commits because she deprives the Soviet people of gold, which could be used for the import of complicated foreign machinery with which the living-standard in the U.S.S.R. could be raised. But due to Orlova's negligence—at this stage we do not want to call it sabotage—our gold is wasted and prosperity is set back.

There is also another aspect to this. Due to Orlova's negligence many people cannot avail themselves of electric light, and have to use candles instead. These might easily start fires and burn down houses. Even if this does not happen, they are spoiling their eyesight and are bound to work less well than they did before. Again thanks to the negligence of Orlova.

Wake up, Anya Mikhailovna! Work as you did before or else account for your crimes to the authorities concerned!

It was a crushing indictment, and I asked the Partorg his opinion of why Orlova's work had deteriorated. 'She simply doesn't care,' he said. Not being satisfied with his explanation, I suggested we went to see her. He did not like it but gave in when I hinted that I might write an article about the matter in my paper.

Anya Mikhailovna Orlova was a plumpish woman of about thirty. She looked ill. When we stopped at her workbench the Partorg told her that I had come from *Vecherniaya Moskva*, and wanted to find out why she had been working so badly of late. Tears surged into her eyes. She did not strike me as a saboteur type.

The Partorg of Elektrozavod began to lecture her about the duties of every Soviet citizen. I soon had enough of this aggressiveness and started to speak to the distressed woman myself. I learned the reason for her bad work. She was not getting any sleep, as she had no place to live.

'Why didn't you tell your Partorg about your troubles?' I enquired.

'I told him, and the Profog, that I had to get out of the house I was living in because it was to be demolished,' she said. Encouraged by my presence, she turned to the Partorg and said: 'You told me you could not do anything for me and I would have to find another place myself.'

The Partorg was temporarily nonplussed. He looked uncomfortable because of the girl's frankness and lack of fear. But some sort of explanation was plainly necessary. 'Well, we have no living accommodation available,' he said, searching for an excuse. 'Had I known, of course, that she is, so to speak, on the street, I would have seen what I could have done for her.' It was obvious to him that I, as a journalist, could print a story that would be embarrassing to him. He promised that he would billet Orlova in the factory's hostel immediately.

Orlova soon got a corner with a bed in the factory hostel. Later on I learned from the Partorg that she had resumed her place in the rank of good workers.

The trouble in the Soviet Union was that the authorities acted in accordance with a 'shoot first and ask question afterwards' theory. Only seldom did they bother to try to find out the root of trouble.

The habit of discrediting 'bad workers' in *Stiengazetas* was not only applied on Soviet factories. One day I read the *Stiengazeta* in the Luks. This was one of the stories that caught my eye:

Although everyone knows only too well that there is a tremendous shortage of crockery all over the U.S.S.R. and that our Soviet factories cannot keep up with the huge demand, there are elements who have no sense of responsibility, who do not take care and who behave like bulls in a china shop—in the real meaning of the word. Although it must sound unbelieveable, there are elements of that sort in our midst right here in the Luks.

It is not the first time that Olga Borisovna Katayeva has broken plates and glasses. However, on 5 June she smashed many dishes and through her stupid carelessness created great hardship and damage to the community.

Katayeva explains that she slipped and that this was the reason for what happened. Can we believe her? Or do we have to come to the conclusion that she was too lazy to wash up and that she, therefore, deliberately smashed the dirty crockery?

Only the future will tell. If Katayeva does her duty and proves that she is an honest and conscientious worker, we might believe her story and forget her irresponsibility.

The case of Olga Borisovna Katayeva illustrates how easy it is to commit acts of sabotage and invent a plausible explanation. Everybody MUST be most watchful, everybody MUST make the greatest effort to work more and to work better. EVERY-BODY IS A SOLDIER OF THE GREAT ARMY OF WORKERS OF THE U.S.S.R. AND HAS TO DO HIS DUTY TO BUILD A STRONG AND PROSPEROUS MOTHERLAND OF ALL THE WORKERS OF THE WORLD!

As I have said before, not all the articles in the *Stiengazetas* discredited a member of their community. In *Iskra Revolucii*, for instance, everybody in every department of the large printing works managed to work according to the production schedule. The management, however, wanted to drive the workers to even better results, and to induce them to increase their output, praises of the following sort could be read weekly:

Comrade Hans Lehmann, of our German Department, this month succeeded in increasing his output considerably, and managed to work 35% above the plan. This is the second month in succession that Comrade Lehmann has increased the norm of the production plan. He has proved himself a truly reliable worker and trusted member of our great Soviet community.

To show how much his effort is appreciated by everyone, Comrade Lehmann will receive a premium of 25 roubles from our works management. No doubt this honour will prompt him to do his utmost to keep his speed of work up, and, even to increase his present production.

We are confident that every single worker of *Iskra Revolucii* will follow in Comrade Lehmann's footsteps.

* * *

The Partorgs in the Soviet Union were suspicious people and assumed that workers who stayed away from work and excused themselves by saying that they had been ill, were malingering. If the absentee did not produce a doctor's certificate, a meeting of all employees was called and the person was publicly cross-examined.

At one such meeting at *Mossoviet Publications Combinat* which consisted of *Rabochaya Moskva*, *Kolkhoznaya Gazeta* and *Vecherniaya Moskva*, the Partorg subjected Fedya Anatolovich Muskyn, one of the proof-readers who had been absent for three days, to the following interrogation:

'You say you have been sick and couldn't come to work?'

'Yes.'

'But you didn't bring a doctor's certificate?'

'The doctor never came to see me though my wife telephoned the surgery and told them that I was sick and had a high temperature.'

'If no doctor saw you, you may not have been sick at all.'

'I had bad cramps and a high temperature.'

'But you haven't a doctor's certificate?'

'Is it my fault that the doctor did not come?' Muskyn said in despair. 'I was very sick, I tell you . . .'

The Partorg believed that he might still catch his man unawares and shot another question. 'Why didn't you see the *Zavdok* when you last left work?'

'When I left here three days ago I was all right,' Muskyn replied. 'I didn't fall sick until the next morning.'

Not one of those assembled doubted that the man spoke the truth. The Partorg sensed this, changed his tone and said in a benevolent voice:

'I will believe you this time, Comrade Muskyn. But remember, if ever you are sick again you *must* produce a doctor's certificate.' He then started a tirade on the theme that Soviet production would be jeopardised if workers stayed away for unimportant private reasons and pretended that they had been ill. He finally concluded: 'I must warn you that if anyone stays away from work in future, comes back and says that he was sick but cannot produce a doctor's certificate to prove it, I will not accept the excuse, and will pass the matter on to the highest level. Let that be understood.'

The eyes of those assembled expressed discontent. Their mouths, however, remained silent.

Another grave offence in the Soviet Union was to be late for work. If it happened three times, it became a very serious matter and could be severely punished—even with imprisonment.

* * *

Whenever the Partorg or any other member of the management wanted to hear his own voice, or display Communist zest, they called a meeting either of a certain department or of all the employees. Most meetings were called during the lunch periods with the result that little time was left for eating. These meetings were not only called for the purpose of criticising or rebuking some member of the establishment. More often than not, propaganda speeches were delivered or production was discussed.

I quickly got tired of these constant meetings. It was worse for me than for most other people because I had to attend meetings at *three* institutions. Due to the fact that I was living in the Luks and had come to the U.S.S.R. on a *Comintern* visa, I had to attend the *Comintern* Party meetings. As an employee of *Vecherniaya Moskva* I had to attend meetings there, and, although I worked only part time at *Iskra Revolucii* I had to take part in their meetings. Some weeks I had to go to meetings every evening in the week. For a Party member not to go to meetings meant near-suicide. I cursed the day I joined the Communist Party . . .

'Why don't you use your brains?' Abram asked me one day when I complained to him about having to attend meetings almost non-stop. 'By belonging to three different organisations you are in a unique position. If there is a boring meeting at *Vecherniaya Moskva* which is likely to drag on till late at night, simply say that you can't attend because you have to be at a *Comintern* meeting, and vice versa. That's simple, isn't it? They will never suspect you.'

One evening there really were meetings being held at the same time at the *Comintern* and *Vecherniaya Moskva*. I took the chance,

E

followed Abram's advice and even showed the circulars to the Partorgs at both places. Both Partorgs told me that, in future, I need not trouble to bring them the circulars beforehand, as it would be quite in order to telephone them or excuse myself at the next meeting.

*   *   *

In the U.S.S.R. they did not have Sundays free as in other countries. They had the *Shestidnievka*.

The slogan, 'SOVIET WORKERS ARE THE BEST BUILD-ERS OF A NEW WORLD!' was seen everywhere. One one occasion a worker whispered to me: 'That poster opposite my machine drives me crazy.' The poster said: 'IT IS THE DUTY OF EVERY SOVIET CITIZEN TO INCREASE PRODUCTION! ONLY ENEMIES OF THE U.S.S.R. WORK BADLY AND SLOWLY! ONLY THOSE NEED EAT WHO WORK HONESTLY!' The worker went on: 'I work like a slave and produce more than is the norm of the plan but I still don't get enough food!'

The managements—prompted by the District Committee of the Communist Party—organised off duty workers, and instead of having a well-deserved rest after a strenuous week, tired workers were transported to building sites and had to help carry bricks, mix cement, and do all kinds of manual labour; or, else were taken to farms, to do ploughing, fruit-picking, and potato digging. The rules called it 'voluntary help.' But coercion was its mainstay.

Some Partorgs and Kultorgs enjoyed organising. Those who were being organised hated it. If there was no help required on a building site or elsewhere, the organisers thought of something else. They organised outings into the country, 'because it is good for the health to breathe fresh air'; they organised visits to museums and made endless speeches which invariably were politically slanted.

Whether the reason for all this was that the Soviet rulers *believed* their people should be occupied practically every minute of their lives, (if nothing else, it would keep them so exhausted as to be incapable of rebellion), or whether it was the powerful urge to *command*, it was typical of existence in a Communist state.

CHAPTER NINE

In an Architect's Flat

DURING the time I worked at *Vercherniaya Moskva*, I came in contact with people from all over the Soviet Union. They ranged from *kolkhoz* peasants and factory workers, to scientists, engineers, and architects. Though on many occasions I spent hours, days, or even weeks in their company, they remained merely acquaintances. I could never risk confiding in them.

There was one exception, however, whom I met quite frequently. He was Yakov Lvovich Messin, a young architect from Bukharest. A member of the Rumanian Communist Party, he had come to Russia a few years previously when things in his own country got too hot for him. He had lived in my country for some time and knew several of my friends.

One day he invited Abram and me to visit him and his wife Mono Reubenovna at their flat. I accepted his invitation with pleasure as it was the first time since coming to the U.S.S.R. that I had been invited to a Soviet household. I knew from my visits to Abram's home that his own ultra-modern flat was not typical of those in which most Muscovites lived. The Messins had been given their flat immediately on their arrival in Moscow before Yakov had become a favoured architect.

As Abram had to remain on duty in the editorial office and I had to attend a *Comintern* meeting, we arranged to meet at the Messins' flat as soon as we were free.

The Messins lived in a little side street, off Kuzniecky Most, which was the best part of Moscow. As I could not find a bell or a knocker, I banged on the heavy door, which was badly in need of a coat of paint.

'Hey, citizen! What's the idea of making such a noise?' a Militia man who had appeared out of the blue, said in a stern voice. 'Go home and be quiet. This is no place for a drunkard.'

'I am not drunk,' I replied, annoyed. 'I want to get in here.'

'Can't you see that the door is locked?'

'That's why I'm knocking,' I retorted.

'Don't you know that *all* front doors are *always* locked?' he went on. My foreign accent probably made him suspicious and he demanded to see my identity card. I showed him my *Comintern* pass. He shone his torch on it and apologized: 'I'm very sorry for having troubled you, Comrade. I couldn't know that you were one of the *Comintern*. You will understand that we must be most watchful.'

'That's all right,' I replied putting my pass book into my pocket. 'You only did your duty, Comrade.'

'I'm grateful that you appreciate my work,' he said, and took me to the back entrance of the house and with the aid of his powerful torch helped me to get across the pitch-dark yard.

The house was a great disappointment to me. It was a ramshackle old building with worn steps and a badly lit staircase. Even in the semi-darkness I noticed that the walls were extremely dirty with what remained of the paint peeling off. There was also a peculiar smell—a mixture of cabbage soup, *Makhorka* smoke, and dirt.

On the second floor I discovered a small card on a door with Messin's name on it. Again no bell or knocker was to be found, so I had to bang with my fist. Presently an elderly woman with a broad peasant face opened the door. I took her to be Messin's maid.

'I've come to see Comrade Messin,' I said.

'Who?' she asked.

'Comrade Messin.'

'He doesn't live here,' she said.

'He *does*,' I insisted, and pointed to the card on the door. 'Look.'

'Ah, you mean the Comrade architect?' Her face lit up. 'Along the corridor. His room is the fifth on the left.'

I was flabbergasted. I had expected the Messins to have their own *flat*, especially as he always referred to coming to their flat. It had never entered my mind that all they had was a room in an old, filthy house.

I could hear people talking behind the closed doors of the other rooms. Some were singing; another one was playing a mouth organ. A small child was crying. From the floor above came stamping as if somebody was performing a Cossack dance. Hesitantly I knocked at the Messins' door. I was prepared to walk into a poor, shabby room.

'Come in, Comrade,' Messin's wife said when she opened the door. 'It's nice of you to come.'

I was surprised to walk into a most pleasant looking room, spotlessly clean. The walls were decorated attractively—though to my mind there were too many photographs of Lenin, Stalin, and other leaders of the Revolution. There were gay folk-weave curtains, and the furniture was comfortable and modern. The lamp which hung from the ceiling in the middle of the room, showed good taste.

'I am pleased to welcome you to our little flat,' said Messin shaking hands with me. 'Let me introduce Mono Reubenovna, my wife.'

'You have a lovely place,' I said after the introductions.

'You should have seen it when we were allocated it,' Mono said. 'Dirty and smelly, even worse than the corridor and staircase. It looked more like a pigsty than a place for human beings to live in. When I first saw it I burst into tears. Really, it was terrible. Yakov and I worked like slaves. Everything you see here—decoration, furniture, and even the lamp—is our own work. But it was worth it, I think. As soon as we close the door behind us, you see, we are in civilised surroundings.'

With about fifty others who lived in the adjoining rooms, they had to use the one and only toilet. The filthy bathroom, she and her husband never used. They preferred the inconvenience of going to the nearby public baths.

Gradually the conversation turned to Messin and his work:

'I really can't compare life in Central Europe with that here,' he told us. 'You see, when I worked in France with Corbusier, he was the famous architect and I a young, unknown fellow, who had just left the Academy. I was a nobody. It was the same everywhere I went. They did the attractive work, I was given the unexciting stuff. But I learned a lot, gathered experience and earned good money, and life was good. We had nice homes wherever we went, and I began to get on—slowly mind, but I was progressing. Had I not been an active member of the Communist Party, I would probably have climbed the ladder more quickly. Who knows? But if one is young and believes in one's ideals one doesn't think so much about a career . . .'

His voice sounded sad.

'Do you regret having come to Moscow?' I asked.

'Certainly not,' he replied emphatically. 'Don't misunderstand me, Comrade. What I mean to say is, that life in Central Europe is, as you yourself know, much more comfortable and luxurious than here—provided you have a job, of course. No, I do not regret having come here because nowhere else would I have such opportunities as I have here. You see, as soon as I arrived, I was invited to work on the project of the sanatorium in Sochi. I worked hard, applied all I knew and had learned from my famous employers and managed to design a sanatorium which was to the liking of the Planning Commission and which won me a first prize.'

He told us that he was now in charge of three other sanatoria and added that when these were finished tens of thousands of Soviet workers would be able to enjoy their holidays in comfort. He spoke in glowing terms of the great work the Soviet rulers did for their people in allowing millions of roubles to be spent on sanatoria, hospitals, nurseries and schools.

I was interested in his work and asked him how building conditions in the U.S.S.R. compared with those in Central European countries.

'It's more difficult here,' he said candidly. 'You see, Soviet people are not as qualified as those in other countries. Then there is the lack of materials to cope with, and unfortunately too often work is held up because there are no bricks or cement. Or because deliveries have gone astray. To avoid grave mistakes being made by the workers, every single stage has to be watched closely by the architect in charge of the site. But we are progressing.'

'Much too slowly,' his wife remarked. 'If we continue at this speed it will be another century before the urgent housing problem is solved.'

'You can't say that, Mono,' Messin corrected. 'It's true that building is slow and inadequate at the moment, but it is also a fact that tremendous building activity is going on and that people whose houses are being demolished because they are no longer fit for human occupation are moving into good modern flats.'

'Don't be a hypocrite, Yakov,' Mono said frankly. 'Only G.P.U. and Party executives get new flats. Workers are transferred from one slum dwelling to another. What about that lovely new block behind Tverskoy Boulevard? You know as well as I that this block is only for G.P.U. and the highest Party officials.'

'Perhaps that block was built by the G.P.U. or Party,' Abram commented. 'That would explain your statement, Mono Reubenovna.'

'I don't know who built it but I happen to know that this preferential treatment towards G.P.U. and Party chiefs is practised all over the country,' she said.

'Rome wasn't built in a day, Mono, I tell you this all the time,' Messin was making an effort to soften his wife's words. 'You must give credit where it is due.'

'Don't try to make things better than they are,' she replied. 'You are not at a mass meeting now. You don't have to deliver propaganda speeches.'

We parted in a cordial way and the Messins invited us to come and have tea with them again soon.

When we were safely out on the street, Abram told me he had cut short our visit, because the discussion had become too dangerous. He insisted on my going to his home, which was nearby, as he wanted to talk to me most urgently. And as we walked along the still busy street, he deliberately chatted about trivia. However, as soon as we arrived at his flat, had closed the door behind us and made ourselves comfortable, he began to speak to me in a serious tone.

CHAPTER TEN

Words of a friend

'I MUST speak to you because I see more clearly than ever that you don't realise what kind of country you are living in,' he began. 'Though you are a member of the Communist Party of your own country, you are nevertheless, still completely European and you seem to think that the privilege of free speech and thought apply equally to people in the Soviet Union. I must tell you how matters stand here in the U.S.S.R., because if I don't, you will pay heavily. I beg you to listen to me carefully. Remember what I tell you.

'Bernard, if you want to survive you must change your entire outlook, you must be on your guard at all times, you must behave as though you were in enemy hands and realise that every unguarded word you utter or every wrong step you make will be held against you.

'You have now been living in this country for a few months. What have you seen? Only a little. You have spoken to people in the Luks, the *Comintern*, in our Combinat, in *Iskra Revolucii*, on the street, in several factories and God knows where else. But what have they told you? Only what they dared to say. Some may have made critical remarks in moments of forgetfulness or depression. But have they spoken to you of hunger Bernard? Or of poverty? Or of fear? No, because they are afraid.

'I did not like the way Mono Reubenovna talked tonight, because I too am afraid. She is either a too-honest Central European Communist like you, or she is a G.P.U. informer who has orders to speak as she does in order to provoke others to reveal their thoughts. A trap Bernard—that many fall into. I had to cut short our visit.

If she is no G.P.U. informer she is in for trouble sooner or later. And once in the hands of the brutes of Lubyanka . . .' He shook his head.

'Don't think that what I am telling you is hearsay. What I am telling you are facts, obtained from most reliable sources, from friends who are high officers of the G.P.U., who have told me what they know from personal experience.

'*Everybody* is spied on. Beautiful girls and simple-looking women, honest-faced men who work hard in factories, and seemingly innocent intellectuals—they all form the enormous army of G.P.U. informers. No, Bernard, don't jump to the conclusion that they do it *voluntarily*. Very few, perhaps, might be G.P.U. informers out of fanaticism, but ninety-nine per cent have been forced into it. If you bear in mind that over a million people are in slave-labour camps, in prisons, or exiled in Siberia, you will understand why most of these informers have to submit to the demands and threats of the G.P.U.

'Remember all this wherever you are. I know it is hard and painful, for a Communist full of idealism such as you, but the only way to survive is to make it a principle of your life never to believe anyone, to see a G.P.U. informer in *everyone*. Play cat-and-mouse with strangers, and never give way to your feelings.

'When I was working in Dniepropetrovsk as a correspondent for the *Kommunist*, they pestered me the whole time to join the Party. My editor as well as the general secretary of the Party District Committee offered to sponsor my application for membership. As you know, I had made up my mind never to join any Party organisation, and not even *Diadia* Movshin made me change my mind. I realised that I had to be extremely careful in what I said, so I told them that I did not consider myself to be ripe for membership yet. They seemed to appreciate my views and agreed that I should remain, for the time being, outside the Party. But behind my back they asked the G.P.U. to keep an eye on me.

'Soon afterwards I met a very attractive young girl, Yolka Petrovna, at an art exhibition, to which I had been sent by my paper. I liked her very much and fell in love with her. Our romance had only lasted for a few months, however, when I accidentally found out that she was a G.P.U. informer. This hit me extremely hard as you can imagine. When she came to my room late one evening, I challenged her:

' "Why didn't you tell me that you are a G.P.U. spy?" I did not care whether she reported what I said or not. I was young and impulsive and at that moment it appeared to me that everything around me had collapsed. "How could you deceive me, Yolochka?" I pressed on.

'She went white and sat down without taking off her coat or cap. "I had to, darling," she whispered, trying hard to hold back her tears.

' "Did they plant you on me?" I shouted at her, deeply hurt and hoping she would deny it.

' "Yes . . ." She could not speak because tears began to stream down her cheeks and her voice was choked.

'That was the last straw. I yelled at her, called her ugly names, even started to shake her, having completely lost my temper. "You pretended to love me so that you could run and report my words and thoughts to your superiors!" I think that if I had had a gun I would have shot her and myself there and then.

'But Yolka begged me to listen to what she had to say. She told me that her father had been arrested by the G.P.U., though he had been an honest worker. He was held and tortured as a saboteur in the cellar prison of Dniepropetrovsk G.P.U. headquarters. Her mother used to send her to take food parcels to the G.P.U. prison. One day she was told that the parcel could not be accepted and she was asked to see the Commandant. He proposed that she become a G.P.U. informer. She refused. He threatened her. She still resisted. This went on for a week or so. Then she was allowed to see her father in the prison hospital. He was unrecognisable. Not only did he look like a sick old man but his teeth were missing, his right arm was broken and in plaster and his face showed other signs of brutal ill treatment. Her father knew that he was beyond help and that death was merely a matter of hours. He begged her to look after her mother.

'When she left the prison hospital she was escorted to the Commandant who grinned at her triumphantly and said that he hoped she had changed her mind and would do what the G.P.U. wanted of her. She told him that she could not understand why he should pick her in particular. He told her that he had picked her because not only was she beautiful but had an extremely appealing way about her which was a tremendous advantage for this type of work, and a very effective weapon. When he sensed that her resistance was still not broken, he threatened that if her answer should be "No" her mother would be arrested and would share the same fate as her father. Then he suddenly changed his tone, smiled at her, and told her that she did not have to make up her mind immediately but that she could let him know her decision in a day or so. She had hardly told her mother that her father was in hospital, when several G.P.U. officers forced their way into the room and arrested her mother.

' "Now you know my story, darling," she said near to a whisper. "The same evening I gave my soul to the G.P.U. The Commandant kept his part of the bargain and released my mother immediately. I hated myself but I had promised my dying father to look after her. Yes darling, they planted me on you. They sent me to the exhibition, gave me your description and asked me to report our conversation, exactly. What neither they nor I could anticipate was that I should fall in love with you. I love you more than I love anything else in the world . . . I told them only what I wanted them to know. I painted a picture of you as a most devoted and reliable Soviet citizen who thinks that he is not yet worthy of being enrolled in the Party and is postponing his application for membership for this reason . . ."

'I believed her. I loved her deeply. I still love her memory . . . Two days later she was dead. An accident they said. Run over by a lorry and killed instantly. I was not allowed to see her body. I do not know, I don't suppose I ever will know, whether her sudden death was really an accident or whether she was killed by the G.P.U.'

For a long time he remained silent. Eventually he shook himself out of his reverie and said:

'Much has been said and written about the atrocities which Ivan the Terrible, Peter the Great and other despots of the past committed. But believe me, Bernard, their's was child's play compared with what is being done by Stalin and his Secret Police. Anyone going on their list is as good as dead. There are no trials before a judge and jury. Life and death are in the hands of fanatical G.P.U. investigators and those sentenced to death are shot in the G.P.U. prisons, without delay. They want confessions, these sadists. They have already made up their minds to ruin a person when they arrest him. They want to be able to close a file with a confession by the accused. They torture their victims scientifically, they use violence and cunning psychology. The exhausted prisoner always gives in and signs. It becomes either a death warrant or a pass to a slave-labour camp, prison, or exile in an unpopulated part of Siberia.

'You have surely noticed that I never talk openly to you in our canteen, even if we are alone. This is because one never knows whether or not there are hidden microphones. I know that may sound melodramatic but I assure you that they will resort to anything. Microphones have already convicted more people than will ever be known ...'

He stopped talking again and seemed to be struggling with some decision. Then he turned and looked directly at me and said: 'There are hidden microphones in your own office, Bernard, behind the Lenin picture on the wall, under the desk, and on top of the bookshelves. Look tomorrow, when you are alone, but don't get caught. And look in your room at the Luks. I shall be most surprised if you don't discover something there.

'I have learned to be a good actor, and I have also learned how to avoid getting into trouble. I *know* that I am being watched by the G.P.U. and I do not doubt that they plant informers on me. Let them! Abram Abramovich Kraskyn talks to them like a walking version of Yaroslavsky's "*History of the V.K.P.B.*" If Yagoda must have a dossier about me, let him. But *I* make sure that its contents reflect nothing but the staunchest *bolshevik* sentiments. It's a strain to keep up. Make no mistake about that.

'When you and I first started to be friendly, I suspected that you were a G.P.U. agent, Bernard. It would have been an extremely clever move on the part of the G.P.U. to use a foreigner. I set some traps to find out. I apologize deeply for my suspicions, but it is the only way to exist—to suspect everyone. Look, when I first met my wife at the *Lenin Library* I suspected her of being an informer. It was a long time before I brushed aside my suspicion. Longer still before I was sure enough to marry her. Trust *no-one*. That is the only motto worth observing. Even blood relationship means nothing.

'My own brother, Salo, is a big shot in the G.P.U.—a Colonel at Lubyanka. He is a fanatical *bolshevik*, lives only for the Party. Since the day we parted, he has followed in *Diadia* Movshin's footsteps and he is now at the top, and has a high position. We love each other deeply as brothers. But I could never disclose my inner thoughts to him. He would not understand. He would have to look on me as an enemy of the State, and would probably disown me. Even if he guesses that many innocent people are wrongly being "liquidated," he can excuse it with the easy explanation that it is "in the interests of the people of the U.S.S.R." He says there is no time to shed tears for the wrongly persecuted individual. His conception of life is "where trees are felled, chips fly." You know, Bernard, it is a despicable thing to be forced to lie even to one's own brother.

'I tell you all this to convince you that you have a chance to survive only if you hide your thoughts. It is dishonest, I know, but so are the methods used by the G.P.U. They are not fools; they have cunning and intelligence.

'If they shadow anyone, naturally enough they do not want that person to know it, so a huge army of "observers" is kept on the streets. They resemble all types of people—young and old, in uniform and in plain clothes, well groomed and badly dressed. They look like any other passer by. This is how they work: one "observer" follows you from the Luks to the next corner. There he "hands you over" to his counterpart. This goes on from stretch to stretch. You see, it's impossible to discover that one is being shadowed. But if you are ever taken in for questioning, not only will they tell you your every move, but show you photographs of yourself to prove it. Hundreds of G.P.U. "observers" are equipped with button-hole cameras to provide the dossiers with authentic photographs.

'Bernard, has it ever occurred to you that the pretty Vira Anatolyevna Razumova who seems to be such an innocent and efficient administrative worker in our Combinat, is a G.P.U. informer? And Nina Ivanovna Prokofyeva, and Sofia Pavlovna Sukevska? I know you flirt with all three of them. But be careful, I beg you. Don't ask me how I know, but simply accept my word for it. Don't break things off with them, that would be silly. But, be on your guard. Never let them guess what you know. It could be fatal. The same applies to Viktor Markovich Kuznietsov. He goes out of his way to make friends with you. He too is a G.P.U. informer.'

Abram had finished. Both he and I were exhausted—he from the amount of talking he had done; I from the shock and disillusion. When I left the flat the weather had changed and it was past three a.m. Abram's words ran continuously through my mind as I made my way back to the Luks. What I had learned was a terrible blow to me. Like other foreign Communists, I had looked upon the Soviet Union as a cradle of Socialism. I had known, before coming to the U.S.S.R., that conditions there were far from ideal, but I had accepted this, as we all did. It was not to be expected that a young country starting from scratch, having gone through a bloody revolution, a devastating civil war and foreign intervention lasting for years, could change into an ideal country overnight. But I had never dreamt that anything like Abram told me was possible.

My ideals seemed to be collapsing like houses of cards. When political opponents in my country had argued that there was no freedom in the U.S.S.R., that there was nothing Socialist in a country ruled by ruthless dictatorship under a form of state capitalism, I had looked on it as unfair fascist propaganda. Now I had discovered the bitter truth of what they had said. I felt like crying. I felt like a child who suddenly realises that it has for ever lost something it had longed for.

My first impulse was to pack my belongings and leave for home as soon as possible. I felt weary and sat down on a bench exhausted. I got up at once, however. My blood was pounding in my veins, and I could not sit still. I had to move, and to do something.

If only Abram could be wrong. But I knew that he had spoken the truth, that things were exactly as he had said. There was no point in shutting one's eyes to the situation.

But perhaps it was only a transitory situation? I had to find out, because perhaps after all the ideals would still have a chance. I decided that I would stay put and see.

When I reached the Luks, there were only a few hours left for sleeping. My nerves were playing havoc with me, so I decided to take a couple of *Veronal* tablets.

Before going to bed I felt it necessary to check on Abram's suspicion that there were hidden microphones in my room. I hoped that he was wrong, but, to my great dismay, found that he had been right. A microphone was neatly hidden behind the headboard of my bed, another behind the embroidered picture above my desk, and yet another in the little ante-room where the wash basin was situated in a recess.

When I went to bed I was tortured by wild dreams, and woke up several times bathed in sweat. I was haunted by G.P.U. men who accused me of being a Nazi spy. Then again I was in the hands of the Gestapo who had discovered that I was a Communist and who proved their accusation by waving my *Comintern* pass before me.

I was glad when the harsh jingling of the alarm clock bell jerked me from the horror world and into wakefulness.

CHAPTER ELEVEN

An Enemy of the People

W HEN I entered the hall of the *Mossoviet Publications Combinat* and
went to the lift to go up to my office on the third floor, I was
surprised to see a new liftman. I had got fond of the friendly
Volodya who was always ready for a joke. I knew he had been in
the Red Guards during the revolution, had fought under Budyenny
for the Soviets and had lost his left arm through a mine exploding.
His eyes always lit up when he spoke about having been praised
for his revolutionary work by the great Lenin himself, and when he
pointed to the *Order of the Red Star*, which Stalin had given him
for exceptional services. Old Volodya was a part of *Mossoviet
Publications Combinat.* I asked the new liftman where he was.

'*Nieznayu*,' was the reply.

The cloak of secrecy (for that was what I was sure it was) had
descended. I decided to try and find out for myself where Volodya
was. I didn't mention my plan to Abram. I got hold of Volodya's
address and telephone number and rang the number from a telephone kiosk. A woman's voice answered and told me that Volodya
was not in. She put the receiver down before I had the chance to
ask any further questions. It was frightening, to say the least, and
for the remainder of the day I couldn't get the liftman out of my mind.

On the way home in the evening, I walked along part of the way
with Abram. Our conversation was tight, but when he was sure
there was nobody within earshot, he said: 'They've arrested old
Volodya. They accuse him of being an enemy of the State who was
planning with others to overthrow the Government.'

I was shocked.

'What nonsense!' I said. 'Volodya, the *Old Bolshevik*, a plotter? It's ridiculous. They must realise this surely and let him go?'

'Once anybody is inside Lubyanka there is rarely a way out,' Abram shook his head. 'Lubyanka is commonly described as "the house with the strange doors which open to the inside but not to the outside." No, Bernard, I don't think we shall ever see him again.'

'Then we must *do* something,' I insisted. 'Lenin knew him. Budyenny was his commanding officer during the revolution and civil war. Stalin himself decorated him with the *Order of the Red Star*. They *must* help. They must be *notified*.'

'I've already tried,' Abram said. 'I even managed to get a message about Volodya's arrest to Budyenny and Stalin through some connections of mine. And what do you think their reaction was Bernard? They refuse to have anything to do with him! They will not interfere with the G.P.U. Nobody will.'

'But he is innocent, I am sure,' I said. 'They can't ruin an innocent man!'

'He is only one of hundreds of thousands of innocent people who are being dealt with by the G.P.U.,' Abram said.

'And his wife and children?' I asked.

'God knows,' he said. 'All we can do is to help them financially.'

The next day every employee of the *Mossoviet Publications Combinat* was ordered to attend a mass meeting. Editors and typists, printers and type-setters, office boys and canteen staff stood next to one another, listening to the speech which the Partorg delivered in a harsh voice.

'Comrades,' he began. 'Our security officers have discovered that a despicable character managed to worm his way into our midst. You all know the little liftman, Volodya, who pretended he was a devoted *bolshevik* and who even managed to deceive the highest authorities. This lowest product of the human race, this wolf in sheeps clothing, this traitor made capital out of his revolutionary past, and managed to conceal that he was on the pay-roll of the Gestapo. The ever watchful eye of our great G.P.U. could not be deceived for long, however. They caught up with him, gathered proof that not only was he spying for the Nazis but it was

F

also his task to sabotage and to plot to overthrow the Government.'

A long tirade about the outstanding work of the G.P.U. whose eyes were everywhere and who could not be deceived by anybody followed. He then went on to speak about foreign spies and saboteurs trying to do their clandestine work in the beloved Soviet Union, and stressed that it was the duty of every Soviet citizen to be most vigilant and to help the G.P.U. in their difficult task of keeping the U.S.S.R. clean of all undesirable elements.

I looked round and thought I could read disbelief on the faces of the crowd. Everybody knew Volodya, everyone liked him. To accuse and arrest this man was preposterous. As a liftman what possibilities did he have of spying or sabotage? He neither had access to the wing in which the printing works were housed, nor was he ever allowed to enter the offices which, when empty, were guarded by an armed sentry. Nobody, however, dared to mention such treacherous thoughts.

Later I heard that old Volodya had been arrested because a distant cousin of his, an engineer in Byelorussia, had been accused of sabotage in his factory. Apart from being a distant cousin there was no connection between Volodya and the engineer. In fact, the two had not been in touch for a great many years. It was, however, sufficient to be a relative of an 'undesirable.'

Volodya would not 'confess' in spite of being tortured in the cellar prison of Lubyanka. We never saw him again, nor were we officially informed as to his fate.

Before I finished that evening's work at *Vecherniaya Moskva*, news reached us that Volodya's wife had also been arrested and the children taken away to some Children's Home. The flat in which they had lived had been sealed with a big red seal of the G.P.U.

For many nights I could not find proper rest, in spite of taking sleeping tablets. I was in a daze and did my work more like an automaton than a thinking human being.

CHAPTER TWELVE

I Meet the Élite

SINCE I had started work at *Vecherniaya Moskva*, I frequently met Karl Radek—in his office at *Izvyestiya*, at the House of the Press (Soviet Journalists' Club in Moscow), at the House of the Writers (Soviet Authors' Club), and at his modern flat off Tverskoy Boulevard. He always had something interesting to say—analyse the characters and activities of Stalin and the *Politburo* members, comment on various Party and Government moves, and divulge much 'inside' information.

Karl Radek was a complicated character. He was extremely intelligent, had a unique memory and felt superior to everyone else. He was an outstanding journalist and writer, and a very fiery speaker who right from the first sentence held his audiences under his spell. But, although he had a great opinion of himself he was nevertheless a person who acknowledged ability in others. If he chose to befriend someone, he was a sincere person—provided one did not attempt to challenge his superiority.

He liked to tell anecdotes, which were always of a cynical nature. Perhaps his best-known, which was whispered all over Russia, was:

'I've heard from Josif Vissarionovich (Stalin) that he has given permission for the Kremlin to be rebuilt.'

'What are they going to do?'

'They're going to make the rooms higher.'

'What for? Everyone says that the Kremlin rooms are very high already.'

'Don't you understand? Josif Vissarionovich is growing to such tremendous heights that, if the rooms are not made higher, he will have to go about on his knees.'

Another well-known Radek anecdote, aimed against the known faulty production of Soviet manufactured articles, went as follows:

At a meeting of Soviet leaders, Mikhail Ivanovich (Kalinin, Russia's President) talked to directors of various factories and asked one of them:

'Did your factory fulfil the production plan, Comrade director?'

'We produced eighty per cent of the plan,' replied the director and added: 'But, during the next months, we hope to do much better because we have now streamlined our aircraft production.'

'And did *your* factory fulfil the production plan, Comrade director?' Kalinin then turned to another factory executive.

'Oh yes, we fulfilled our plan by a hundred-and-fifty per cent,' came the prompt reply. 'But we must still improve our output because the demand for our products greatly exceeds our production.'

'What are you producing?'

'We make cards which say BROKEN DOWN! and OUT OF ORDER!'

Radek was the author of most of the anecdotes he told, and Bukharin, who was Editor of *Izvyestiya*, liked these anecdotes so much that he had them duplicated in pamphlet form and distributed among trusted friends.

A hard worker, Radek consumed pints of strong coffee and chain-smoked while working. He also liked his food, and ate mostly at the House of the Press or the House of the Writers, both of which regularly provided excellent food in their dining rooms. Best of all he preferred to have elaborate meals at his flat, which his different mistresses prepared for him. When he tired of one mistress and installed another, he used to say: 'I got fed-up with her cooking. But I was lucky. I've found an excellent cook. You must come for supper one day, to find out that I am right.'

Drink was another thing Radek lived for. He consumed vodka, brandy, rum, and wine in large quantities, and there were many occasions when I saw him empty a two-pint bottle of vodka after dinner. But I never saw him drunk; nor did anyone else I ever met.

When explaining anything, Radek would always point his index finger in front of his listener's face. He rarely sat down when speaking, but preferred to walk about, his hands either stuck in his trouser pockets, or his thumbs anchored under his braces. He rarely accepted invitations to strictly social parties. 'I am too busy to be able to waste my time gossiping or flirting,' he used to say when rejecting a social invitation. But he seldom turned down an invitation to take part in a discussion group, regardless of whether it was during the afternoon, evening, or the early hours of the morning. And, apart from being the centre of a discussion, he also liked to focus the attention of the females on himself. He loved to score successes with women.

When he and I got to know each other better, Radek talked more freely; he spoke about Stalin and other Soviet Party and Government leaders in a way which the *Politburo* and the Secret Police would have classed as 'high treason.' His instinct seemed to assure him, however, that none of his friends would ever denounce him, and it was in fact so. When he was eventually arrested, it was not because someone had talked, his arrest was made on direct orders from Stalin because the Master of the Kremlin was determined that the time had come to silence this man who could perhaps become more dangerous to him than anyone else.

It was shortly after I first met Karl Radek and heard from him things about Stalin which, with the exception of Stalin's oldest friends, no one else knew, that I first thought of one day writing a Stalin biography. Radek had invited me to his flat for a supper which his girl-friend of the moment—the beautiful Yevgeniya Pyatakova*—had prepared for us. During the conversation after supper the theme centred on Stalin.

'Whether one agrees or disagrees with what Stalin does,' Radek said, 'one must credit him with one thing—he lives for the Party and the Party alone, and he will always do anything which he considers to be in the interests of the Party.'

'What one can't tolerate is that he commits his brutal crimes under the pretence that he acts in the interests of the Party,' Yevgeniya cut in. 'I, personally, can never forgive him for having murdered Nadiezhda.'**

*Sister of Yuriy Pyatakov—Stalin's boyhood friend and member of the Kremlin's Inner Circle.
**Stalin's second wife.

'What do you mean by saying Nadiezhda was murdered?' I said surprised. I knew, of course, that Stalin's second wife had died in November 1932, but I had always accepted the Communist Party version about her death. 'How could she have been murdered when she is supposed to have died of appendicitis?'

'What are you talking about?' Radek took over. 'You don't really believe the official Party version of Nadiezhda's death?' When I explained that I knew nothing other than the Party account he put me wise by telling me the actual facts: 'Stalin's marriage to Nadiezhda ended on the fifteenth anniversary of the Great October Revolution. At the finish of a concert, which she attended with Stalin, she learned that a fellow-student of hers had been arrested and was to be shot. As soon as they arrived back home, she demanded that Stalin give immediate orders for the release of her friend.'

Radek stood up and went across the room to his book case, and handed me Kolenov's book, *The Way To Power*, which had recently been published in Prague and Warsaw.

'Read this,' he said. 'Here you have an authentic account of what in fact took place.'

I read to my amazement:

'You dare to order me what to do, you worthless——!?' Stalin shouted, wild with rage, and using unrepeatable expressions. 'I will teach you how to speak to me! I will force you to your knees! You will be so timid that you will eat out of my hand!'

'You have taught me enough during our married life!' she shouted back. 'I have had enough of you, you tormentor! Yes, tormentor, that's what you are! You torment your own son, you torment your wife, you torment the whole Russian people! I am leaving you, I am, whether you agree or not!'

'You are over excited,' Stalin said, and went to his cabinet to fetch a drink for her. 'Here, drink this, it will soothe your nerves.'

A little later the guards outside, who had overheard every single word, heard a bump and a glass breaking. They rushed into the room. Nadiezhda was lying on the floor—looking very beautiful in the black dress which she had worn at the concert. 'How do you know Kolenov wrote the truth and was not merely trying to throw mud on Stalin in order to discredit him?' I asked, returning the book to Radek.

'I heard exactly the same version from Mekhlis, Pauker, Redens, and several others,' Radek replied. Before I could make any comment, he added: 'I hope you won't query the reliability of these men because it would mean that you doubt the honesty and integrity of both Stalin's private secretaries and closest confidents, and of his brother-in-law.'

Radek was obviously eager to acquaint me with all the facts of the Nadiezhda Alliluyeva-Stalin mystery.

'The cause of her death was kept secret, and it was rumoured that she had been killed in a car crash,' he went on. 'Then it was stated that she had died of appendicitis. Finally it was announced that she had been very ill. Not one of these rumours and announcements was convincing because too many people had seen her alive and healthy at the concert half an hour before her death. Stalin then spread the story that his wife had been sick and in spite of doctor's orders had ventured out too soon, resulting in the return of her illness and in her death.

'She was given a state funeral on the 11th of November. Stalin walked behind the bier all the way from Red Square to the ancient cemetery of the New Maiden Monastery where she was buried not far from the graves of the first wife of Tsar Peter the Great, his sister Sofia, and many others of the old Russian nobility.'

Radek re-filled our glasses with vodka and added cynically:

'Stalin managed to put on a magnificent performance for the Russian people—they were convinced that he was a mourning husband and grief-stricken man. But, as soon as he returned to the seclusion of the Kremlin, he went to a party which was already in full swing. I was there, and heard him cracking jokes and laughing, and dancing as if nothing had happened. Nadiezhda was buried— this chapter of his life was closed as far as he was concerned. The Man of Steel had no time for tears or mourning but he had time to persuade a pretty young typist of the Central Committee to spend the night with him.'

The unknown parts of Stalin's life was one of Radek's pet

subjects, and realising that at that time I knew only the idealised official Soviet biography version of Stalin, he spoke at length about how Koba* had committed burglaries to provide the *bolshevik* movement of Tsarist times with printing presses; how he organised brothels and protection rackets to fill the coffers of the Party; and how he had carried out the daring Tiflis Treasury robbery to finance the revolutionary cadres. He also told me that Stalin was perhaps the best toxicologist in the world, and he dwelt at length on Stalin's experiments with all sorts of poisons. This knowledge Stalin thus gleaned he afterwards used in order to rid himself of various comrades and friends who stood in his way.

Some of Radek's fascinating and intriguing facts about Stalin seemed to me so incredible that I suspected exaggeration and invention. But when I later spoke with Madame Lunacharsky, Mekhlis, Nadiezhda Krupskaya, Yuriy Pyatakov, Sergo Ordzhonikidze, Mikhail Kalinin, Rosa Kaganovich-Stalin, Abel Yenukidze, and many other people close to Stalin, they all told me in different words the very same facts about Stalin.

*   *   *

Yevgeniya Pyatakova loved Radek and even when their affaire came to an end and he made the pretty Pioneer-leader Musya Chernikhova her successor, she remained his sincere friend. Through her I met Madame Lunacharsky, the widow of Soviet Russia's first Peoples' Commissar for Education and, at her flat, got to know several leading Soviet intellectuals and politicians.

Madame Lunacharsky, a lady of great charm and intelligence, held weekly discussion groups in her flat, which was situated in the corner house of Trubnaya Square and B-Boulevard. These were attended by top people and were commonly known in Moscow as Madame Lunacharsky's Teas. Yet, although much 'inside information' was divulged at these discussions and much was said that the Secret Police would class 'anti-Kremlin attacks' or possibly even 'high treason,' it would be wrong to assume that Madame Lunacharsky's teas were a centre of the anti-Stalin or anti-Soviet

*Stalin's pre-revolutionary *nom de plume*.

opposition. It was just that articulate and intelligent people met periodically for the free exchange of ideas, information and opinions.

As far as I was concerned, Madame Lunacharsky's teas were a happy hunting ground for learning the truth about many things, and meeting Party and Government personalities as well as many leading Soviet intellectuals. Some of them eventually invited me to their homes. I always chose my words carefully so that no one could ever denounce me to the Partorg or the Secret Police. I always remembered Abram's warning words and, although I sometimes reproached myself for the life that I was living, I realised that this was the only way to survive.

The most important political top-brass who regularly attended Madame Lunacharsky's teas was Lev Mekhlis—Stalin's closest collaborator and confidant. Almost from the moment I first met him, a friendship developed between us and, throughout my stay in Russia, we met regularly.

The great Mekhlis was only 5 ft 5 in, but somehow he seemed to be taller. He had an interesting face with intelligent brown eyes, and was a likeable fellow who had the gift of being able to tell any story in an amusingly sarcastic manner. He was rapidly going bald at that time, but Stalin's private secretary Pauker secured for him a toupée from Paris, which he wore to impress the 'weaker sex.' Always afraid that the wig would move and give his secret away, he kept his right hand close by, pretending he was smoothing it down.

Mekhlis was a real man about town—very fond of gay parties. He was a good dancer, successful with women, and was known for having innumerable love affairs. He was interested in literature, theatre, film, and music. Among his friends were Eisenstein, Gorky, Mayerkhold, Tolstoy, and other famous Russian intellectuals. His closest friend was Mikhoels, leading actor and director at the Jewish State Theatre in Moscow and, being close to Stalin, and therefore powerful, he saw to it that *Pravda* and other newspapers published excellent reviews of Mikhoel's performances.

A typical example of the lengths Mekhlis would go in supporting a friend was the occasion when Mikhoels planned to stage

Shakespeare's *King Lear*. Kaganovich, Molotov, and other *Politburo* members criticised Mikhoels for choosing a 'reactionary' play, and tried to stop the production. Realising that he alone would not be powerful enough to avert the danger that threatened his friend, Mekhlis secured Stalin's support with the result that Mikhoels was allowed to carry on. And when the reviews were enthusiastic as well, *King Lear* settled down to a long run.

Mekhlis was never involved in a scandal and always managed to remain friends with his former mistresses. Like the other Kremlin dignitaries he was also a natural show-off, but somehow this weak point in his character was not so obvious and hateful as it was in some others. Probably because he was well-mannered and jovial.

★   ★   ★

Another man I met at Madame Lunacharsky's teas was Klim Voroshilov—the Peoples' Commissar for Defence. He was a great bore who had only one topic of conversation—how the *bolsheviks* had fought during the revolution and the civil war. His pet subject was the fight for Tsaritsin,★ and, due to the fact that he repeated his long narrative so often, we knew his story almost word for word.

Although Voroshilov was a devoted supporter of Stalin, he nevertheless criticised his master—especially when drunk. He would try to convince his listeners that Stalin had made many fatal mistakes during the fight for Tsaritsin and that he, Voroshilov, had been the actual but unacclaimed brain behind the *Bolshevik* successes. The ex-blacksmith Voroshilov had neither the intelligence nor sufficient strategic knowledge to direct military operations—the *bolshevik* successes at Tsaritsin were the work of a number of ex-Tsarist officers. So nobody believed Voroshilov's story—it was too stupid to be accepted.

Voroshilov always wore his uniform and always kept his cap on. However, when thinking, or when put off balance by an unexpected question during discussion, he would take his cap off with his right hand and, still holding the hat, scratch his head with the same hand. Then he would replace the cap and continue speaking.

★Later Stalingrad and now Volgograd.

He was a very heavy drinker who usually consumed vast quantities of vodka. Although he was accustomed to drinking, there were several occasions when he had to be carried out, singing and swearing.

I remember one particular occasion during a function at the House of the Writers when Voroshilov drank almost non-stop. Those around him noticed that he had said too much, and arranged for caviare with chopped raw onions and eggs★ to be brought. As soon as the dish was placed before him, he put his hand into it and stuffed the caviare into his tunic pocket. His friends tried to carry him out but he became violent, swore and fought. When he was at last overpowered and taken out, the organisers warned all of us not to speak about what had happened, if we wished to avoid trouble. But a few days later, when I attended Rosa's Salons, everyone who had been at the House of the Writers was asked for details. The news had already travelled.

Voroshilov himself let it be known that he did not find social parties enjoyable. If he came to any gathering, he was merely interested in plenty of vodka and pretty women. And, as soon as he thought he had had enough to drink, and having picked out a woman to his liking, he left. The woman invariably left with him, or shortly afterwards.

Stalin and the other Kremlin dignitaries considered Voroshilov a valuable propaganda show-piece and useful *Politburo* member simply because he blindly supported everything the Master of the Kremlin and his confidants planned and suggested. Soviet propaganda had therefore built up Voroshilov as an 'outstanding military leader.' He looked good in his uniform and was popular with the public. His private life was, of course, kept a well-guarded secret from the masses.

★   ★   ★

I found that I was soon accepted as one of the circle because of my attendances at the Teas. Aleksey Tolstoy, the then top Soviet writer, for instance, invited me to spend my free day at his country

---

★The Russians use this if someone has had too much vodka, because it absorbs the alcohol and quickly revives the drunk.

villa; and the Soviet composer Dunayevsky, the famous theatre producer Mayerkhold, and other equally prominent figures of the Soviet intelligentsia insisted I stayed at their homes too. Before long, I was able to mingle freely with the Soviet élite—thanks to Madame Lunacharsky.

I had made friends with Mark Kolosov, editor of the publishing house *Molodaya Gvardiya*. When I submitted the contracted script of my book, he suggested I should approach Lenin's widow, Nadiezhda Krupskaya, to write a Preface. Madame Lunacharsky arranged the appointment, and I met Krupskaya at her modest flat in a delapidated house a stonesthrow from the *Comintern* in Makhovaya Street.

Lenin's widow was frail with grey hair and very lively eyes, and in spite of her advanced years, was still very attractive. I was amazed to find her living in a dingy flat, furnished with a few ramshackle items.

As if she had read my thoughts, Krupskaya said that she had not chosen the ugly furniture, nor the hovel of a flat, and stressed that the Housing Committee was responsible for all this. She added that someone in a very high position must have thought that by forcing her to live like this, he would punish her for having opposed certain Kremlin leaders when fighting for her rights during Lenin's illness, and after his death.

I was not really surprised that, having only just met me, she told me all this as a sort of introduction. It was commonly known in Moscow that Krupskaya was an outspoken and fearless woman, saying without hesitation what was in her mind. She never concealed her hatred for Stalin and, although her pointed attacks were sometimes harmful to him, he nevertheless dared not to order the Secret Police to make 'the brainless shrew,' as he called her, disappear. Nadiezhda Krupskaya was too much a symbol of Leninism with the Russian people and several top Kremlin dignitaries. If anything had happened to her, it could have been the start to a nationwide upset which would have dangerously cracked the foundations of the Communist Party and the Soviet Government.

A few days after our first meeting she telephoned me at *Vecherniaya Moskva*, saying she had read the script, approved it, had written a preface, and invited me to have tea with her.

Nadiezhda Krupskaya had a very alert brain and a great sense of humour. Although she liked to talk in detail about her life with Lenin, and about the part they both had played in the struggle for world revolution, she did not live in the past. Holding the function of Head of the Soviet Children's Movement, she kept in touch with the younger generation saying that it kept her young.

A valuable friendship developed between us, and during my numerous visits to her flat I gleaned many unknown details about Stalin and other Soviet leaders. Krupskaya had a remarkable memory. She had a priceless collection of Lenin's notes which he had made about his close comrades, and a great number of letters from pre-revolutionary *bolshevik* leaders. She had also managed to save the first editions of Lenin's works which contained all those passages that had been ruthlessly deleted from later editions, because they revealed too much about the real Stalin.

'I wonder how long these historic documents will be preserved,' she said one day in a matter-of-fact tone. 'Every time I come back to my flat after an outing, I expect to find it burgled . . .'

'Perhaps they don't know that you keep everything here,' I remarked.

'They know,' she said. 'Not once, but several times, Vissarionovich sent word to me to let him have everything. He even offered me money and an adequate flat, and when I persisted in refusing, what did he do? He ordered that I be sacked from my post as lecturer at Moscow University, because he wanted me to live on my pension of a hundred and fifty roubles a month—less than half of what a factory worker earns. But he does not dare to order the *State Publishing House* to keep my books out of print, or instruct the journals and newspapers to reject my articles, because he knows that it would create unrest among the people. So I am still able to live decently.'

The only Kremlin top-brass who came to visit Krupskaya regularly was Vyacheslav Molotov.

It was during one of my visits that I first met Molotov, and on this occasion I learned that his father, who was a second cousin of the famous Russian composer Skriabin, had shared his schooldays with Al Jolson's father, who later emigrated to the United States and became the well-known Rabbi Moses Jolson.

Molotov, usually dressed in a well-cut dark suit, looked more like a Western school teacher than a Russian *bolshevik* leader. His dark hair was neatly brushed and his moustache carefully trimmed. He had penetrating eyes, which he fixed on me whenever he said anything to me.

He never engaged in lengthy or frank conversations with me. Even in merry, social surroundings, he was always reserved. It was difficult to make contact with him. But when he felt inclined to converse for a few minutes, it was amazing how knowledgeable he proved to be on almost every subject. And, speaking quite slowly, he almost managed to conceal his slight stammer.

The easiest way to secure Molotov's company was to suggest a chess match—provided he considered the challenger a worthwhile opponent. Chess was his great hobby and he was an excellent player. His eagerness for this game was such that if he attended some gay party and spotted someone whom he knew to be a good chess player, he retreated with him to some quiet corner and seemed to forget all the others round him. Another hobby of Molotov's was music; he was a great admirer of Beethoven, Mozart, Schubert and Tchaikovsky.

I was never so friendly with Molotov as to be invited to *his* flat in the Kremlin which was next to Stalin's. But from Mekhlis I knew that Stalin and Molotov hardly ever went to each other's flats—they preferred to discuss Party and other matters in Stalin's private office. Radek claimed that Molotov, who created the impression that he was a family man and devoted husband, had many love affairs with pretty artistes with whom he spent much time at his dacha near Moscow.

One day, when Molotov had left after his usual short visit to her flat, Krupskaya said about him:

'Sometimes I can't help feeling sorry for Mikhailovich. There's no doubt that he has one of the finest brains in the Kremlin, but where does it get him? Ever since he met Vissarionovich and was dragged under his spell, all he has been allowed to do is play second fiddle to him. But mark my words, the time is bound to come when the worm will turn.'

Pouring out two fresh glasses of tea from the steaming *samovar*, Krupskaya continued:

'Vissarionovich has taught Mikhailovich everything—deceit, toxicology, and much else besides. I hope I'll live to see the day when Mikhailovich sees daylight and makes use of Vissarionovich's own weapons for doing away with him.

'Already at school Mikhailovich's pet subject was mathematics, and in later life his political moves and chess games resembled mathematical calculations. One day it must dawn on him that if he applies the same mathematically calculated surprise moves which he makes during a game of chess, he can relieve the Russian people of their tormentor.'

Nadiezhda Krupskaya's prediction proved to be right—it was Molotov who was responsible for Stalin's death in March 1953. But, unfortunately, Krupskava did not live to see her prophecy come true.

CHAPTER THIRTEEN

The University of Communism

ONE morning the Luks duty officer handed me a grey coloured envelope with my name typed on it. Recognising it as coming from the *Comintern*, I opened it and read it at once.

Take notice that you are requested to appear at the offices of the *Comintern* on July 26, 1934, at 10 o'clock in the forenoon.

You are to bring this letter with you and hand it to the officer on duty, and you are also to take special notice to appear at the time stated.

D. M. Manuilsky.

At first I thought that I had read it wrong for the letter, which was undated, requested me to appear at the *Comintern* in just under two hours. I had to be at *Vecherniaya Moskva* at that time, and, as it happened, my presence that morning was essential, for I had to select contributions in foreign languages, and there was no one else there who could do this. On the other hand the letter was signed by the head of the *Comintern*, which meant that I *had* to be there.

I went back to the duty officer and asked him when the letter arrived for me, suspecting that it had been there for some days and that they had forgotten to give it to me, which would have been nothing unusual in the Luks. He assured me, however, that it had been delivered by a despatch rider a little while before.

When I telephoned my editor to tell him about my summons, he was furious and shouted into the telephone:

'What do they think they're doing? You have your duties to

Vecherniaya Moskva, Bernard Frederickovich; you know that the Press Department asked us to publish more foreign material.'

I explained I had only just received the summons, and I read the letter out to him. He started to swear and I suggested he should communicate with the Press Department and ask them to arrange a postponement with Manuilsky. He did not like the idea, however, especially as he knew that technically the head of the *Comintern* was above the Press Department, so he advised me to go to the *Comintern* but to do my utmost to get back to the office as quickly as possible, promising that he would send a car there so that no unnecessary time would be wasted in travelling.

At the *Comintern* I handed the letter to the duty officer, and was escorted to an office on the first floor. It was a fair-sized room the windows of which afforded a view over Red Square. Dmitriy Manuilsky was sitting at a table covered with a red cloth, on the ends of which were busts of Lenin and Stalin. Next to the head of the *Comintern* were my section leader Birne and a man whom I had never seen before, dressed in a khaki tunic covered with all kinds of decorations. The three of them sat with their back towards the windows.

'When did you join the Party?' Manuilsky asked me straight away.

'In April 1932,' I replied.

'You are a very young member,' Manuilsky continued.

I decided to play the innocent. 'Yes, I am twenty-three,' I said.

'I know your age,' he snapped. 'I referred to your Party membership.' He consulted a file in front of him and went on: 'Before you became a member of the Party you were a member of *Komsomol*?'

'No,' I corrected him. 'I never joined the *Komsomol*.'

'Why not?'

'At that time,' I replied, remembering the argument Abram had used when being pressed to join the Party, 'I did not think myself worthy of joining the *Komsomol*. First I wanted to study Marx and Engels, Lenin and Stalin . . .'

'Did you do that?'

'Yes. I went to the *Marxist Workers' School*.'

'Would you say that you have a fair Marxist education?'

G

'I still have a lot to learn,' I said non-committally.

Manuilsky's cold eyes were fixed on me. 'The Central Committee of the Party regarded you as a worthy member and sent you to the U.S.S.R.,' the head of the *Comintern* continued.

I did not make any comment.

'We are watching your activities as a journalist and a writer,' he continued. 'You are successful—you are quite well known by now. But don't think that you are of any importance and that you can do what you please. Success is not everything. There is one thing, and one thing only, that matters: fullest devotion to the Party and the most orthodox discipline.'

I said that that was how I too felt.

'You have always to remember that a *bolshevik* must not be conceited,' he said. 'You still have a lot to learn and I only hope that you realise this.'

'I do,' I said and continued to play 'Dialectical Materialism' as well as I could. 'I utilise much of my spare time to study the works of Lenin and Stalin, and I have also started to study Yaroslavky's *History of the V.K.P.B.*'

'I am pleased to hear that,' Manuilsky replied. For the first time his voice sounded friendlier. 'Why don't you sit down?' he said and consulted his file once more. Without looking up, he asked me: 'What would you say if we sent you to a course at *Lenin School*?'

'If the Party considers that I deserve the best political education, I will prove that their trust has not been misplaced,' I said, using Abram's tactics.

'It has been decided that you will attend *Lenin School*,' Manuilsky continued. 'However, we do not wish to put *Vecherniaya Moskva* into an awkward situation, so we have decided that you will attend the evening classes.'

He still had a lot to say but I finally left with instructions to report to the secretary general of *Lenin School* at 19.00 hours on the 31st July 1934. Birne and the other man had not said a single word all the time but shook hands with me, and wished me success, after Manuilsky had done so.

★   ★   ★

I reported dead on time at *Lenin School*, which was a few steps from Arbat Square. It was housed in a large building not easily seen from outside because of a high stone wall around the grounds. Those who passed the entrance had no idea what this building was, as there was no plate or sign to indicate that this was the world-famous *Lenin School*. The fact that there was an armed guard outside gave no clue either, as it was a common sight to see guards watching unimportant buildings in the U.S.S.R.

One of the guards took me into the building and I was shown into the room where I was to meet Comrade Lebediev, Commandant of the school. Lenin's slogan, in large white letters on a red background, was on the wall. BOLSHEVIKS ARE SOLDIERS OF THE REVOLUTION! it said.

A number of people of both sexes were already assembled. The only one I knew was Beatrice Georgovna.

'You're quite a stranger,' said Beatrice in a cordial way. 'Haven't seen you for quite a time.'

'I am still about at the Luks,' I replied, 'but I am extremely busy.'

At that moment Lebediev entered. He was a tall broad-shouldered man with clearcut features and brown hair beginning to grey at the temples. He was dressed in an embroidered Russian shirt-blouse, hanging over his G.P.U. trousers which were tucked into black leather jackboots. He lost no time in addressing us:

'Comrade Party members, I am pleased to see that the Executive Committee of the Communist International has decided to send you to attend our courses and it gives me great satisfaction to find that many more of you have been selected than anticipated. This is an extremely wise decision of Comrade Manuilsky who, having consulted our great teacher and leader, our beloved Josif Vissariono-vich Stalin, decided to send every suitable comrade to these important courses so as to be certain that as many fully schooled Party members as possible are available for leading functions in most of the countries of the world. I therefore propose a toast to our great teacher and leader, our beloved Josif Vissarionovich Stalin.'

We all shouted 'Long live Comrade Stalin! Long live Comrade

Manuilsky!' When the shouting was over we all sang the Internationale.

Lebediev then told us that we would have to attend the school
every third evening at 19.00 hours, regardless of whether it was
anyone's free day or not. Our first lesson would commence on the
3rd August, the next one would be on the 6th, and so on. He made
it clear that we were to attend punctually and were not allowed to
miss a single lesson, as there was a *Comintern* ruling that this schooling
had preference over any other Party activities. He also told us that
the duration of the schooling was estimated to last about eighteen
months and that the greatest specialists, such as Manuilsky, Radek,
and other leading members of the Party—not forgetting some outstanding members of foreign Parties—would deliver lectures. At
the end of his speech he expressed his conviction that the schooling
would bear rich fruits, and that it would be one of the stepping
stones to *bolshevik* revolutions in many capitalist countries.

After Lebediev had finished his speech, his elderly secretary
Simonova, who told us that she had been a friend of Lenin, and was
also a great friend of his wife Nadiezhda Krupskaya, informed us
that we all had to be registered. Her assistant, a pretty young girl,
handed out detailed questionnaires which we had to fill in then and
there. Over a hundred questions had to be answered. It seemed to
me a ridiculous waste of time, as all these details were already known
to the *Comintern*. Before we were allowed to leave, little passes
with our photographs, bound in red cloth, were handed to us with
the warning that we had to take the utmost care of them since it
would be regarded a most serious crime to lose or mislay them.

In a way I was annoyed that for the next eighteen months I would
have to attend *Lenin School* every third evening. On the other
hand, I now had the opportunity of getting fully acquainted with
the moves and tactics of the Executive Committee of the Communist International. I knew, of course, that *Lenin School* in Moscow
provided the Communist Parties all over the world with their highest
level executives and that its pupils formed the Central Committees
of the foreign Communist Parties. I also knew that when the courses
were finished and the students were due to return to their countries,

a special selection was made resulting in some remaining in the service of the *Comintern* to work as special links between the Executive Committee and the Central Committees of the foreign Parties. They also had to travel from country to country and to act as special *Comintern* instructors. Exactly how this was practised, however, I did not know, and I was glad to have the opportunity of finding out.

★ ★ ★

It was one of the greatest experiences I have ever had. *Lenin School* exceeded the estimated eighteen months and did not finish before the end of April 1936. The aim was to acquaint us with the complete history of the international revolutionary movement, to teach us revolutionary strategy, and to prepare us for leadership of revolutions in capitalist countries. Some of the lectures which—as Lebediev had promised—were delivered by the 'best brains of international Communism,' were most interesting and valuable. Because of my previous attendance at the *Marxist Workers' School*, I had a fair knowledge of the history of the revolution and I discovered that at *Lenin School* the famous lecturers omitted historical happenings which did not suit their purposes, and in some cases even indulged in inaccuracies in order to paint the picture they wanted. There were others, beside me, who were aware of this, but they were 'dialectical materialists' and made a mental note to accept the version taught at the University of Communism as the official one.

Russian *Bolsheviks* always regarded themselves as the most experienced avant-gardes on World Communism. They had proved this by turning Tsarist Russia into a Union of Soviet Socialist Republics.

Strategy and Tactics was designed to teach us how to behave in times of underground activity. We would be able to continue our *bolshevik* activities even under the most difficult conditions, provided we worked right, our lecturer stated. He was the well-known Smirnov who had taken an active and leading part in the 1917 revolution in St. Petersburg and who from then onwards had held a high position in the U.S.S.R.

'Comrades,' Smirnov addressed us one evening, 'the most important thing for a *bolshevik* is to be ready for any situation. Only then can you complete the most difficult task and deceive your enemies. What would you do if the Party in your country was illegal, you were on your way to meet another important comrade who was not known to the Fascist secret police, and you discovered that a detective was trailing you?.'

'I would try to shake off the detective,' answered Gavrilovitch, a Yugoslav delegate.

'Excellent,' Smirnov exclaimed. 'How would you do it?'

'I would jump onto a passing tram. If the detective did the same, I would jump off at some cross-roads and disappear.'

'Very good—provided that a tram came along the street. But what would you do if it was a little side street where there is no traffic at all?'

'I would run as fast as I could and try to get away.'

'And what if the detective runs faster than you?'

'I would try to hide somewhere and do everything possible so that he would not find me.'

'That is no good, Comrade,' Smirnov criticised. 'Remember, you must meet your contact. You know him by sight but you don't know his name or where you can find him if you miss him. Only when you meet will you arrange when and where you meet next. It is of the utmost importance that you keep in touch with one another. On the other hand you must not lead the police to him.' He looked up and asked: 'What would you do?'

'That's difficult to say,' replied my compatriot Bremer. 'I think this depends on the circumstances. Sometimes one has to make one's decision on the spur of the moment.'

'That's a good answer. Yes, a *bolshevik* has always to make his decision on the spur of the moment if need be,' Smirnov confirmed. 'However, your answer is not fully satisfactory. You are walking along an ordinary street where there is nothing unusual. No traffic, no cross roads, only two rows of houses. What would you do in such a situation, Comrades?'

'You say that the comrade I am to meet must not be disclosed to the police under any circumstances, that the police don't know who he is and want me to lead them to him?' Seidler, a German delegate, repeated. When Smirnov nodded, Seidler went on: 'If I satisfy myself that I cannot shake off the detective then I must do something drastic to save this important comrade. When I see him approaching in the distance, walking among other passers by, I make sure he sees me. But before he gets the chance of disclosing his identity, I jump under a passing car or lorry. He is then warned and the police will still not know who he is as there are many other people on the pavement. He can then use the commotion to get away safely.'

'Very heroic indeed,' Smirnov praised the German. 'However, what a waste of a valuable life! No, Comrade, your plan is no good. We need every experienced *bolshevik* and can't afford to weaken our ranks with unnecessary heroism.' He looked up and said triumphantly: 'There is a much simpler answer to the problem. I once was in a similar position in 1908 in St. Petersburg. I found the solution on the spur of the moment. I did not have to kill myself to warn my comrade. I shook the *Okhrana* agent off and was then able to meet my comrade and arrange our next *rendezvous*.'

Everybody was eager to hear how this famous figure of the Russian revolution had done this.

'When I realised there was no chance of running away, I began to think hard,' Smirnov went on. 'Suddenly I saw that decorators were busy on one of the houses. Quickly I dashed into the yard, took some of the chalk and put it on my hair which I quickly arranged the way the peasants wore it. My dark hair was now grey and I picked up a stick in the yard and walked into the street with a bent back, pretending to be an old peasant.' He looked at us triumphantly and concluded: 'You see, Comrades, there is always a solution to every problem! I managed to shake off the *Okhrana* agent and to meet my comrade.'

We were all disappointed with the great solution. We had expected something brilliant. Bremer pointed out that this method was doubtless an excellent one in the times of the primitive Tsarist Russia, but in our country it would not do because the present day secret police were not such stupid *muzhiks* as the old time *Okhrana* agents. Though Bremer had actually said what all of us thought, Smirnov was obviously offended.

'I will not have any stupid criticism from anybody,' he said testily. 'If you don't want to listen and to accept what you are taught in this institution, then don't come here.' He puffed at his *papiros* and continued in an angry voice: 'Won't work? How ridiculous! My method was copied in Belgrade and Vienna, and successfully too. You wouldn't know—you were probably still in your cradle.'

My rebuked compatriot attempted to pacify Smirnov, and pointed out Lenin's teaching that 'life is discussion.' However, this only made matters worse. Smirnov threatened him that should he ever dare to criticise anything else he would not last long at the University of Communism. Nobody guessed then that this was actually the beginning of Bremer's sad end in the Soviet Union.

This lecture, though delivered by one of the most famous leaders of the Russian revolution, was not a typical example of the generally high standard of the courses. Manuilsky, for instance, lectured on the work *Comintern* instructors, whose job it was to travel all over the world to supervise the campaigns of the Central Committees of the various Communist Parties. He spoke at great length and was most emphatic about the necessity of every *Comintern* instructor being fully versed in Marxist-Leninist-Stalinist theory, as well as being a perfect master of strategy.

During the many evenings which this lecture lasted, Manuilsky confronted us with all kinds of situations which had arisen in the past, and advocated the study of every mistake which had been made so that these could not recur. He was a very good speaker who chose his examples cleverly and succeeded in making his lectures most interesting. At the end he disclosed technical difficulties with which the *Comintern* was faced when sending their instructors into the capitalist world.

'One of our greatest problems is the question of passports,' he told us. 'Most of our instructors, like Georgi Dimitrov, Fritz Geminder, Anna Pauker, Herta Kuuzinen, and many others, are, unfortunately, known by name to the police forces in the capitalist world and cannot, therefore, travel under their own identities. Of course, they can enter foreign countries as harmless students, tourists, or business people, but to be able to do so they must have proper passports. Naturally, Soviet passports cannot be used. We could, of course, print foreign passports in the U.S.S.R. but this is not entirely satisfactory. First of all, there is the question of making the paper, then there is the difficulty of perfectly forging signatures. Thirdly—and this is the most important point—there is the numbering of the passports. If for one or another reason a mistake were to be made, the security police of the country concerned might detect it and that would mean the end of the instructor. This we cannot risk.'

Manuilsky said that the secret police of all foreign countries worked closely together, especially when their activities were directed against *Comintern* instructors. He stated that the *Comintern* too had people in the police forces, and even in some Ministries, Consulates, Legations, and Embassies. These people managed from time to time to obtain blank passports, but not enough. He concluded:

'We utilise the passports of those comrades who have come to work at the *Comintern* and which have not been marked by our frontier commandants. On these the entry visas into the U.S.S.R. are not entered into the passport but are given on separate sheets of paper. These passports are so-called 'clean ones,' and all we have to do when using them for any of our instructors is to take out the photograph of the owner and replace it with the one of the instructor who is to use it. We have specialists who are able to put that part of the rubber stamp which was on the photograph of the real owner on to the photograph of the instructor. Nobody is able to detect the doctoring.'

I failed to understand the reason for all this. If any one of my compatriots needed a passport but could not, or did not want to, apply for one in his own name, all he had to do was to get someone else's documents. There were always plenty of comrades or sympathisers ready to oblige the Party. The passport was then issued in the name of the person whose documents had been submitted, but the photograph used was that of the person who actually wanted the document. Of course, I did not say anything of that because it might have been to my disadvantage to appear that I knew more than Manuilsky.

★   ★   ★

The last part of the course was our training as saboteurs, organisers of strikes, and disturbances. Colonel Norkyn, an explosives expert, taught us how to use dynamite and other explosives, how to assess the amount to be used, and how to fix and detonate it. Marshal Budyenny lectured on how to organise and lead armed riots, how to fight in streets, and how to storm buildings and other strongholds. The well-known Sergo Ordzhonikidze★ lectured on *Dialectical Materialism* and did his utmost to train us to be as flexible and as adaptable as possible, and to be ready to take up leading *Comintern* positions.

★   ★   ★

When all the lectures had come to an end, we had to undergo oral and written examinations. The examinations lasted six evenings of nearly five hours each, and the problems set were from the previous twenty one months study. Like all examinations, this one was a fierce ordeal. The fact that none of us were full-time students made it all the harder.

Finally the last evening arrived. This they called the parting evening. We were now to hear the result of the examinations. This was supposed to be a festive affair.

The head of the *Comintern*, Dmitriy Manuilsky, presided and made a long speech about the importance of the course. He then expressed his thanks to 'our great and wise leader, our beloved Josif Vissarionovich Stalin' for having given us the opportunity of taking part in such an important and historical event.

Afterwards Lebediev, in his capacity as commandant of *Lenin School*, announced the results. To my great surprise, I had 'passed with honours.' (Out of fifty eight students, eleven had passed with honours, thirty three had passed outright, eight were allowed to

★With Stalin, Ordzhonikidze had organised *bolshevik* resistance in Tiflis about thirty-five years before, and was one of Stalin's closest friends, a leading member of the *Politburo*, and People's Commissar for Heavy Industry.

take another examination, and the remaining six had failed.) Lebediev considered the results 'fairly good.' Quite a good dinner was served afterwards, yet it was spoilt by the long speeches our ex-lecturers thought it their duty to deliver.

The festivities ended with dancing and drinking right up to the early hours of the morning.

When at last I walked back to the Luks at day-break on that April morning in 1936 I realised that much of what I had learned at the University of Communism would help me to keep out of trouble during my stay in the U.S.S.R. I would use their own methods against the N.K.V.D.—the methods I had spent nearly two years learning.

CHAPTER FOURTEEN

The Turning of the Tide?

IN the late summer of 1934 several serious changes had taken place in the U.S.S.R. It was announced, for instance, that the G.P.U. had ceased to exist and that its activities had been taken over by the N.K.V.D. Everywhere I heard the opinion expressed that the news about the terrible activities of the G.P.U. must have reached Stalin's ears, and that he had terminated their reign of brutality and terror by decreeing that the N.K.V.D. take over. 'From now on everything will take a turn for the better,' many predicted.

As if to confirm the view of the masses that a new era was being ushered in, a shop at the corner of Gorky Street and Soviet Square was opened over night. They named it *Gastronom*.

It was like a miracle. The newly decorated *Gastronom* shop was full of all sorts of food, its windows for once used for displaying goods, and not as a repository of flags and political pictures.

People flocked to this shop by the hundred to look at the loaves of white bread, the big blocks of fresh butter, whole hams and all the other foods. But who could afford to pay ten roubles for a small loaf of white bread,* fifty roubles for a pound of ham, or sixty roubles for a pound of butter? A skilled worker earned between 145 and 350 roubles gross per month. His net income was considerably lower. Nevertheless, the Muscovites were happy to be able at least to *look* at the food even if they could not afford to buy it. Long queues formed and old and young streamed into the wonder shop to see for themselves.

Shortly afterwards a new cafe, *Krasnyi Mak*, was opened in the

*About eighteen times as much as black bread from their local bakery.

little square behind Bolshoi Theatre. This café was in striking contrast to the dirty little places all over the capital. *Krasnyi Mak* was a cosy, and well-decorated place. The community of foreign journalists and writers, composers and conductors, artists, scientists, doctors and other intellectuals made it their second home. Though only light refreshments were served at high prices, it was very pleasant to sit there, to read the paper or to meet English, French, German, and other well-known figures of the Communist intelligentsia.

Soon the *Gastronom* at the corner of the Soviet Square, and the *Krasnyi Mak*, behind the Bolshoi Theatre, were not the only places of their kind.

A few hundred yards from the first *Gastronom* another one was established, opposite Luks. *Café Moskva*, at the corner of Gorky Street and Tverskoy Boulevard was opened. It had ultra-modern chromium steel arm-chairs with beige upholstery and round tables with black glass tops. It was possible to get a good Vienna *Schnitzel*, a rump steak, a Georgian *Shashlik* and similar dishes there. One could even order a glass of quite good coffee—an unusual treat for it was impossible at that time to get coffee anywhere else in Moscow. At about the same time another *Gastronom* was opened between *Café Moskva* and the Luks. This was the biggest food store in Moscow and was housed in the once exclusive Yelisseyev Store where the Tsarist nobility used to shop.

Gradually prices began to tumble. Butter, for instance, which only a short while before had cost sixty roubles a pound, went down to fifty, thirty-five, twenty, and finally ranged between sixteen and twenty according to quality. The shops opened at 9 o'clock in the morning and stayed open until 10 or 11 o'clock at night. Some stayed open all night. The shops were always crowded, and people spent every spare rouble they had on food.

Wherever I went, in factories or offices, I heard people speak of their hopes that the tide was now turning in the U.S.S.R. Muscovites saw a tremendous improvement in conditions with more and more food reaching the shops, even before the harvest had been brought in. This, and the abolition of the hated G.P.U., was, as most of them thought, the first stepping stone to a free and real Socialist life . . .

CHAPTER FIFTEEN

Stalin's Third Wife

AFTER the poisoning death of Stalin's second wife, Nadiezhda, a new woman appeared on the scene who was the cause of much speculation and much gossip. Foreign newspapers wanted to know who she was, and when they found out, they wanted to know whether she and Stalin were married. Moscow correspondents tried to find out by every means known to them. They always ran against a wall of silence. Certain of their Russian colleagues knew the story, and could have told it. But for some reason or other, Stalin clamped secrecy on the facts of his third marriage. He forbade the official Soviet photo agency, *Soyuzfoto*, to release photographs of the woman; and whenever he attended a function, though she too was there, her name never appeared in reports.

Her name was Rosa Kaganovich. She *was* Stalin's third wife.

But lest any of the foregoing give the impression that Rosa Kaganovich-Stalin lived the life of a recluse, let me say at once that nothing could be further from the truth. I got to know her well, and, through her, met Stalin himself on a great number of occasions. You may have noticed I did not claim to have got to *know* Stalin; I don't think *anyone* got to know Stalin.

But, to go back, when Rosa first appeared (and she was seen by many a diplomat, tourist, and foreign correspondent) she was a mystery to the outside world. All they saw was a trim-figured tallish (5 ft. 8 ins.) woman holding the hands of Stalin's children, Svyetlana and Vasiliy; a woman that most of them presumed was Stalin's mistress.

Records in the registry office of the Oktyabrsky District in

Moscow, however, proved that Stalin and Rosa were married soon after the death of Nadiezhda Alliluyeva (Stalin's second wife). In the spaces reserved for the signatures of witnesses appear the names of Abel Yenukidze (an old friend of Stalin) and Lazar Kaganovich (Rosa's brother). Stalin and Rosa Kaganovich had been introduced to each other by Molotov. The occasion had been a birthday party— Stalin's.

Rosa Kaganovich had been very much an active intellectual before she met the Russian leader. She'd been a librarian at the *State Library*, lecturer on literature at Moscow University, literary and film critic for several Soviet newspapers and journals, editor of the *State Publishing House*, and a successful authoress. When Stalin asked her to marry him, she knew exactly what confronted her. As Lazar Kaganovich's sister, she had been very close to the Kremlin hierarchy and counted Kalinin, Mekhlis, Malenkov, Radek, and other 'Inner Circle' personalities among her friends. She knew about Stalin's affaires with other women and about Nadiezhda's death by poison, but, having been fascinated by Stalin and fallen in love with him, she was content to devote herself to Nadiezhda's two children Vasiliy and Svyetlana, and to Stalin's adopted son Boris. She knew she would be powerless to stop Stalin's womanising. This too was something she was prepared to accept.

There were certain conditions though that Rosa had clarified before her marriage. Accustomed to being active in public life, she made it clear that she must be allowed to meet all her friends without restriction, and to continue her literary and musical activities. To everyone's surprise, Stalin agreed to her conditions, and kept his part of the bargain throughout their married life.

The Kremlin, of course, was not a practical place for Rosa to meet all her friends, so Stalin arranged for his wife to have her own private flat *opposite* the Kremlin. She was not subjected to secret police supervision. Rosa was thus able to meet her friends every third day in the week, and continued her social life as before. Her literary and musical meetings were known amongst the Soviet élite as Rosa's Salons. To be invited to them was a unique privilege.

Rosa was also allowed to do something that Nadiezhda had always longed to do but never dared—she replaced the Tsarist furniture in their Kremlin home with less valuable modern pieces. The only items she did not touch were the old Oriental carpets and heavy curtains. She knew Stalin loved these.

Abram Kraskyn, who was proving such a good friend to me, was one of those who was a frequent visitor at Rosa's Salons, and he told me much of what went on and what was said. This Rosa Kaganovich-Stalin certainly seemed to be a woman to meet. I mentioned to Abram that I would like an introduction. Weeks went by. I didn't press it with him. I knew that when the time was right, Abram would do the necessary, and since I was already on familiar terms with Radek, Madame Lunacharsky, Lev Mekhlis and several others of the Moscow _élite_, I felt confident I wouldn't let him down.

One summer's afternoon, Abram said: 'Would you like to come and meet Rosa today?'

There was no real need to ask.

Rosa herself hadn't yet arrived by the time Abram and I got to her flat on the Eastern side of Red Square. She had, however, sent Lev Mekhlis to hold the fort and tell her visitors that she had been delayed and would come as soon as possible.

Abram showed me round the flat. It consisted of two spacious communicating rooms and one large, almost square one. They were all furnished with contemporary furniture, the floors were covered with thick carpets, and in the communicating room stood a grand piano and a radiogram. On a long sideboard were tempting refreshments—Russian salads, Continental sandwiches, cakes and pastries. Next to the refreshments were bottles of vodka, zubrovka (a strongly spiced vodka variety), brandy, rum, and wines, and on a separate table stood a samovar to provide tea.

Shortly after our arrival, Rosa's guests began arriving. Radek was first; then came the famous Soviet poet Boris Pasternak; and a little while later, Nikolai Bukharin, Mikhail Koltsov, Aleksei Tolstoy, and Sergo Ordzhonikidze.

Then Rosa Kaganovich-Stalin arrived. She was slim, and tastefully dressed. She had auburn hair, grey eyes, a straight nose, lovely skin and white teeth, and she had a smile for everyone. When Abram introduced me to her, she said:

'I am happy to meet you, and I want you to know that Abram's friends are also mine. I hope you'll come often.'

From the very beginning she seemed to be a warm, friendly, highly intelligent woman, and a most loyal wife.

★   ★   ★

Rosa's Salons always kept to literary discussions and music sessions but while there were no out-and-out political discussions, plenty of information about the Kremlin and the country in general was aired. For it was only natural that, during the breaks for refreshments, Rosa's guests should speak freely with each other.

When the Secret Police arrested huge numbers of innocent people and tens of thousands were tortured and shot in the Secret Police prisons, Rosa openly admitted that she abhorred the purges. But she never criticised Stalin. He was her husband and, she said, no one could expect her to stick a dagger in his back. She was aware of his faults, detested his terrorising, was against his merciless destruction of former friends; but, apart from condemning these acts and attributing them deliberately to the Secret Police, she never openly blamed him. 'I am his wife,' she would say. And she was indeed a loyal wife to Stalin.

She was extremely fond of classical music, and would listen for hours to gramophone records of Beethoven's symphonies, his violin concerto, Schubert's 'Unfinished' Symphony, and Mozart's 'Eine Kleine Nachtmusik.' On one occasion invited young Busya Goldstein (then the top young Soviet violinist) was to give a recital. He played Beethoven's violin concerto, while she watched and listened entranced. On another occasion, yielding to persuasion, she sang Schubert's and Tchaikovsky's songs, accompanied on the piano by the famous Dunayevsky. She could sing well in a good contralto voice.

Stalin himself often came and happily joined in the discussions of Soviet literature, especially when Tolstoy initiated them. On one occasion, he praised a new song a composer had just played on the

H

piano, and commanded the well-known Marshak to write a lyric for it. Later he joined in the dance which always rounded off the discussions or musical performances, and finally ended the evening by taking the floor with his wife, who was an excellent dancer.

I met Stalin many times at Rosa's Salons, and soon came to the conclusion that he was an extremely strange character and a completely unpredictable one. However much I tried, I was never able to understand his way of thinking or behaviour. Once, for instance, when I met him at Rosa's, he chatted freely for half an hour or so. Less than a week later, I greeted him with the customary Russian '*Zdravstvuytie.*' He ignored me completely, as though I were a block of stone.

On another occasion, the Editor of *Vecherniaya Moskva* presented me with a motor car, and a special testimonial document personally signed by Stalin 'in recognition of outstanding work.' I was very flattered and surprised, and on the following day I sought out Stalin at Rosa's, and thanked him profoundly. He cut me off and snarled: 'Don't break your neck!' Barely a fortnight later, *he* sought me out (again at Rosa's) clapped me vigorously on the back, was full of *bonhomie*, and insisted loudly that I give him an autographed copy of a book of mine that had just been published. There was no knowing what way he would react from one moment to the next.

I discreetly mentioned my inability to understand him to Rosa. She listened thoughtfully. After a while she said: 'You're not the only one who finds it hard to understand him.'

But if Rosa's Salons provided a problem figure in the shape of Stalin they provided compensations in the persons of men like poet Boris Pasternak, a quiet kind man of great scholarship and understanding. At his flat I met Tolstoy, Lugovskoy, Marshak, Ehrenburg, Koltsov, Sholokhov, and many others. On occasions our discussions on literature stretched into the early hours of the morning. Soviet writers and poets are voluble talkers.

But one meeting nearly brought disaster for the lot of us.

Pasternak had sent out invitations to a group of his friends to come to a party at his country villa. All accepted, and the villa was crowded with prominent writers, poets, journalists and artists.

Aleksei Tolstoy, who was among the crowd, had brought a huge samovar filled with vodka and a large tea-pot full of brandy. Everyone else also provided substantial supplies of vodka and zubrovka, and, needless to say, considerable quantities of alcohol were consumed.

Lugovskoy suddenly suggested that we should all show our skill as sharp-shooters; he had a Mauser pistol and several rounds of ammunition in his briefcase. Spotting a large picture of Stalin on the wall of Pasternak's living room, he exclaimed that it was an excellent target. We were all too drunk to realise the danger, the madness of it, and followed Lugovskoy's example and shot at the Stalin picture, aiming at the eyes, forehead, mouth and heart.

One of Pasternak's country neighbours heard the shots and, mistaking the jubilant shouts (when someone scored top marks) for shouts for help, called the police. Finding that the shooting target had been the Stalin picture and suspecting that anti-Stalin de- monstrations were being staged at Pasternak's villa, the policemen turned the matter over to the Secret Police.

Had it not been for Rosa Kaganovich-Stalin and Lev Mekhlis, we would all have met with certain death. Realising the seriousness of our situation, Abram telephoned Rosa and explained what had happened. She immediately mobilised Mekhlis, drove with him in an official Kremlin car to the villa and managed to arrive before the Secret Police Colonel had a chance to dump us in Lubyanka. After a long discussion, the Secret Police Colonel complied with Mekhlis' request to 'ignore the local police report and close the matter.' He was convinced that Stalin's private secretary was acting on Stalin's personal orders. He even returned the bullet-ridden Stalin picture and the Mauser pistol with the remaining rounds of ammunition to Pasternak. But his warning to us before he left was frightening.

Stalin, of course, never knew about the incident.

*　　*　　*

Stalin's marriage to Rosa Kaganovich came to an end in 1938.

Voroshilov one day mentioned the 'Kaganovich dynasty' and shortly afterwards the chief of the Soviet Secret Police, Yezhov, accused the Kaganovich brothers, Mikhail, Moyshe, and Yuryi, who occupied high positions in the Soviet administration, of 'subversion, speculation, and even sabotage.' Being married to their sister and therefore a member of the Kaganovich family, it vitally and personally concerned Stalin.

As soon as Rosa heard about these unfounded accusations against her brothers, she did her utmost to protect them. She detested Voroshilov as a 'malicious gossip' and told Stalin she would not tolerate Voroshilov's drunken accusations. Stalin not only stopped investigations but arranged for Mikhail, Moyshe and Yuryi to be given highly paid sinecures in the country.

Alhough he had given way to Rosa, the ruthless and fickle, Stalin had tired of her. This was a golden opportunity for him and he contrived a divorce. Rosa disappeared without trace . . .

Rosa's brother Lazar remained the only Kaganovich in the limelight. His interests and life were dedicated solely to Stalin and the Party; there was no room in his heart for his sister, brothers. relatives or friends.

CHAPTER SIXTEEN

I Meet President Kalinin

BEFORE coming to Russia, I had often heard its President, Mikhail Ivanovich Kalinin, described as 'a simple-minded peasant, a political nothing.' It was a description that baffled me, because I found it difficult to swallow the idea that one of the highest posts in the land could be held by an ineffective simpleton.

Even after spending some time in Russia itself, I found that the idea persisted that Kalinin was a dullard. Not *everyone* thought so, but enough to constitute an appreciable body of opinion. I decided to reserve my own views until such time as I could meet Kalinin and judge for myself. At the same time I didn't hold out much chance of a meeting.

But in September 1934 the opportunity came my way.

That year the agricultural paper published by *Mossoviet Publications Combinat* was awarded the *Order of Lenin* in recognition of its services, and a banquet was held on the anniversary of the publication's founding to celebrate the honour. Journalists, department heads, agricultural correspondents, even leaders of collective farms from various parts of the Soviet Union were invited. When my own invitation arrived, I was intrigued to discover that members of the*Politburo* as well as the President of the U.S.S.R. had also been invited.

The presence of senior *Politburo* members would ensure more than a full measure of boredom (at least for me, because I was now well beyond saturation point as far as listening to long dry speechs was concerned), but it would be worth enduring in order to get a close look at Kalinin.

As it happened, most of the senior *Politburo* members sent excuses

for not being able to come.* So at least there would be more time
for eating and drinking. And a better chance of getting closer to
the President.

When Mikhail Ivanovich Kalinin began to talk, everyone's
attention was upon him. He was a small old man with lively eyes.
In contrast to most speakers on occasions like this who stood up in
order to punctuate their speeches with gesticulations and table-
thumpings, Kalinin remained seated.

'My dear comrades,' he began, in a voice that was pleasant to
listen to and remarkably youthful for a man of his years, 'I am
greatly honoured at being invited to join you. I like mixing with
people and I like good food and drink. I don't know what else I
should say. To speak about the important work this paper does
every day would be a sheer waste of time. A lot has been written on
this subject in *Pravda*, *Kommunist* and other Party publications. It
would be pointless my going over what has already been said, so
don't let's spoil this occasion with lectures. I am sure everybody
came here to celebrate. So let's celebrate. Let's eat and drink and
dance.' He raised his glass and added: 'To your health and happiness,
comrades.'

Kalinin had set an example. The others could not very well deliver
long speeches now. They cut themselves down to a few words each.
The brevity was heartily welcomed by everyone.

It began to be a very enjoyable evening.

After the banquet was finished the tables were removed, and the
orchestra, which during the dinner had played light background-
music, turned into the nearest Russian equivalent of a jazz band.
Soon the floor was full of couples dancing to gay swinging music.
Because there were far more women than men here, many of the
women danced together.

As I was the only foreigner at the party, Abram, who was friendly
with Kalinin, made this an excuse for bringing me into the
President's company and introduced me. As I stood waiting, I
looked at this tiny man and tried to visualise him as the extraordinary

*They looked with disdain on *Mossoviet Publications Combinat* because of its basically non-
political set-up.

revolutionary I knew him to have been. It was easy enough to understand his immense popularity with the ordinary people, for he was
still a warm and modest man, and he had a face and eyes which told
of a great sense of humour.

'I am glad to know you,' Kalinin said shaking hands and inviting
me to sit down at his table to drink vodka with him to our friendship. 'I know your country,' he told me when he had emptied his
glass. 'I have been there, to a conference, long before the Revolution.
What a beautiful capital! Especially when the sun falls on the
ancient roofs and the cupolas of the churches.'

'I wonder what will happen to all those churches when our
foreign comrades are strong enough to make a successful revolution,'
said the editor of the agricultural paper who was standing behind
my chair and had heard Kalinin's words. 'I only hope that they will
have sense enough to burn them down.'

'How can you talk like a stupid scribbler of *Bezbozhnik*, comrade?' Kalinin objected. 'The churches I spoke of are monuments of
art. They are examples of a true *culture*. They are reminders of
ancient history. I sincerely hope that our foreign comrades will be
sufficiently *intelligent* to save these beautiful places. They ought to
be turned into museums. I am sure they will. Not *everything* that
has been built by enemies has to be destroyed, you know.'

There was nothing of the simpleton about this man. The vehem-
ence with which he spoke, his appreciation of beauty, and his complete slapping down of the toadying editor added up to something
far more than a dullard. Maybe the accents were peasant. But there
was no doubting the intelligence.

The editor, red-faced, excused himself and left us.

'It is really astonishing that some of our new Soviet intelligentsia
talk such rubbish,' Kalinin said. 'If these torch bearers were compelled
to clean lavatories, our Soviet culture would greatly improve.'

Another couple of vodkas, which we drank together, sealed the
friendship between Kalinin and myself. He insisted that I should stop
addressing him by the formal 'Comrade Kalinin' saying that he
was Mikhail Ivanovich to me and, according to the old Russian
custom, he kissed me to show he was my friend. He also gave me a

card with his name and Kremlin address printed on it and wrote on the back a request to anyone whom I might approach to give me every assistance; underneath he put his signature. I treasured this card and later made frequent use of it.

The Soviet President was in an excellent mood that evening. He joked and laughed and entertained the whole company.

'Don't let's sit here like dummies,' he suddenly said and stood up. 'Let's enjoy ourselves, let's dance.'

He picked out a pretty young girl and started to foxtrot skilfully on the crowded floor.

Before we parted company, Kalinin asked me to keep in touch with him and not to hesitate to contact him if I thought he could help me in any way. This he said in his car in which he had insisted Abram and I should ride with him. We got out then, and he waved as the car pulled away.

*   *   *

The Soviet President was loved by everyone because he was so human and genuine. He spoke the simple language of the people. He never barricaded himself behind closed doors as did most of his Kremlin comrades. Instead, he encouraged the people to come to his office for a chat or tell him about their troubles if they needed help. Numerous cases are known where Kalinin helped peasants and workers, and afterwards invited them to a meal in a restaurant, and rounded off the evening with a visit to the ballet or theatre. His 'Living with the people,' as he called it, was not a calculated publicity stunt—it was a reflection of his true nature.

Shortly after I first met him, he invited me to visit him at his flat in the Kremlin—a few doors from Stalin's household. I was surprised to find the Soviet President living in a small two-roomed flat which, like Krupskaya's home, was furnished with tasteless and uncomfortable odds and ends from palaces of the ex-Tsarist nobility. Kalinin must have noticed something in my attitude, because he said: 'Yes, I know how ugly and awkward these museum pieces are, but why should I use my position as President to get modern furniture when so many millions of my people live in awful poverty?'

I said nothing. But there was so much that I wanted to say.

'You'll have to excuse me for a little while,' he said, 'I haven't quite finished the meal yet . . . I hope you like Vienna *Schnitzel?*'

'You invited me for a drink . . .,' I began.

'Food and drink go together, don't they?' he chuckled. 'My motto is: always eat if it's worth eating.'

I followed him into the adjoining room where, on a large table, stood three Primus cookers with pots and frying pans on them. 'You haven't got a kitchen?' I asked, surprised.

'Only the communal one at the end of the corridor, but I never use it because I can't stand the housewives nosing about so that they can tell their husbands what I'm eating.'

He poured out two large glasses of vodka, and when he had emptied his in one gulp, continued:

'I can't stand the food in our Kremlin dining-room. Fortunately I am quite fond of cooking, so I decided I'd get a cooker put in here to prepare my own food in privacy. It took a lot of trouble to get it, and it was a beauty of a cooker, but when the factory delivered it, the engineers weren't allowed to install it because of some stupid regulations. I could have had it out with the Kremlin commandant, but I didn't want to make a fuss out of such a trivial matter.'

During supper, to which he had also invited Rosa,* Radek, Pyatakova, Redens, Krupskaya, and Abram, he seemed pleased to hear us praising the food which he had so elaborately and tastefully prepared on his Primus cookers.

'Unfortunately it's not quite as nice as I would have liked it to be, because the meat isn't as good as it used to be,' he remarked, and added critically: 'The trouble is that the collective farmers nowadays have no time to do their work properly. They have to attend too many compulsory meetings.'

'Don't let Lazar hear you say that,' Radek joked, referring to Rosa's all-powerful brother who, this very day, had delivered a speech in which he had attacked 'all those who try to find some sort of an excuse to avoid attending the usual Party and production meetings in factories, offices, collective and State farms.'

'Oh, forget him and his boring propaganda speeches,' laughed

*Stalin had gone to Sochi with his children.

Rosa, who classed her brother as the most conceited and dogmatic *Politburo* member of them all. 'His success has gone to his head,' she said.

'Comrade Party members!' said Kalinin, doing his best to imitate Kaganovich's typically *Bolshevik* way of speech. 'Complete and unqualified devotion and obedience to the Party and Government is the unquestionable MUST for every disciplined and loyal comrade!' He pointed to his Vienna *Schnitzel* and added, with his usual chuckle: 'So, obey orders from highest quarters and eat your food before it gets cold!'

Kalinin's very funny mimicry was greeted with howls of laughter.

There was hardly an occasion when the Soviet President did not take the opportunity to make fun of his Kremlin comrades. Like Radek, he liked to tell jokes. One, which he specially relished and which later was attributed to him all over Russia went as follows:

A peasant met Stalin in Moscow. When Stalin asked if he knew with whom he was speaking, the peasant replied: 'Of course, with Comrade Stalin.' Stalin asked why he was so sure since they had never met before, to which the peasant, scratching his head, replied: 'Well, I know you, Comrade Stalin. Everyone knows you. Wherever I go, I see your pictures. Even our pigs know you, Comrade Stalin! We have your pictures hung up in their sties!'

Stalin and his devoted confidants, Molotov and Kaganovich, were displeased with Kalinin's 'un-*Bolshevik*-like' behaviour; they often criticised him for 'playing the fool' and 'behaving like a clown.' Rosa Kaganovich-Stalin, who was a good judge of people, however, rightly said of Kalinin: 'He has an intelligent brain and is a genuine, sincere friend.'

During the whole of my stay in the Soviet Union, I kept in touch with Kalinin. He never changed. He remained the warm likeable Russian who liked to joke, and who was not afraid of speaking about things which other *Politburo* members guarded as secrets. Above all, I liked him as a friend.

In June 1946, my friend, the Old *Bolshevik*, Mikhail Ivanovich Kalinin, was murdered.

According to Stalin's trusted confidant Lev Mekhlis, Kalinin had dared to try to persuade his master not to execute General Vlasov, insisting there was not sufficient evidence to prove that the hero of the Battle of Moscow was a Nazi collaborator. An angry scene took place in Stalin's office in the Kremlin on the 1st of June 1946. Two days later came the official announcement:

'Mikhail Ivanovich Kalinin, President of the U.S.S.R. until his resignation two and a half months ago, has suddenly and unexpectedly died . . .'

CHAPTER SEVENTEEN

Men and Supermen

THE shelves in Moscow's shops stayed empty. Except in the *Gastronoms* and *Mostorgs*, that is; but these, as far as ordinary citizens were concerned, were no more than places of disillusionment and provocations. Certainly the *Gastronoms* and *Mostorgs*, with their fine displays of goods, were always crowded with people; but few of the people had enough money to make purchases. Only the privileged ones could shop there. The others just came and looked, and went away disgruntled and hungry.

For the latter it was back to the Co-operative and State shops, back to queueing, back to endless disappointments. But there was a new spirit stirring in the people towards the end of 1934. No longer were they swallowing *all* their grumbles. Little rumbles of discontent could be heard where before there would have been acceptance, or at least surly silence.

One day in October of that year I myself was at the centre of an incident which had the effect of bringing a tiny open rebellion into the lives of some fellow shoppers. It was not so much *what* they said —but that they did it at *all*.

I was passing *Magazine 87* when I noticed the long queue which sucked out of its door and along the pavement. 'Fresh herrings are being sold,' I was informed what this particular queue was for. I was not pushed for time, and decided to queue up for some of these fresh herrings.

Now one of the things I had temporarily forgotten was that, in Moscow, shops never provided paper for wrapping up purchases. So when I eventually got to the assistant and ordered two pounds of herrings, I asked her if she could spare me a little piece of paper to wrap the wet fish in.

'We have no paper,' she said tartly.

'I can't very well take the wet fish just like that,' I said. 'Surely you have a small piece of paper you could spare me?'

'I told you we haven't,' she snapped. 'If you don't want the herrings, it's all right with me, comrade.'

Every Soviet shop was provided by the authorities with a Book of Complaints or Satisfaction, because anyone who had either cause for complaint or satisfaction was expected to write it in the book. I asked the assistant to let me have the book.

'You don't really mean to complain in the book that we haven't any paper, comrade?' she said, instead of producing the book.

'Give me the book, please.'

'But, comrade . . .'

'Give me the book, please,' I insisted.

She produced the book and handed it over. She mumbled something about it not being her fault that the shop had no paper.

When the book was in my hands, I stepped back, opened it and tore out the two middle pages, and wrapped the herrings with them.

I suppose in a way it was a foolhardy thing to have done, but I was angry at the stupidity of the system, and had no intention of carrying wet herrings in my hands through the streets. The shop assistant looked horrified at me. Her horror increased when some of those behind me followed my example. They passed the book from one to the other, and I was amazed at their daring. The girl managed, however, to save part of the book by wrenching it out of the hands of the last one, who also wanted a page or two.

As I walked away from the shop, many of those in the queue, who had seen what had happened, said: 'Well done, comrade!' And their resentment at their plight came into the open. They grumbled openly.

* * *

One evening in the following month, as I left *Vecherniaya Moskva* and passed Lubyanka N.K.V.D. Headquarters where big white lettering on a red poster repeated Stalin's slogan, INCREASE

PRODUCTION AND BUILD A PROSPEROUS U.S.S.R.,
a young man in working clothes, one of a group of five, said in a
loud voice:

'If we had more to eat we could work better!'

The sentry in front of Secret Police Headquarters pretended not
to have heard these treacherous words, and merely requested the
group to move on. They did so but, encouraged by the N.K.V.D.
sentry not having taken drastic action, another workman shouted:

'It is high time Stalin did something for his people, and saw to it
that we get better wages so that we can buy bread and clothes!'

'I am fed up with being hungry all the time!' a woman passer-by
joined in. 'I can't bear to see how undernourished my children
are . . .'

'Give us bread!' somebody shouted. 'We are hungry and cold!'

A few blue-capped N.K.V.D. officers, who were always around
the building, thought that the time for action had come; they dispersed the spontaneous demonstration, but without using force. No
arrests were made there and then. However, whether those who had
said what they thought were trailed by plain-clothes agents I do not
know. But by Russian standards, they were behaving dangerously.

Some days later, Abram invited me to have supper with himself
and his wife at their flat. He said his brother Salo (the N.K.V.D.
colonel) would also be there. During the supper, Salo talked of
unrest and dissatisfaction all over the Soviet Union. He said people
were grumbling in the Ukraine, in Byelorussia, in the Soviet Far
East, in fact, all over Russia. I was surprised at his admission, but
then came his explanation.

'It's a Trotskyite conspiracy,' exclaimed Salo. 'It's being done for
the purpose of disrupting our everyday life by enticing the people
to create unrest and by so doing pave the way for imperialist
aggression against our motherland.'

It was quite obvious he believed what he was saying. He was
completely mentally won over to the accepted Party line.

'I don't think you are right, Salo,' Nina contradicted him. 'I
hear people grumble while they queue for their rations, travel on the
bus, or go to the library, but they don't behave like people who have

been *enticed* by anybody. They sound like people who are forced by sheer desperation. They can't get, or can't afford to buy the necessities of life. That's a brutal *fact*. That's not enticement. I still believe that they interpret Comrade Stalin's words "We need sound criticism" in their own simple way.'

'You don't seem to see things as they are, Ninochka,' her brother-in-law replied. 'You are an intelligent woman and I would have expected you to realise that the Enemies of the People always concentrate on discontent. Because they can entice discontented people to sabotage more easily than the ideologically reliable and stable ones.'

'If you maintain that all those who grumble are *enticed* by the Enemies of the People, you're actually implying that our enemies have almost complete control over our population because, wherever you go, you can hear grumbling,' Nina went on.

'I don't say that *all* people who grumble and publicly criticise the Party and Government are dancing to Trotsky's tune, but I do say that considerable numbers of them are,' Salo explained. To prove his point, he told us about the riots which had taken place in the previous week in Chelyabynsk. Factory workers and women shoppers had demonstrated in the centre of Chelyabynsk and had shouted their demands for larger food supplies, better housing, and higher wages, and when the number of the demonstrators had swelled to a few hundred, they had plundered whatever there was in the warehouses and distributed it amongst the people.

'Here you have a perfect example of how the Enemies of the People manage to entice good Soviet citizens to riot against the Party and Government,' Salo exclaimed. And, looking at Nina, he went on: 'Don't think that I am jumping to conclusions. Demonstrators who were afterwards arrested made written statements in which they described how known oppositionists, whom they named, encouraged them to demonstrate and riot, by cunningly using the temporary food shortage as an effective bait. And the same sort of thing has been happening all over. In every single instance, the arrested rioters made written statements that they had yielded to Trotskyite persuasion. It's an all-Soviet conspiracy to rock the Party and Government on their foundations. Stern measures must be taken if we want to prevent real trouble in our motherland.'

'I think it's wrong that the news about all this is kept secret,' Nina remarked. 'If everybody *knew* about the methods of these Enemies of the People it would fortify us all.'

I was not quite sure whether Nina really meant what she said or whether it was a clever attempt to ridicule Salo.

'No, it musn't be made public,' Salo replied. 'If it were, Hitler and the rest of the imperialists would make capital out of it. That could have a very dangerous effect on all Communists in the capitalist world, something we can't afford because we need their active support. As far as our own people are concerned, it must also be kept secret because it could create uncertainty among them. For this reason, foreign agents who are arrested are tried by Military Tribunals and secretly dealt with.'

Shortly afterwards, Abram introduced me to two more N.K.V.D. men, Mironov and Molchanov who played most important roles during Stalin's blood purges. They were both very likeable men and had I not known the positions they held in the N.K.V.D., I would have fallen for the temptation to accept them as the friends they pretended to be and talked with them openly. Briefed by Abram, however, I said nothing that could at any time or in any way be held against me.

One acquaintance led to another. I became fairly friendly with Stanislav Redens who was married to the sister of Stalin's second wife, Nadiezhda Alliluyeva. He was Chief of the N.K.V.D. of the Moscow Region.

A fanatic *Bolshevik* of Polish origin, he had been a prominent member of the Cheka since the establishment of the Soviet secret police after the Great October Revolution, and, having been close to Stalin and other Kremlin dignitaries, he was perhaps my most important source of information. I met him frequently—at Radek's flat, at Rosa's Salons, and at many other places—almost up to the day he met his sudden end.

Despite the fact that he was a most devoted *Bolshevik*, a ruthless secret police chief, and a determined supporter of Stalin's *Politburo*, he was killed in cold blood on the 30th of September 1936, a week before his friend Karl Radek was arrested on charges of complicity in the Trotsky-Zinovyev plot. Redens' end was characteristic of the Soviet secret police terror. The circumstances surrounding it, which Mironov, Molchanov, Chertok, and other N.K.V.D. dignitaries confirmed, was as follows:

When Stalin sacked Yagoda as Head of the N.K.V.D. on the 29th of September 1936, and appointed in his place Nikolai Yezhov, the new Chief of the Secret Police installed himself at Lubyanka with three hundred specially picked henchmen. His first act was to compile a list of suspects who were to be purged from the N.K.V.D., to root out Yagoda's people. Men who a short while before had sentenced innocent people to death were now shot in the cellars of Lubyanka.

One of the most striking examples of the Lubyanka blood-bath was when Yezhov assembled a number of senior N.K.V.D. officers. When they had been surrounded by reliable guards brought from the provinces, he shouted at them: 'You people here are all gangsters, spies, traitors, and saboteurs! You have all become mercenaries of the imperialist warmongers!' They were then shot like mad dogs.

As soon as Redens heard about this, he went to see his ex-brother-in-law, Stalin, to try to induce him to stop this incredible barbarism. Stalin only shrugged his shoulders and repeated his usual phrase, that where trees are felled chips fly. Redens was no longer one of his intimate friends.

Encouraged by Ordzhonikidze, Yenukidze, and others, Redens went to Yezhov's office. After some heated words had been exchanged between the two in the presence of Yezhov's deputy, Redens spat in Yezhov's face. Yezhov drew his pistol and shot Redens down . . .

* * *

I also got to know the 'great' Lazar Kaganovich who, because it was difficult to detect any signs of humanity in him, reminded me of Molotov. In Kaganovich's opinion, it was only worth his while to speak at gatherings at *Pravda* and *Izvyestiya*, and Universities and Colleges, or at the largest and most important factories. He turned

J

down other invitations. He had an enormous ego.

An intelligent and fiery speaker, he frequently talked too long; but in spite of his conceit, he was nevertheless one of the *Politburo* members most popular with the Russian masses. Stalin chose Kaganovich as a kind of 'avenger.' If some 'plot' was 'discovered' anywhere and Enemies of the People were blamed for shortcomings, Lazar Kaganovich was ordered to speak to the people promising that Stalin and the *Politburo* would mercilessly stamp out any injustice. So the masses came to regard him as a 'watchdog' for their well-being.

Although propaganda had built him up as the enemy of corruption, he himself was not above suspicion. But accusations against him were always suppressed.

He was a fanatical supporter of Stalin's policies. It paid him—in power and popularity.

He had no manners—at the table for instance, he would scratch his head with his fork. Rosa would call him a 'pig' and rebuke him for his uncouth habits. 'Lazar,' she said, 'is intelligent, but has no character. He's too easy influenced and always ready to discard his own opinion if Josif (Stalin) has different ideas.'

The only one of Stalin's closest confidants and drinking companions whom I did not meet at this time was Nikita Khrushchev, who then held a modest post as Secretary of the Moscow Party Committee. Rosa would not invite him to her Salons because she said of him, 'he is a primitive peasant who laughs too loud, spits in company too often, and clowns badly.' But, Khrushchev could frequently be found in the company of Voroshilov, Budyenny, and other heavy drinkers, because they admired him for his liquid capacity.

However, later I met Khrushchev on several occasions at his office in the Party Committee on official business. I had to go to him several times to secure clearance for articles we wished to publish. He always had his stock answer ready: 'I will give a decision in a day or so.' He was afraid to sanction anything or to commit himself.

'I'm afraid, Comrade Khrushchev, we can't wait a day or so,' was my usual reply. 'If we don't publish this article in our next issue, it won't be of interest.'

'I will give my decision in a day or so,' he would repeat, as if he had not heard my objection.

'I'll have to take it to the Press Department . . .'

'You can't without my signature,' he would then exclaim and remind me of the Press Department's rules: 'Your article concerns Moscow Party matters and consequently must first be vetted by the Secretary of the Moscow Party Committee before the Press Department can consider if it's suitable for publication.'

On most occasions I would go to the Press Department first and explain why I had come without Khrushchev's signature. And, more than once, when the Censor-in-Charge was in a talkative mood, he would mumble: 'Oh him, we know him,' and add that Khrushchev did it to other newspapers as well. Sometimes the Censor-in-Charge put his big rubber stamp, FIT FOR PUBLICATION, on it without referring me back to Khrushchev. But, if for one reason or another he did not approve it, but did not wish to prohibit publication openly, he would insist that Khrushchev's signature must be obtained. It was an elegant way of preventing publication, because it was common knowledge that Khrushchev's 'in a day or so' never came!

At that time, Khrushchev lived with his family in one of the Moscow Party blocks, near the *Comintern* hotel. However, during the super-purges he was transferred on Stalin's direct orders to the Ukraine to conduct the blood-purge. And, acting on his master's direct orders and not being required to make any decision of his own, he quickly earned Stalin's admiration for his ruthlessness. He became commonly known as 'The Butcher of the Ukraine' because of his merciless wiping out of innocent men, women, and even children.

★　　★　　★

Winter had come early to Russia that year, and in November the fierce frost and thick snow made matters more difficult than ever. Everywhere, sparsely clothed women of all ages cleaned the frozen snow away and throughout Russia volunteers were forcibly. recruited to give up their rest-day and help the workers to fulfil their production plan.

Our Partorg at *Vecherniaya Moskva* accounced without prior
warning that volunteers were required for building the Moscow
Underground Railway. Everyone was ordered to report to
Dzierzhinsky Square the next day at six o'clock in the morning.

It was a bitterly cold morning and, although I had a fur coat, cap,
and fur-lined boots, I felt the icy wind creeping through my bones.
I was only one of the very few who were adequately dressed—the
majority of the men and women only had padded jackets which
looked as if made from grey cotton quilts. Quite a few did not even
have these, or proper shoes. At the building site on Dzhierzhinsky
Square, where the excavation work for the Underground was in
full swing the workers grumbled, because they did not like the idea
that newspapermen and office workers had been ordered to come
to their site. 'You have no experience of this sort of work; you are
only in our way and hinder us in getting on with the job,' they
complained and suggested we should dig in another part of the site.

During the lunch break, they were friendly and hospitable and
insisted that we share their tea. But their 'tea' was only clear boiling
water, which they drank even without sugar because they had none.

Kolka, a young workman, sat next to me and busied himself
with unwrapping his lunch. All he had was about a pound of the
usual black sour-tasting bread and a raw onion! Yet, when he saw
that I did not have any food, he offered to share his 'dinner' with me.

'Is that all you have?' I asked.

'Well, yes,' he confirmed. 'It's what I usually have.'

Looking round, I saw that most of the workers had approximately
the same quantity of bread. Some had pickled cucumber instead of
an onion; some had bread only.

'Why don't you go to the canteen for a proper meal?' I asked.

'Canteen?' he said surprised. 'We haven't one. When they sent
us to work here they promised we'd have a canteen. It's always like
this.' After a while, he said: 'It's really the limit the way they force
us to work like this. We work twelve hours a day because we must
do four hours overtime to fulfil the production plan, but we can't
buy ourselves enough food and proper clothing. It's time comrade
Stalin was told what's actually going on in our country so that he

could set matters right.'

Poor Kolka. He also belonged to the millions of Soviet citizens who firmly believed that if Stalin knew about their plight things would change rapidly.

I suddenly remembered Salo's, Mironov's, and Molchanov's allegations that the masses grumbled because they were enticed by Enemies of the People.

I allowed myself a little smile.

CHAPTER EIGHTEEN

Shots in Leningrad

On the 1st of December 1934, Abram and I were on late duty at the *Rabochaya Moskva* because some of their editors were down with flu. Right out of the blue we received a most alarming news flash from the TASS correspondent in Leningrad. It said:

SERGEI MIRONOVICH KIROV SHOT DEAD
Our beloved member of the *Politburo*, Sergei Mironovich Kirov, close friend of our Great Leader Stalin, was shot dead this afternoon in his office in Leningrad. The sudden tragic death of the Secretary of the Leningrad Party Section is a great loss not only to the Party but also to all the people of the Soviet Union.

His murderer has been arrested, the gun still in his hand. This gangster of the name of Nikolayev managed to slip through to Comrade Kirov and to shoot him in cold blood.

The motive for this brutal murder? Gangster Nikolayev states that he killed Comrade Kirov because he was having a love affair with Nikolayev's wife.

We got this announcement ready at once, compiled a life story of Kirov, and selected photographs from our archives, so that everything was ready for publication.

Just when the front page was made up, the Editor received a telephone call from the Press Department, ordering him to scrap everything, have the printing destroyed, and return all galley and page proofs together with the Tass message to the Press Department.

He was ordered to wait for the official version and instructions as to how the paper was to be made up.

The new material arrived just one hour before the paper was due to go to press, and although we had several Linotype machines we were of course fighting an impossible battle against time. We had six large-size pages to get ready.

At last, nearly three and a half hours later, *Rabochaya Moskva* did go to press. The front page, which was framed by thick black lines, showed a very large picture of Kirov. The following is what we were told to print:

COMRADE SERGEI MIRONOVICH KIROV BRUTALLY
MURDERED

On the afternoon of December 1st, 1934, our beloved Sergei Mironovich Kirov was shot dead in his office by a gangster named Nikolayev.

By this brutal act of murder, the enemies of the Soviet Union have shown that they will stop at nothing to undermine our régime and install their own capitalist and fascist thugs.

These devils will not, however, have any success, since the nation stands united behind our beloved leader Josif Vissarionovich Stalin.

It is necessary to stress that every citizen should be most vigilant, and should report anything he considers dangerous to the authorities. Now, more than ever before, everyone should work closely with the N.K.V.D.

Death to Fascism and its despicable, cunning lackeys! Long live our Party and its great and wise leader, our beloved Josif Vissarionovich Stalin!

Then followed the life story of Kirov, supported by photographs from his early youth up to the time of his sudden death. There were also long articles warning the people that the Enemies of the State would try to stage a campaign of murder, sabotage and chaos, but the ever-watchful N.K.V.D. with the full support of the people of the Soviet Union would destroy these plans, etc. etc.

Neither *Rabochaya Moskva* nor any other newspaper in the Soviet

Union said anything about Nikolayev's real reason for killing Kirov. One of our *Rabochaya Moskva* colleagues who had been on duty on the evening of the 1st of December and who was a close friend of the Tass correspondent whose initials had appeared on the message, tried to contact him on the telephone for further information. He could not get through to the Tass man, and was told by the duty officer that any further news would be issued only through the usual channels—those of the Press Department.

Abram and I were not satisfied, and we decided to try to get the real truth of the story. I had a vague idea that even the original Tass version was a fake. Through our connections in high places we uncovered the real facts behind Kirov's death. We checked and cross-checked. This was what we found out.

Sergei Mironovich Kirov, Party Secretary of the Leningrad District,* had, in the summer of 1934, unearthed a conspiracy in the garrison of Petrozavodsk, and discovered that the head of the conspiracy was the Chief of the Local Government. The result was that fifty-six Party members were executed.

In August 1934, trouble arose in Sverdlovsk where the Secretary of the Urals Committee and his assistant had organised an Opposition Centre and made contact with similar centres in Leningrad, Moscow, Kiev and Tiflis. It was the same Kirov who unearthed this lot.

A close friend of Stalin, Kirov was furious at his findings. Correspondence which he found described Stalin as a 'Genghis Khan', 'a miniature tyrant' and 'an immoral tyrant'. This, to Kirov and his associates, was the worst form of treason. But equally bad was the discovery of a budding revolt inside the Party itself. All sorts of trusted executives were involved. Even the Secret Police were mixed up in it. It was at their printing works in Sverdlovsk that thousands of illegal pamphlets had been turned out. The link? The Head of the Secret Police in the Urals (he was a friend of Yagoda) was leader of the Opposition Centre.

When Kirov revealed the details of the plot to Stalin, action was quick and merciless. 350 people were shot dead.

*Which included Soviet Karelia.

But now it was Yagoda who felt imperilled by Kirov's activities. After all, a certain amount of smear was already attaching itself to his name because of the fool in the Urals. Comrade Kirov might start insidious whisperings into the ears of Stalin, and then perhaps one day he, Yagoda, would be sent for, denounced, and shot.

Yagoda decided to act. He started by trying to persuade Stalin that Kirov was an adventurer who would stop at nothing. To support his statement he produced a dossier he had compiled which disclosed that Kirov had married an ex-Denikin spy who, soon after her marriage, had stolen some secret military papers and disappeared. But Stalin knew *Yagoda's* past, and had not forgotten that before the Revolution this man had attempted to penetrate into Sverdlov's wealthy family by marriage; that some jewels had disappeared; and that from then on their door was closed to Yagoda. Stalin also had a very great affection for Kirov. He took the dossier from Yagoda now and when he accompanied him to the door of his Kremlin office, said:

'I warn you, Yagoda that I hold you entirely responsible for ensuring that the contents of this filthy thing which you call a dossier shall never become known to anyone.'

He saw Yagoda out, then went back and burned the dossier himself in the stove in his office.

Shortly afterwards, Kirov was shot in Leningrad by an N.K.V.D. man named Nikolayev.

The murder of his friend was a great blow to Stalin. He immediately suspected that Nikolayev had shot Kirov on higher instructions because of the fear that sooner or later the Party Secretary of the Leningrad District would either become the head of the Secret Police or, at least, 'clean it up.' Stalin's suspicions were strengthened by the fact that Nikolayev had apparently not tried to escape and had immediately confessed that his act was one of jealousy. But the story didn't ring true to Stalin. He felt sure it was a fabrication invented for Nikolayev by Yagoda. So he immediately decided to travel to Leningrad to interrogate Nikolayev in person.

When Yagoda turned up at the Moscow railway station saying

that he wanted to accompany him, Stalin lost his temper and shouted: 'On this journey I have no need of you or your services!'

However, the head of the N.K.V.D. would not accept defeat. He demanded an engine to take him to Leningrad. The station commandant, however, refused. Yagoda then remembered that he had an aircraft at his disposal, and though it was old and slow it got him to Leningrad before Stalin.

Thus when Stalin interrogated Nikolayev, using violence as a persuader, the murderer stuck to his story insisting that he had killed out of jealousy because the Party Secretary had been his wife's lover. But Stalin never accepted this story and became more than ever convinced that Yagoda was directly or indirectly behind the plot.

He decided to exploit the death of his friend Kirov for his own purposes. A gigantic purge began. In Leningrad alone, nearly five hundred victims were shot. Thousands of prisoners all over the country were exterminated. As Stalin had no faith in Yagoda, he entrusted Nikolai Ivanovich Yezhov with the sifting of the leaders of the N.K.V.D. Mass executions took place in the prisons of the N.K.V.D. all over the country. The victims were members of the Secret Police, Party executives, innocent citizens and even peasants.

That then is the true story of the murder of Sergei Mironovich Kirov whose death triggered off Stalin to begin the greatest blood bath the world has ever known.

No one who was not in the U.S.S.R. at that time can imagine the extent of the terror. The 'Black Ravens'* were on the move day and night as especially selected N.K.V.D. officers arrested suspects in factories, offices, institutions, hostels. They also came to the Luks. Always in the early hours of the morning. I would hear their nailed jackboots stamping in the corridors, the doors banging, their shouting and cursing. Nobody knew whose turn would come next. It went on for weeks and weeks.

Tens of thousands were shot after 'confessions' had been extracted by the most brutal methods. The civilised world was later shocked by the brutality which Hitler's Gestapo used, but the Nazis were

*Closed police vans.

only copying what Stalin's henchmen had already done. Hundreds of thousands were sent to prisons. Millions to slave-labour camps.

Eventually, no one dared even to whisper the word 'hunger,' or to complain of the cold, or of their bad wages and living conditions. The Soviet people lived under a reign of fear. The grumbling ceased again, and no more men shouted their protests outside the Lubyanka or anywhere else.

CHAPTER NINETEEN

'Scientific' Methods

THE single-minded brutality of Josif Stalin didn't end with the initial burst of executions. History wasn't yet finished with him; nor he with so many who were still alive.

Therefore when Kirov's successor—Zhdanov (he was a protegé of Kaganovich and Molotov)—came to Stalin with the proposition that *anyone* who had had even the slightest contact with the Opposition faction should be liquidated, the Georgian listened patiently.

'As long as a single follower of Trotsky, Zinovyev, Kameniev, or any of their like remains,' Zhdanov said, 'there is a danger that they could one day stage a *putsch* to overthrow you. Let me root them out and exterminate them.'

After a while Stalin gave his verdict.

No, he said, it would not be enough that these people should be merely exterminated, confessions should first be obtained from all of them. They would have to be shown to the whole of the Russian people as vile plotters against Stalin and against the Party. Then they could be exterminated with impunity, and Stalin and the Party would appear justified to the Masses.

And while on the business of confessions, it would be as good a time as any for the N.K.V.D. to modernise their methods, to introduce some more science into their activities.

Kaganovich and Molotov, the yes-men, wholeheartedly agreed with their chief. Comrade Stalin, as always, was so right.

At that time, Stalin's intimate friend Sergo Ordzhonikidze, one of the most important members of the *Politburo*, was convalescing

at Kyslovodsk. Stalin went to see him and told him of his plans.
But Ordzhonikidze was appalled. 'I can't accept the execution of
these companions of Lenin, under such a disgraceful accusation,'
Ordzhonikidze replied. 'We would discredit our Party both in the
U.S.S.R. and abroad if we did as you suggest. The Committee
would not survive such executions.'

'The unity of our Party, its absolute unity, is the only guarantee
of victory,' said Stalin. 'These people conspire even in prison; they
are living just to overthrow us. They will utilise the least setback in a
war to attack us. It is precisely their reputation as Lenin's old
companions that makes them more dangerous than the émigrées
abroad. They could destroy the Party itself!'

Pacing up and down he went on:

'If there is ever the least possibility of conspiracy on the part of the
N.K.V.D. and Yagoda, they will deliberately set themselves up as
the spiritual leaders of the revolt. Then it will be too late. Face
facts Sergo.'

Ordzhonikidze kept quiet, but he was worried.

'They would destroy us, if they could—so we must destroy them
first,' said Stalin.

But Ordzhonikidze was not convinced.

*   *   *

On the 28th and 29th of December 1934, the 'Trial of the Fourteen'
(also known as the Nikolayev-Rumyantsev case) took place. All
fourteen accused were condemned to death.

On the 15th and 16th of January 1935, the 'Trial of the Nineteen'
was held. Zinovyev, Kameniev and seventeen of their comrades
were charged with 'seeking to restore Capitalism, general counter-
revolutionary activity, and political and moral responsibility for the
assassination of Kirov.' They were all sentenced to imprisonment.

On the 23rd of January 1935, came 'The Trial of the Twelve
Leningrad N.K.V.D. officials.' P. D. Medvyed, ex-head of the
Leningrad N.K.V.D. and other high officers were charged with
failure to prevent Kirov's assassination. Their sentences were light—
they were deported.

In the spring of 1935, a second Kameniev trial was held in secret. About thirty defendants were in the dock, and they were all sent to prison. Kameniev's sentence was increased by five years.

* * *

The desire for more scientific methods of interrogation became one of Stalin's obsessions. He knew all about Yagoda's methods, but became increasingly convinced that better results could be obtained in new ways.

Yagoda's tortures (which were not primarily his, many of them having been copied from other countries and other ages) deserve to be recalled.

One 'persuasion' was to strap the victim into a dentist's chair and drill his teeth right through to the nerves without filling them. The 'patients' begged on their knees to have their teeth extracted, even without an anaesthetic. Their torturers laughed and told them that a dentist would relieve them of their pain as soon as they signed a 'confession.' When they could not stand the inhuman pain any longer, they 'confessed.'

Another method the N.K.V.D. sadists enjoyed was the old Asiatic one of strapping the victims on to a table, and then allowing a goat to lick the soles of their bare feet. Not only were the inquisitors amused but the victims readily gave in.

Quite common also was the practice of bringing the wife, husband, children or parents of the accused into the N.K.V.D. prisons. When the accused refused to 'confess,' the Red inquisitors began to torture in the most brutal way the family in the presence of the arrested. To save their loved ones further suffering the accused 'confessed' to crimes which they had not committed.

Stalin's 'scientific' methods were, however, of a different nature. The victims were questioned for hours, being forced to look into a dazzling light. If this did not produce any result they were led into the corridor and made to stand with their hands behind their backs with their faces to the wall for many hours. They were then led back and questioned again in the blinding light. Interrogators changed and fresh ones took over. If the accused still refused to 'confess' he was led away to a cell. He was given no food or drink. Exhausted he fell on the bunk, dead tired. The moment he had fallen asleep, the guards who had watched him came to fetch him. Everything, exactly as before, started all over again. If the accused was 'stubborn,' it went on for days on end. Sooner or later came the moment when the victim, deciding that death was better than this torture, signed the 'confession.'

There were some, however, who still refused to 'confess.' Another method was then applied. The accused was brought into a room which resembled a court where an N.K.V.D. Tribunal was sitting at a table covered with a red cloth.

'Are you now willing to confess to your crime?' the 'presiding judge' asked. 'If you do, it will be considered in your favour and the highest penalty will not be imposed upon you.'

The prisoner who had endured the terrible tortures before, usually did not fall for this trick.

'Very well then. You are sentenced to death. The execution is to take place immediately.' And while the prisoner was being slowly led out of the room, the 'presiding judge' said to the others, so that the prisoner could hear it: 'This fool thinks we need his confession. If he had known that all the others have already confessed he would not have thrown his life away.'

This was deliberately said to change the attitude of the prisoner and finally extort the requested 'confession.'

If the prisoner still did not give in he was taken before the firing squad. The 'presiding judge' repeated his sentence. The executors were called to attention. When the command 'Fire!' was given, blanks were used. The prisoner was led to his cell to be again woken up just when he had fallen asleep. And this went on and on—until he either 'confessed' or was brutally murdered. Some amazingly managed to survive, and this is how the truth about this method leaked through to the outside world. The accuracy of the accounts was confirmed by N.K.V.D. executives who entrusted these secrets to their friends.

Stalin was still not satisfied and insisted that 'scientific' methods should be improved. He planned mass trials of popular Opposition leaders, and his dream was that ways should be found which would make these enemies of his 'confess' that they had planned to overthrow his government, to wipe out the *Bolshevik* Party and to reinstate capitalism. He dreamed of mass trials which would be staged in public without a hitch and give the widest publicity.

Like a producer he directed a huge performance and rehearsed on human guinea pigs secretly so that he could see whether his methods would be successful. He even prepared a special prison in Lefortovo, near Moscow (to which Yagoda was not admitted) where his most trusted henchmen tried out his methods.

'We have not yet succeeded in breaking the minds of the confessors,' Stalin said. 'They are still able to *think*. This is very dangerous because they might revoke their confessions and could use the open court as a forum for their propaganda.

'We must find an effective drug which will transform their minds as if under hypnosis,' he continued. 'We must not make the same mistake the Gestapo did with Van der Lubbe at the *Reichstag* trial. They made an idiot out of him, and this convinced the world that he was poisoned. Our injected confessors must at least appear to be normal.'

Soviet specialists immediately began to perfect the drugs. Scopolamine was one. People in the *Politburo* prison of Lefortovo and in many other N.K.V.D. prisons were injected. Some research on this line was even carried out at the Kremlin Hospital.

Step by step Stalin's 'scientific' methods made headway, and the day when the first public trial could be staged was not far off.

I. MAKSIM GORKY AND STALIN

To give his 'treason trials' conviction in the U.S.S.R. and abroad, Stalin approached the famous writer Maksim Gorky, to get him to cloak the farce with his authority and pen. Gorky refused and by doing so paid for his defiance with his life.

2. ROSA, STALIN'S THIRD WIFE

At the age of thirty-five, Rosa Kaganovich gave up her own public life to devote herself to being a housewife. In return, Stalin allowed her to meet all her friends without restriction, and to continue her literary discussions, and musical evenings, at weekly gatherings which were known as *Rosa's Salons*.

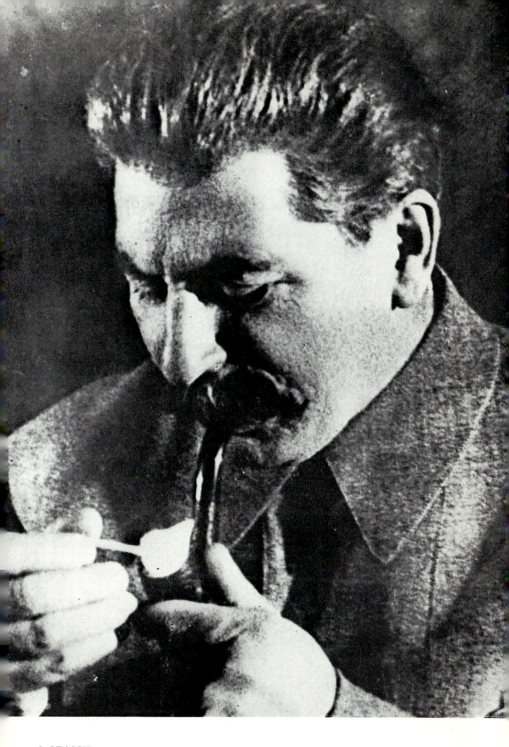

3. STALIN

The man with the world on his mind. Nevertheless, he often found time to attend *Rosa's Salons* and happily took part in the discussions of Soviet literature. He also enjoyed joining in the dances which always rounded off the discussions or musical performances.

4. LAVRENTIY BERIA—LAST HEAD OF STALIN'S SECRET POLICE
Beria recorded a most authentic account about Stalin's death in a Memorandum which he entrusted to faithful friends—to be circulated only in the
event of his own death. After he was shot, the Memorandum was made
known and the world learned the full truth about Stalin's end.

5. MIKHAIL SUSLOV
'Young Mikhail' at the time when he attended the University of Communism.
He was one of Stalin's youngest protégés, survived all purges and super-
purges, and is now one of the most important and feared Kremlin dignitaries. His nickname in the Russian Party hierarchy is 'The String Puller.'

6. GENRIKH YAGODA

Stalin's number one henchman during the blood purges in the Thirties. However, when he dared to defy his Master, he signed his own death warrant. On Stalin's orders, the ex-head of the Soviet Secret Police was accused of poisoning Maksim Gorky, tried in March 1939, and—executed.

7. NIKOLAI YEZHOV

Stalin's mighty Secret Police chief was given *carte blanche* when he succeeded Yagoda. Yezhov's bloodshed took on such dimensions that no one in Russia felt safe. But he too became Stalin's victim. He was interned in a lunatic asylum and on the day of his arrival he was found hanged on a tree.

8. (*above*) TRADE UNION BUILDING IN MOSCOW
Home of Stalin's Marionette Show Trials in the Thirties.
(*below*) LUBYANKA
Moscow headquarters of the Soviet Secret Police in Dzhierzhinsky Square.
In its cellar prison, thousands of innocent citizens have been tortured and
murdered.

9. SOVIET WOMEN AT WORK

Soviet women of all ages work in collieries, salt and ore mines, tunnelling, on building sites, road and rail constructions, as lumberjacks, etc.

(*above*) Soviet women doing heavy manual work on a railway line.

(*below*) Soviet women–lumberjacks.

10. FUTURE RED ARMY OFFICERS

Ground warfare is taught in Soviet schools, beginning at the age of eight years.

(*above*) Ground warfare instruction of ten-year-olds in the Kalinin Elementary School in Moscow's Lenin District.

(*below*) Soviet Red Army recruits at the ceremony of swearing the Oath of Allegiance.

11. MAY DAY PARADE
(*above*) Military parade in Moscow's Red Square.
(*below*) Demonstration of Soviet youth in Moscow's Red Square, following
the military parade.

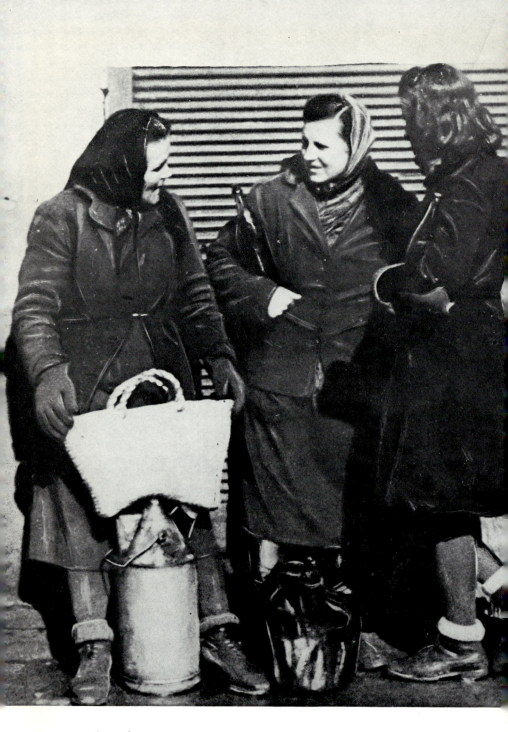

12. 'FREE' MARKET

Collective farmers travel to Moscow, Leningrad, Kiev, and other Soviet cities and towns to sell their products at inflated prices. Some of them do lucrative business because they are allowed to sell products which official shops do not have. Here is a group of women-farmers who sold all their products in record time on the 'Free' Market.

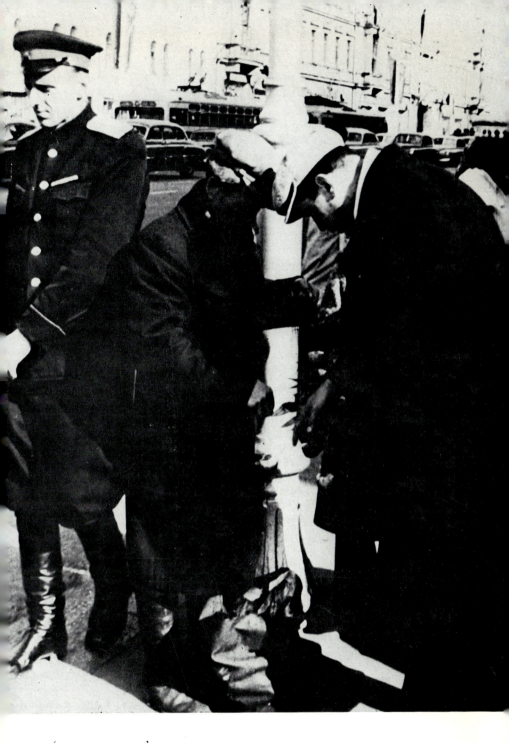

13. 'LAW BREAKERS' IGNORED

This black-market operator (*left*), at a busy street corner in Moscow, sells a scarce item to one of the Soviet Union's constant searchers for daily living needs. A Soviet officer, accustomed to such sights, turns a blind eye to the 'law breaker'.

14. BORIS PASTERNAK

The famous Russian poet and author was often praised in the Soviet Press for his 'qualities of quiet scholarship and poetic reflections which have gone into his literary works'. Nevertheless, he was eventually considered 'a slanderer of Communism' and—suddenly died.

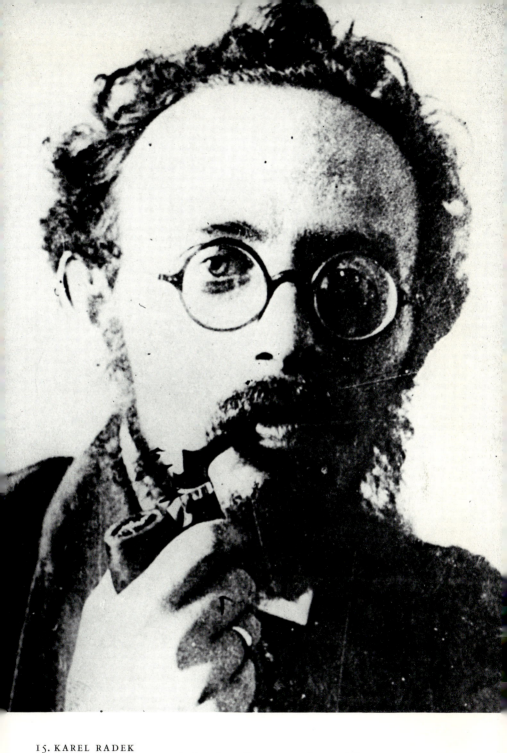

15. KAREL RADEK

One of the most distinguished and intelligent members of the Soviet hierarchy. But he knew too much and had to be silenced. In this particular instance, however, Stalin kept his promise and spared his life, for, under a new identity, he was still of considerable value.

16. ABOARD A SOVIET CRUISER
Between duty, a Soviet naval officer explains to his sailors the cruisers route
and strategic moves during the manoeuvres.

CHAPTER TWENTY

Everything's the Best in the World

ONE of the things that I was finding increasingly annoying (as well as extremely stupid) about the Russians was their obsession with claiming that everything in Russia was 'the best in the world.' This sort of groundless boasting was all the more remarkable when it appeared in articles or cropped up in conversations which were based on the morale-building statement that 'while the Capitalists may have certain things which we just now have not yet, *we* shall soon have them—but better.' Of course. It went without saying really. But they still never lost an opportunity of saying it!

At that time the Russian people were being duped on a scale that was staggering to contemplate. What I could rarely understand was the *point* of it. Russian manufacturers became adept at copying Western products; but they would never admit it. Great elaborate webs of lies were spun and dispensed—and believed.

When I was assigned to go to Leningrad to cover the launching of the first ever type-setting machine to be made in Russia, I wondered what new deceptions I'd come across. In actual fact, I was aware of one even before I started.

The factory I was to go to was named after one Max Hoeltz. Now Max Hoeltz was already a legendary figure at the time. The only thing was, I knew the truth about Max Hoeltz, an unpalatable truth for myth-makers and those they would seek to mislead.

Max Hoeltz's name was linked with the German Revolutionary Movement, and the rank and file comrades revered his memory. What a tragedy, they said, that he should die under such sad circumstances while bathing in the Volga. The truth of the matter

K

was that Max Hoeltz had been *murdered* by drowning—murdered by those very same people who afterwards created the myth of accidental death. Poor Hoeltz, who fled Germany when the pressure became too great, arrived in Russia to a chorus of praise and a barrage of publicity. Unfortunately for everyone concerned, he began to believe his own publicity, and became an increasing embarrassment because of his loudly trumpeted critical views. In the end it became necessary to shut his mouth, and it had to be done for ever. Death, as always, was the most final of all ways to accomplish this; but Hoeltz's manufactured popularity had already grown to such an extent as to preclude an ordinary arrest and death sentence.

So one day, while he was in a boat, Max Hoeltz was tipped into the water, the boat deliberately capsized, and an outspoken German Revolutionary ceased to exist. But those who were responsible didn't stop there. Now that their source of embarrassment would trouble them no longer, they set to work to perpetuate his name and his heroism. And one of the things they did was to name a factory after him. This was the factory to which I was to travel to report on the unveiling of the new type-setting machine.

I hadn't been in Leningrad before, and at the airport at Moscow, I was surprised to see the familiar sight of a Douglas airplane on the tarmac. Surprised because it was bearing the insignia of the *Russian* airline, and it was engaged on internal flights.

Before boarding, I was introduced to the pilot, and when the conventional pleasantries were over, I said: 'By the way, what make of plane is this?'

He looked surprised.

'An A.N.T. of course,' he answered. 'Designed by Anatol Nikolayevich Tupulevsky.'

I knew he was either lying, or else the victim of official hoodwinking.

He said: 'You're a journalist? Would you like to see over the plane? It might give you material for an article in your paper on a magnificent Russian aircraft.'

I said yes, I'd like to see the plane. I followed him aboard. Everything about the aircraft was just as I remembered from many flights I had made around the Continent in Douglas twin-engined air-liners.

At the end of our little tour of inspection, I said: 'And you say this is an A.N.T.?'

'Yes,' the pilot said proudly. 'The best in the world, and at least twenty years ahead of anything the Western capitalists can turn out.'

There seemed little point in arguing. Nevertheless I said: 'Well, outside the Soviet Union, this plane is known as a Douglas.'

The pilot became angry then and told me I was talking rubbish, that I was making a mistake, that Anatol Nikolayevich Tupulevsky had designed this plane. I shut up. It would have been highly dangerous to point out the obvious answer—that Tupulevsky had copied in almost every detail the plane produced by the Douglas company.

It is easy enough to successfully practice deception on people wallowing in ignorance.

Almost as soon as I arrived at the Max Hoeltz factory later that day, I was subjected to the inevitable lecture by the Partorg. In the company of the factory chief, trade union organiser and chief engineer, he began to spew forth almost word for word, the contents of an article which had recently appeared in *Pravda*. It was to the effect that the designers and engineers of the Max Hoeltz factory had invented a type-setting machine vastly superior to anything produced anywhere else in the world. (I nearly said: 'Of course, *naturally*.')

We then trooped in solemnly to view 'this wonder of Soviet invention and design.' Imagine my feelings when all I saw was what looked like an old-fashioned Linotype machine such as we were using at *Iskra Revolucii*. When I mentioned this, I was laughed at.

'No, no comrade,' the Partorg said. 'You are wrong. It may *look* like your Linotype machine, but it is quite different.'

Then I said I'd like to try it. (I was a qualified type-setter). They agreed to let me try, but within seconds, the machine was working chaotically. One matrix after the other fell.

The Partorg tried to retrieve the situation. He said: 'Well, it's not anyone who can work one of these. It takes an experienced operator.'

I showed him my qualifications.

He said: 'Just wait until I get the designer.'

The designer came and started to operate the machine. He had set no more than about fifty words when again the machine went haywire.

The Partorg blustered. The designer—a German—sweated, and finally the Partorg resorted to a safe standby reason for the failure. 'Sabotage!' he said. 'It must be sabotage!'

I was hustled away from the machine and the word sabotage was bandied about with great frequency. It was a dicey situation for the Partorg—a fiasco in front of a visiting journalist. They would have to try to retrieve the situation somehow. Knowing all this, I found their efforts almost pathetic. But when they asked me if I would like to see Leningrad, I thought I might just as well take advantage of the situation.

The resultant car tour of the city was very enjoyable. It struck me as being a fine well-laid-out place, modern in its design, and yet not devoid of character and places of historical interest. We drove along Nievskyi Prospekt, saw the Smolny, the Winter Palace, the Fort of Kronstadt—and all the time my hosts were being as charming and attentive as possible.

They even took me to the river Neva and enticed me to go for a swim. I didn't need much persuading, but I cursed the mosquitoes that plagued me while I was undressed. All the swiping and slapping in the world wouldn't keep them away.

And finally it was time for me to leave and catch my plane back to Moscow. The Partorg and the designer were bending over backwards to be pleasant; the Partorg regretted the 'unfortunate business of the machine;' between them they almost begged me not to make them look fools in my article. I played them along, kept them in suspense. But I knew that I hadn't a snowball's chance in Hell of getting the facts published anyway.

★   ★   ★

When I awoke next morning I discovered that my left foot was terribly swollen and hurt when I touched or moved it. As there was no doctor in the Luks, I telephoned my office for advice. They instructed me to go to Botkyn Hospital and promised to send a car to fetch me. With great difficulty I managed, helped by the driver, to hop along the long corridor on my right foot as far as the reception hall of Botkyn Hospital. Though they had been advised by the First Aid Department of *Mossoviet Publications Combinat* of my arrival, I had to wait in the crowded reception hall. The foot was becoming more swollen by the minute. After nearly an hour I was called.

'Very serious, very serious,' the doctor said as soon as I hopped into his surgery. He hadn't even looked at my foot! 'I tell you, comrade, it's very serious,' he repeated. He was wearing a dirty overall, and looked more like a porter than a doctor. 'I'll have to ask the specialist for his opinion,' he said, and left me alone in the room.

A few minutes later he came back with a youngster who looked no more than twenty-one. This was the specialist? He touched my foot, looked very serious and gave his verdict:

'The comrade casualty doctor is right. It's very grave. I'll have to operate on you immediately.'

'What is it then?' I demanded. 'What exactly is wrong with my foot?'

'Blood poisoning,' he replied without hesitation. 'You're in danger of your life, comrade. No time must be lost.'

'What do you propose to do?' I enquired.

'Amputate,' he said curtly.

I was horrified.

'Not the whole of your leg,' he said. 'I think we should be able to save it from the knee up. Don't worry, you'll be under anaesthetic, you won't feel a thing.'

'You're absolutely right,' I said. 'I won't feel a thing, because you're not amputating *my* leg!'

He tried to plead with me at first to be reasonable, then became abusive. But I wasn't having any fuzzy-faced youngster amputating my leg on what seemed to me to be little more than an ignorant whim. I got up to go.

'If your leg isn't amputated as soon as possible, you'll die,' the 'specialist' said.

'I'll take that risk,' I said. 'It's my leg, and my life.'

'So you know better than the doctors, is that it?' the casualty doctor said. 'What do *you* propose to do, if I may ask?'

I said I intended to fly back to my own country as soon as possible and seek medical attention there.

'Back to a Capitalist doctor?' he sneered. 'Well let me tell you comrade, you'll be given the same diagnosis and prognosis, and it will be too late. You are a fool I think. And if you were not an editor of *Vecherniaya Moskva*, I might be tempted to think you were something else.'

The car had waited for me so I asked the driver to take me to Kremlin Hospital which was considered to be the best in the U.S.S.R. Strictly speaking, I was not really entitled to go there. However, I knew that employees of the *Comintern* belonged to that hospital and I hoped that my *Comintern* and Luks pass would open the doors for me. In fact, it worked.

Again I was seen by a casualty doctor who decided to call a specialist. Presently an elderly gentleman with a little grey beard looked at my foot which by now was even more swollen.

'I'm afraid it will have to come off,' he decided. 'There's no point in trying to save it.'

'Am I in danger of life?' I wanted to know.

'Oh, no,' he assured me. 'We haven't any beds free at the moment. But you needn't worry. You will be all right for a couple of days.'

That was all I wanted to know. There was still time (although perhaps only barely enough) to fly home. *If* I could get out of Russia. I knew that would be an enormous problem, because I was not in possession of an Exit Permit, and these took nearly a week to get, even with top official aid.

As soon as I got back to my room, I phoned Beatrice, my colleague and friend from the *Comintern* Section. I told her my plight, and what I proposed doing. She sympathised, and said that Russian doctors were amputation-happy; but that I should not try to get away. It would be futile, even dangerous, she said.

'Stay there, and I'll see if there are any foreign doctors in Moscow at the moment,' she said. 'If I can locate one, I'll try to get him to see you as soon as possible.'

I lay there looking at my swollen foot, thoughts of blood-poisoning, amputation and death racing through my mind. I don't know how long I waited. I must have dozed off, but I awoke to the phone's instant ringing. It was Beatrice. She had tracked down a German doctor named Fried, she said, and he would be with me inside an hour.

I had known a Dr. Fried before coming to Russia. Could it possibly be the same one? If it was, I would be in luck, because the Dr. Fried I'd known was a first rate medical man.

Fifty-five minutes later there was a knock on my door, and I opened it to admit 'my' doctor Fried.

He examined my foot carefully, but within seconds he straightened up, smiling. 'There's not much wrong with that,' he said. 'Once I've taken the sting out, you should be all right.'

'Sting!' I said.

'That's right,' Fried said.

'But what about the blood poisoning, amputation, the danger to my life . . .'

'Nonsense, or ignorance, perhaps both,' he said, spreading his hands.

'But I'd have lost a leg if I'd let them have their way!' I said. 'And all over an insect sting. What are they, pork butchers masquerading as doctors?'

He was a good Communist. He was also a good doctor. He didn't say anything. But his expression, and in a way, his silence, said everything.

He gave me a solution which I was to add to warm water to bathe my foot. The swelling began to go down almost at once. On the next day I was able to get my shoe on; four days later my foot was back to normal.

I tried to persuade my Editor to let me write up my experience in the paper. But he refused. 'It would harm the reputation of Soviet medicine,' he said. Some reputation.

I went to see the Medical Chiefs of the two hospitals, and told them how, in each of their hospitals, I had nearly had my leg amputated because of an insect sting. I got no satisfaction. Both of them backed up their doctors. 'The diagnosis of the doctors *must* have been correct,' they said. 'But sometimes nature works its own cures. It must have been so in your case.'

I ought to have known. How *could* they have been wrong? After all, like anything else Russian, they were the best in the world.

CHAPTER TWENTY-ONE

Russian Law

WHEN my Section Leader, Birne, told me that my time at the Luks was at an end, he was in effect telling me that my connection with the *Comintern* was over too. It was a serious thing to be told, because a natural follow-on would be to be told that I was to leave Russia altogether. Although this wouldn't have left me heartbroken, it would most certainly have caused me a certain amount of fear. I was well enough acquainted with Russian methods by this time to know that my 'disappearance' could be quite easily arranged; and my death could be one more 'tragic accident.'

All this was going through my mind as Birne talked.

'. . . so your accommodation at the Luks will have to be surrendered, comrade,' he was saying again, and he paused. He looked levelly at me, and I thought, this is it, this is where he tells me to leave Russia. But no, he wasn't saying that at all. He was saying: 'However, if you yourself want to stay on in Moscow with *Vecherniaya Moskva*, the *Comintern* will not object. But you will have to find your own living accommodation.'

Trying to find a suitable flat in Moscow in those days was every bit as bad as trying to find one in England at the time of its worst housing crisis. There were some available all right; but at black market rents that put them away beyond most people's range.

I decided to ask my Editor to help. He was a person of influence. Surely he would be able to do something. He tried. He telephoned the Housing Commandant of *Mossoviet Publications Combinat* and pressed him hard, saying I was an 'essential executive who cannot be replaced at the moment' and pointing out that I might be forced to leave Russia for the want of some rooms to live in. But he drew a blank. There was nothing available.

In the end I resorted to an advertisement in *Vecherniaya Moskva*. In one day I got fifty replies, and I went by car to most of those who had replied before I found an apartment worth taking. Some of the rooms I was offered were filthy, many dilapidated, most of them only cubby-hole size. But at one apartment in a modern block, I thought I had struck gold. I had too, in the shape of the buxom blond girl with the inviting eyes who opened the door for me.

I had reckoned that rent for an apartment would cost me a minimum of a couple of hundred roubles a month. But the girl made me an offer—co-habitation at nineteen roubles a month! Maybe I should have accepted. Especially in view of some of the other females who made me similar offers. Most of them were what the Americans call 'homely.'

In the end I got a room in a flat in a ten year old block. The flat was owned by an elderly couple named Rissing. The old man had been an engineer; his wife was confined to a wheelchair; their savings were gone; their old-age pension kept them barely above starvation level. So they were letting a room of their flat. They were looking for a steepish rent—three hundred roubles a month—but the place was close to my office, and in a good area. I accepted, and moved in.

Two months later I was in court over my room. What happened was that one morning an Inspector from the District Housing Committee came to see me and wanted to know how much I was paying for my room. I knew that it was illegal to charge exorbitant rents, but I was sorry for the Rissings and did not mind helping them by paying the three hundred roubles a month. So I told the Inspector, that it was none of his or the Housing Committee's business what I was paying. The Rissings had *bought* the flat and according to the Housing Law could do whatever they pleased with it.

Shortly afterwards I was summoned to appear at the District People's Court. The charge against me was possession of my room. The Rissings were not summoned.

'How ridiculous!' exclaimed my Editor when I showed him my summons. 'I'll come with you to the court and tell them that you are one of our key workers, that you must have a room as otherwise you could not work for us. I will also arrange for a high executive from *Mossoviet* to appear and make it clear to the judge that it would be damaging for *Vecherniaya Moskva* if your room were to be taken away. After all, *Mossoviet* is above the District Housing Committee. I am pretty sure that the judge will rule in your favour.'

'That's all very well,' Abram said later, 'but I think that you ought to have a lawyer. He can question the Housing Inspector in court, and can call our Editor and the *Mossoviet* executive. A lawyer can do all kinds of things which neither you nor any of your supporters could do.'

Together we went to a District Lawyers' Office to get a lawyer assigned, who would be able to take my case on. There was no private legal practice in the U.S.S.R. and one had to take a lawyer assigned by the office clerk. The fee generally speaking was very low.

'What do you want?' a bored woman enquired when we arrived at the District Lawyers' Office. She was obviously annoyed that we had interrupted her reading.

Abram did the talking. It was important for me to get not just a lawyer, but a good one, and this was not always easy, because Soviet lawyers were in the same category as clerks and received a miserable monthly salary. He called the woman *golubchik*,* offered her a cigarette, invited her to have dinner with us in the restaurant of the House of the Press and promised her that I would give her a signed copy of my book. So he managed to soften the little dictator of the District Lawyers' Office and she assigned me Comrade Matvyeyev who was considered to be one of the best defenders and cross-examiners in Moscow.

Matvyeyev was a thin little man with a very intelligent hollow-cheeked face and burning eyes. He was dressed in a shabby suit—not surprising considering the ridiculous salary he received. As soon as he heard the story, he said that he would be delighted to take my case on. Abram slipped him a couple of hundred roubles.

*Little pigeon – an affectionate expression widely used in Russian.

Delighted, Matvyeyev assured us that he had not the slightest doubt that he would win the case for me. Abram casually mentioned that there would be another three hundred roubles to be collected if we *did* win.

On the morning of the hearing, I went with Matvyeyev, Abram, my Editor, the *Mossoviet* executive, and the Rissings, and sat in the District People's Court which was housed in a dirty and badly ventilated room on the second floor of a dilapidated house. The yellowish paint was peeling off the walls. Large pictures of Stalin and other Soviet leaders hung everywhere, and an oblong red-draped table was placed in front of two windows which looked as if they had not been cleaned since the 1917 Revolution. A few electric-light bulbs without shades lit the room, and opposite the red table, about twelve long wooden benches were placed, for the people who had been summoned. The benches were full. The over-spill were standing.

A young fellow in a khaki blouse suddenly shouted: 'Everybody rise!'

Two men and one woman entered. The first, who was the judge, took his seat at the centre of the red-draped table, and the other two sat on either side of him. The judge had some legal qualifications but the two others were laymen who had come from some factory or office to form the People's Court.

'Valeryan Grigoryevich Gorbatov,' the fellow in the khaki blouse called out.

A man of about forty years of age, dressed in threadbare overalls, stepped towards the table, facing the judge and his assistants.

'You are charged with having been late for work,' the judge addressed the man. 'What have you to say in your defence?'

'According to the work's clock I was two minutes late,' the work-man replied in a clear voice, 'but the work's clock is always five minutes fast.'

'I am not concerned with that,' the judge replied. 'As far as the works are concerned you were late. Have you anything else to say?'

'As far as the right time is concerned I was three minutes early because on that day the work's clock was five minutes fast.'

'That's enough!' The judge banged the table with his fist. 'It is regrettable that a man of such an excellent working record has to be brought before the People's Court. You should be ashamed of yourself!' He whispered something to the other two and said: 'If you had not such an excellent working record I would send you to prison for a period of at least eighteen months. However, taking your record into consideration, I will sentence you to six months imprisonment. The sentence is not to be served in a prison, but at your factory. That means that you are to work as before but that twenty per cent of your earnings will be deducted as a fine. As far as your criminal record is concerned, however, you have been sentenced to six months.'

'That is not fair,' the man exclaimed. 'One can hardly call this People's Justice.'

'One more word and I will change your sentence to the full eighteen months *in prison*,' the judge shouted. 'Next case.'

'Otto Fritzovich Braun!'

This was a tall and broad-shouldered man in his late twenties.

'You are charged with not having fulfilled your working norm and with having produced a greater percentage of rejects than is usual,' the judge addressed the defendant. 'What have you to say in your defence?'

'Nothing, Comrade Judge,' the accused replied with a strong German accent. 'The charge is as idiotic as our director.'

'If you don't stop speaking in such an aggressive way I will have you removed from this court and will pronounce sentence in your absence,' the judge said angrily. 'You are standing before a People's Court and are requested to show respect to Soviet Justice.'

'Since I was a small boy I have always respected everything that has been connected with the Soviet Union,' the man replied fearlessly. 'My father fought together with Karl Liebknecht in the German Revolution and is now imprisoned by Hitler because of his Communist activities. My brother who was a leading member of the German Communist Party, was murdered by the Gestapo because of his illegal Communist activities. I was arrested by the Nazis because I took over from my brother and was a link with the illegal Central Committee of the German Communist Party. On my transport to a concentration camp I managed to escape, and with Comrade Wilhelm Piek's help I was granted asylum in the U.S.S.R. I am a skilled toolmaker and I know my job.'

'I can't see what you and your family's past has to do with the charge against you,' the judge stopped him. The two others whispered something and he then said: 'I think it best in the interests of Soviet Justice that I should grant you legal aid so that you can be represented by a lawyer. Case adjourned for seven days.'

Case after case was called. A woman worker was sentenced to eighteen months in prison for having been half-an-hour late for work. A factory director got three years hard labour for having spent too much money on improving the works canteen. An elderly turner who had worked all his life was sentenced to one year's prison for having spoiled his precious machine. A bus driver got two years because an official car had crashed into the back of his vehicle. The bus driver was ordered to drive his bus and receive only eighty per cent of his earnings. And so it went on.

I was getting annoyed. My case should have been the first and we had been requested to be at the People's Court at precisely ten o'clock in the morning. However, there was no sign of my case coming on.

Then, suddenly, the fellow in the khaki blouse called my name.

'This is an application by the District Housing Committee for possession of a room,' the judge said when I stood in front of him. 'What have you to say in your defence?'

'Comrade Judge,' my lawyer said before I had a chance to say a word, 'I have been instructed to represent my client, and I submit that the application for possession of my client's room is not only preposterous, but also malicious. It may even be proved to be an act of sabotage. I shall call witnesses of the highest standing to prove this.'

'Very well then, Comrade Matvyeyev,' the judge said. He knew the lawyer. 'Let's hear what you have to say.'

Matvyeyev, who was an excellent speaker, told the People's Court all he wished to say, then called my Editor, then the *Mos-*

soviet executive, and ended up by saying that it was an outrageous act of bureaucracy on the part of the District Housing Committee to demand that a well-known journalist and writer, an indispensible editor of *Vecherniaya Moskva*, should be asked to give up his room. A room over which they (the District Housing Committee) had no jurisdiction whatsoever.

'I thank you, comrades,' the judge said, turning to Matvyeyev, my Editor, and the *Mossoviet* executive. 'It is very good of you to have left your important jobs to come to the People's Court to help Soviet justice.' He then called the Housing Inspector and said in a stern voice: 'You have heard what has been said. What have you to say now?'

'In accordance with our law this comrade is not entitled to have the room as he is helping an exploiter to make Capitalist profits,' said the Inspector. 'All that has been said here about the defendant has nothing to do with the issue. Our Soviet law . . .'

'Are you trying to teach me the law, comrade?' the judge said angrily. 'All I want to hear from you is why you summoned a well-known journalist and writer?'

'Because he would not collaborate with me,' the Inspector answered.

'So you summoned him!' The judge raised his voice. 'You were the cause of the Editor of *Vecherniaya Moskva* having to leave his important job to come here, of a high *Mossoviet* executive having to abandon his activities, to prove to this court how ridiculous your application is! Comrade Matvyeyev said that your action, is among other things one of sabotage. The court will decide whether that is the case, and whether you should be prosecuted.'

However, the Housing Inspector was no fool. He brought up clever arguments, managed at some stages to create the impression that his case was a good one and answered very carefully and convincingly when cross-examined by Matvyeyev.

Finally the court left the room to discuss the case in private and arrive at their verdict. They were out for over half-an-hour. The judge then announced:

'The People's Court have arrived at the following conclusion.

The application of the District Housing Committee is herewith rejected. The defendant is entitled to keep his room, and the District Housing Committee has, forthwith, to allocate the room to him so that on their records he is entered as the rightful owner. As far as the charge of exploitation is concerned, it has not been proved that the citizens Rissings charge an exorbitant rent, and they remain, therefore, the rightful owners of the rest of the flat. It is also ordered that no prosecution against the Housing Inspector be instituted as the People's Court has come to the conclusion that, although he acted unwisely, he acted in good faith.' The judge closed the folder on his table and said: 'Next case.'

I had much pleasure in paying my lawyer a hundred roubles above the promised sum.

A few days later I received from the District Housing Committee a decree confirming that the room was my property.

CHAPTER TWENTY-TWO

Militarism and Suspicion

IN 1935, with numbers of people 'disappearing,' talk of purges on the lips of frightened people, and the continued verbal attacks on the 'would-be Capitalist aggressors' heard on all sides, the whole climate of existence in Moscow was one of fear and suspicion. 'We must be prepared to fight' was the theme that recurred in speech after speech. 'Our people must learn the ways of war,' they said; and they set about teaching the people just that.

All over the country, men and women of all ages were organised and given training. And one day Abram told me it was our turn next—we of *Mossoviet Publications Combinat.*

'I know how you feel,' Abram said, 'but you'd better not object. Fall in with their plans, otherwise . . . well, I don't have to tell you, do I?'

In due course a Red Army colonel and a group of junior officers arrived, a mass meeting was called, and the Partorg stood before us and told us the purpose of the visit. Then the colonel stood up, berated the West, eulogised 'our beloved Josif Vissarionovich,' said the mighty Red Army, Air Force and Navy were the best in the world, but that the civilian population too must be ready to defend the glorious Motherland. The Partorg of course led the clapping.

Afterwards, we were informed that our training would not interfere with our work.

'Long live our great and wise leader who will take us on to victory!' they shouted. And the cheers rang out again.

And so it was that I was taught to shoot pistol and machine gun, and how to throw hand grenades. And when that was done, I was

L

taken up twenty-five times in a dilapidated aircraft, and made to jump (terrified) off a wing, counting three seconds before pulling a rip-cord. After these twenty-five jumps I was passed out as a trained parachutist. But I wasn't unique. There were many others who did the same thing. And anyway, one of the girls who worked in our office—Sonya Davidovna—qualified before I did.

One of the so-called privileges attached to qualifying as a parachutist was membership of the *Workers' Aviation Club*. Keen parachutists were delighted at this of course, because it provided them with plenty of opportunities of indulging in their hobby. There was one other reason which attracted the males to the club— Lyubov Abelovna Yenukidze. She was a beautiful twenty-year-old Georgian girl who was Russia's ace parachutist, holder of many records, and an instructor at the club. But most of all, she was very much of a woman.

*   *   *

When we were informed that the Black Sea fleet was to engage in manoeuvres, *Vecherniaya Moskva* sent me to Sebastopol to cover the story. On arrival there I reported at the Press Centre and was given an order (written) to go to the Intourist Hotel. The letter was addressed to the Commandant and requested him to allocate a room to me.

'You will have to come back later in the evening,' the reception clerk told me, when he had looked at the order.

I knew this was the usual practice in the Soviet Union, even if rooms were available. They liked to make people wait. 'I want a room *now*!' I said, and made it clear I knew the Press Centre had booked rooms.

'You will have to wait,' said the reception clerk.

'Call the Comrade Commandant, please,' I said.

'What for?' the reception clerk looked up. 'I am in charge of allocating rooms. The Commandant is busy with much more important matters.'

'Call the Commandant, please,' I repeated. 'And I would advise you not to be awkward if you wish to avoid trouble.'

As always, the threat worked. Regardless of whether it was in

Moscow, Leningrad, or as now, in Sebastopol, people were afraid. As soon as one was firm, they at once imagined one might have influential friends and that this might be dangerous for them.

'The Comrade Commandant will be coming in a minute,' the reception clerk told me as he replaced the telephone receiver.

A little later a jolly looking man in his early sixties, came to the reception desk. It was the Hotel Commandant. As soon as he saw the order from the Press Centre he told the reception clerk to give me the key to a room on the first floor. He apologized for giving me a double room and said there was no single room available.

My luck in having a nice room, with windows overlooking the sea, did not last long. I had hardly settled in when the telephone rang and the Commandant asked whether I would care to have a drink with him. I met him shortly afterwards in the hotel bar.

'I wonder whether you would do me a favour,' he asked over a glass of vodka. He told me that in the whole hotel there was not a single bed free, with the exception of the one in my room, and that he just had to find accommodation for one more person. 'I thought that you might be willing to help me,' he concluded. 'He is a very nice person . . .'

I did not really mind. 'Who is it?' I asked.

'That comrade over there,' said the Commandant and pointed to a young-looking man in the uniform of a Rear Admiral.

'I'm sorry,' I replied firmly. Sebastopol was a frontier town, and I had to be even more careful than in Moscow. With the purge still raging in full force all over the country I could not risk being accused one day (when it suited the N.K.V.D.) of pushing myself on to a high naval officer. All sorts of sinister (and baseless) constructions could be put on it.

'But why not?' The Commandant was surprised at my refusal. 'He is . . .'

'He is a Rear Admiral of the fleet,' I completed his sentence. 'That is why.'

The Commandant could not, or would not, see my point, so I told him I would be agreeable to sharing my room with the Rear Admiral only if he brought me confirmation in writing from the

District Headquarters of N.K.V.D. to the effect that I had been *asked* to share my room. I had to do this in order to safeguard myself. An hour or so later I received a letter written on the stationery of the N.K.V.D. Headquarters Sebastopol, bearing a big red rubber stamp next to the signature, in which they confirmed that the Soviet Navy would be obliged if I would let Rear Admiral Ilya Markovich Danilov share my room.

'Satisfied?' the Hotel Commandant asked.

'Yes,' I said. 'To you it may seem trivial, to me it is important. Comrade Danilov may now share my room.'   ·

In order to take every possible precaution, I wrote a letter to Abram, asking him to forward the N.K.V.D. confirmation to my Consulate, in case I should ever be accused of spying. I sent it off by registered post.

The Rear Admiral turned out to be a very pleasant fellow, and as we had plenty of time on our hands because the manoeuvres were delayed for some reason, we decided to take advantage of the lovely summer weather and went to the beach. Danilov had a weakness for the fair sex and quickly made the acquaintance of two attractive girls.

The four of us spent the whole afternoon on the beach, and we invited the girls to come with us to a dinner and dance at our hotel.

'Have you ever been on a battleship?' Danilov suddenly asked, while filling our glasses. When we told him that we had not, he said: 'I will make arrangements for you to go over my ship to-morrow. I think you will find it interesting.'

The next morning a motorboat took us to his flag-ship, and he showed us all over it. I was under the impression that both girls, who had told us they were textile workers, were bored with looking at guns, machine rooms, the radio room and the armoury. Only when we sat down in the ship's dining room and had some food and plenty of drinks, did they thaw out.

Danilov was a fellow of tremendous energy and insisted on taking us for a sightseeing tour in his car when we returned to the town. Because he was such a high-ranking officer, we were allowed to look over the camouflaged fortifications encircling this important harbour. I found this marvellously interesting, but the girls just seemed bored and when Danilov suggested we should continue sight-seeing, they said they were tired and asked us to drop them at their hostel. When at last we retired to our beds, I couldn't sleep, though I was very tired. My room-mate was more fortunate—he snored away happily.

Suddenly I was aware of someone carefully turning our door handle. I had locked it from the inside and the key was still in the lock. I wondered if someone had made a mistake and was trying the wrong door. But then I heard a scratching noise which convinced me that a burglar was trying to enter our room. I woke the Rear Admiral and told him in a whisper what was going on. He was wide awake immediately. He took his gun and a powerful torch and whispered to me that we would arrest the burglar as soon as he came into the room.

A little later the key was pushed out of the lock and fell with a cushioned plop on to the carpet. Then another key was inserted from the outside and the door opened inwards very slowly and quietly. There was no light in the corridor and we couldn't see who was there. Danilov sat bolt upright and switched on the torch.

'Stay where you are, or I'll shoot!' he shouted. 'You are under arrest.'

'Shut up!' a commanding voice said from the door. 'We are N.K.V.D. officers.' At the same moment the man who had spoken switched on the light and commanded: 'Put the gun away!' He then told us to get out of our beds and dress. 'You are under arrest.'

'What is this all about?' Danilov protested. 'You must have made a mistake.'

'The N.K.V.D. never makes mistakes,' one of them, a major, replied.

'I must telephone my headquarters,' said my room-mate. 'This is outrageous.'

'You will not telephone anybody!' the major commanded. 'Hurry and get dressed.'

These two were experts at searching a room. They did not overlook a scrap of paper and even took some old bills and notes which someone who had occupied the room before us had left behind. They took my typewriter, fountain pen, wrist watch and lighter, my wallet with all my money and various papers. They emptied all the pockets of our suits.

'Come on now,' the major commanded. 'And don't try to escape —it would cost you your lives.'

In the corridor were four more N.K.V.D. officers with drawn revolvers. They ushered us into their waiting car and sat next to us.

No word was spoken during the journey to District N.K.V.D. Headquarters. I racked my brain to find some clue as to why we had been arrested. It was pointless. I was nevertheless glad that I had obtained written confirmation from the N.K.V.D. that I had been approached to share my room with the Rear Admiral. I was quite sure Abram would take whatever steps he could.

On arrival at District N.K.V.D. Headquarters we were immediately separated. I was taken to the third floor and told to wait in the corridor. 'Stand over there,' an N.K.V.D. man ordered me. 'Face the wall, hands behind your head. Don't turn round, and don't rest your head on the wall.'

No one who has not been forced to stand for hour after hour in one position, facing a wall, can even begin to understand what it is like. The hands, arms, feet and head feel heavier every minute. One begins to *feel* every part of the body, each joint of every finger.

After an hour or so I started to break out into a cold sweat. My body began to itch unbearably. I had an irresistable urge to scratch myself. The guard who was watching noticed the movement of my hands and shouted:

'Put those filthy hands of yours back! *At once*, or I'll blow your brains out!'

The hours stretched out interminably.

Daylight began to creep into the corridor, and just when I was on the point of collapse I was led into the office of an N.K.V.D. Colonel. I could hardly walk, and my temper was now fully risen.

'What's the idea of bringing me here and making me stand in front of the wall like a criminal?' I demanded.

'It is I who ask questions here,' the colonel said. 'Sit down.' He offered me a papiros and remarked: 'That will soothe your nerves.'

I inhaled the smoke eagerly. 'I am entitled to know why you treat me like a criminal,' I said, but this time I had control of my voice.

'You are charged with being an accessory to Japanese espionage,' he said.

I was flabbergasted. If I had not known so much about the methods of the secret police I would have laughed. But it was no laughing matter. 'That's ridiculous!' I said. 'A Japanese spy? I don't even know any Japanese people.'

'I did not say that *you* were a Japanese spy,' the colonel corrected me. 'I said that you are an accessory to Japanese espionage.'

He was quite serious. I knew I was in a very tight spot.

'I object most strongly,' I said. 'I demand an immediate investigation to clear me of such a preposterous allegation.'

'That's just what I'm doing,' my interrogator replied. 'Tell me,' he went on, 'what you know about Ilya Markovich Danilov.'

From the start I had suspected that the Rear Admiral might mean trouble for me. Now here it was. I could have kicked myself for having consented to share my room with him. I told the colonel exactly what had happened, pointing out that District N.K.V.D. Headquarters had *requested* me to share my room with him, and that I knew nothing about the man at all.

'You arranged your alibi very cleverly right from the start by insisting on the request from the N.K.V.D., didn't you?' the colonel was saying. 'As soon as you had it, you introduced Danilov to two girls whom you knew to be Japanese spies. You suggested that all of you go to the battleship. *You* also suggested a sight-seeing tour of the defence bunkers. Very neat, comrade. Two girls wouldn't arouse suspicion. But they weren't just two ordinary girls. They were spies.'

'I am amazed at your invention, Comrade Colonel,' I said, trying hard to control my temper.

'Enough!' He banged on the desk with his fist. 'You know I am right. Prepare a statement in your own writing immediately.'

I copied his method and banged on the desk. 'I won't be insulted

by you or anybody else,' I said coldly. 'Ring Comrade Kalinin
now, and tell him that I have been arrested.'

'How do you know Comrade Kalinin?' he asked. The name of
the President of the U.S.S.R. had obviously impressed him.

'Ask him.' I decided to bluff as much as possible. 'Go and ring him.
At once. I've had enough of this. And tell him also that your major
took all my things away and . . .'

'All your belongings are in a safe place,' the colonel interrupted.
'Even the card Comrade Kalinin gave . . .' He stopped short,
realising that he had said too much. He offered me another papiros
and while lighting it said: 'You insist then that your story is correct?'

'Yes.'

'Your friend Danilov has made a statement in which he makes a
liar of you,' he shot back. 'What have you to say to that?'

'That *he* is the liar, if what you say is true.'

'Maybe he is; maybe he isn't,' the colonel said casually. 'But he is
a Soviet Rear Admiral. You're only a foreigner about whom we
know very little . . .'

'I asked you to ring Comrade Kalinin,' I shouted. 'Telephone
Comrade Manuilsky in the *Comintern* as well.'

'How do you know that we haven't already done so?' the colonel
said. 'Tell me what you know about the two girls.'

'I know nothing about them. We met them on the beach. I never
saw them before.'

'You introduced them to your friend?'

'I did not. *He* picked them up.'

'So you say that he knew them,' the colonel said quickly. 'Tell
me more about it.'

'I did not say that he knew them,' I replied. 'I said that we met
them by chance on the beach. Danilov liked them. That's how it
started.'

'Now listen to me.' The colonel raised his voice. 'If you want to
leave this building alive, tell me the truth.'

'That's what I am doing,' I said firmly. 'But it seems to me that
you want me to tell you lies.'

'I could apply other methods,' the colonel shouted. 'We know how to deal with little lice like you.' He banged the desk furiously and shouted: 'Are you going to make a statement or do we have to deal with you in our way?'

'All you seem to be able to do is to shout and threaten,' I said. 'But you will be sorry, I tell you.'

He stared at me cold-eyed for several seconds. He wasn't sure what to do. Maybe I had some influential friends. He knew too well that bullets were always ready in Soviet guns. He decided to change his tactics, and told me that he had conclusive proof that the two girls were Japanese spies, and that the N.K.V.D. had tapped a telephone conversation between one of them and the Japanese Consulate. In support of this he played me a recording; there was little doubt that the voice was that of one of the girls. She was describing the ship and the fortifications of Sebastopol in detail.

'What have you to say now?' said the colonel, switching off the recording. 'Do you recognise her voice?'

'It sounds like her,' I had to admit, but added: 'Of course, I cannot be absolutely certain.'

'It is her voice all right,' my interrogator said, and then, speaking to a guard over the intercom, he told him to bring in the girls. 'You will be able to ask them yourself.'

A minute or so later the two girls were brought into the office. They too had obviously been through it.

The colonel switched on the record, played a little of it and asked one girl whether this was her voice. Without hesitation she admitted, it was and added that she had signed a statement. The other girl confirmed that she had been present while her friend telephoned The colonel asked the guard to take them away.

'What have you to say now?' he said to me as soon as we were alone. 'Now you have proof that your excursion to the battleship and the fortifications was made exclusively for the purpose of supplying the Japanese with vital military information. Are you now prepared to admit that you are an accessory to Japanese espionage?'

'No, I am not,' I replied. 'I cannot dispute the fact that the girl has described what she saw but I had nothing whatsoever to do with the whole affair.'

'You suggested the trip.'

'I did not! I've told you so before,' I said.

'We can call Rear Admiral Danilov. He will confirm that the whole plan was suggested by you.'

'Yes, call him,' I assented. 'I don't think a Rear Admiral of the Soviet fleet would sink so low as to lie in my face.'

My interrogator did not comment. He gave instructions to a guard over the intercom and, a little later, Danilov was brought in, his hands handcuffed behind his back. I could hardly recognise him. There was blood on his face, both eyes were black, and he limped heavily. The colonel did not ask him to sit down but shot a question at him at once:

'You made a statement that this comrade suggested the trip to your ship?'

'No, I did not,' the Rear Admiral replied. 'I did not make any statement at all.'

'Who suggested the trip to your ship?'

'I did,' Danilov answered firmly. 'It was a mistake, I know, but . . .'

'Liar!' The colonel jumped up and hit him between the eyes. 'I'll teach you to speak the truth.'

Danilov staggered under the attack, but his voice was firm. 'It is true. I suggested this unfortunate trip . . .'

'Take him away!' my interrogator shouted to the guards. Then he turned to me: 'Do you still refuse to admit you are an accessory to Japanese espionage? It would be in everybody's interest if you . . .'

'Wait till Yagoda hears about . . .'

'You know him?' he interrupted me, and for the first time I noticed a frightened look in his eyes.

I did not know Yagoda, nor did he know me, but I decided to continue with my bluff. 'Telephone him and find out,' I said. I was terrified he would call my bluff.

'Perhaps I will and perhaps I won't . . .'

'You *must*!' I demanded. 'Go on, telephone him now! And Kalinin and Manuilsky as well.' I took the telephone receiver from its rest. 'If you won't I will.'

He grabbed the receiver from my hand and replaced it on its

rest. 'You cannot disturb Comrade Yagoda at this hour of the morning.'

'Can't I?' I laughed.

'It isn't necessary, I assure you, comrade,' he insisted. 'I can see that you had nothing to do with the whole affair. But as a member of the Communist Party you must understand we have to interrogate *every* suspect.

'I agree that you have to investigate every *suspect*, but I will not stand for the treatment you've meted out, keeping me for hours in the corridor with my face to the wall, and having that ape of a guard threaten to blow my guts out if I moved. I will tell not only Yagoda but also Kalinin and others of how I have been dealt with at the Sebastopol N.K.V.D. Headquarters.'

'That, surely, will not be necessary,' the colonel said in a persuasive voice and offered me another papiros. 'I am sorry you were treated like that. I will see that the culprits are severely reprimanded. Will you make a statement to the effect that Danilov suggested the inspection of his ship and the fortification bunkers so that the Japanese could get the secret information they were after? That's what it boils down to, isn't it?'

'It does not!' I was not prepared to help him to convict the Rear Admiral. 'Danilov made his suggestion out of sheer bravado, merely to impress the girls.'

'Rear Admiral Danilov had no right to take you or anyone else over his ship and show you the bunkers without permission,' the colonel said. 'He commited an act of great negligence, and will have to be severely punished.'

The argument continued for some time. I managed, however, to leave the office without having made any statement, and with a letter confirming that my arrest had been a mistake.

It was nearly eight o'clock in the morning when an N.K.V.D. car delivered me back at my hotel. I felt as if I had aged twenty years overnight. It had been a very close affair.

CHAPTER TWENTY-THREE

The Glories of an Organised Holiday

WHEN I got back to Moscow after the alarming events in Sebastopol, it was to be upraided by Abram. He called me all sorts of a fool for having had anything at all to do with Danilov. Poor Danilov—if only Abram could have seen him as I saw him. But then again, Abram knew his Russia too, knew of the things that happened to me, knew of the machinations of an organisation eager for scapegoats and determined to find them.

As it happened, Abram had telephoned me at the hotel in Sebastopol only two hours after my release from custody, but it wasn't until I returned to Moscow that I learned the N.K.V.D. had phoned my Editor, Partorg, and Abram for details of me. They made it sound like a routine check, never intimated that in fact I was even then under arrest.

'What does it take to teach you a lesson?' Abram said after I had told him the whole story.

'But Danilov was such a *nice* character——,' I began.

'How often do I have to tell you, don't get involved with *anyone*,' Abram cut in.

However, despite the attentions of the N.K.V.D., my journalistic work must have attracted some notice, and was praised, and within a few weeks I was informed that Abram and I were being rewarded with *putyevka's* for a one-month holiday at a luxury recreation home at Yalta. Abram in fact did not want to go. He wanted to spend the time with his wife and son at their *dacha*. But he was forced to accept the *putyevka*, and was refused vouchers (which he had offered to pay for) for his family. By virtue of some persuasion and a swop, I managed to arrange my holiday for the same time as Abram.

During the train journey to Yalta, I bought a roast duck and a loaf of bread from a peasant woman who was selling them. I didn't need them there and then, but I'd learned that in Russia one could never tell when need would arise.

The train was late arriving at our destination, and we arrived at the recreation home to be sharply told by the receptionist that our rooms had been disposed of.

There followed one of those angry exchanges which were now so much a part of my life; rudeness on the part of the woman behind the desk, anger and frustration from Abram and myself.

'Whoever you've given the rooms to,' I said, 'move them out. They're not entitled to the rooms.'

'I'm the one who decides this,' said the receptionist angrily. 'You should have been here on time.'

'We didn't keep the train late,' Abram interposed. 'Here are our vouchers; please allot us our rooms.'

The receptionist mumbled something to the effect that no room was vacant but some would be available in a day or so.

'What do you propose to do?' Abram asked her.

'I don't know yet,' the receptionist said candidly. 'I'll have to think something out. Perhaps you can come back in an hour or so.'

It was the same old story.

I asked the way to the dining room, but was told that it was too late for dinner, and that no restaurants or snack bars were open in Yalta at this time of night.

We went and sat down at a table in the reception hall and unpacked the duck and the loaf of bread. Abram produced a bottle of light Caucasian wine from his suitcase and we spread the lot on the table and started eating, to the obvious displeasure of the receptionist and another unpleasant looking woman who joined her.

After a while we were called to the reception desk and told that there just weren't any rooms available, and that the best arrangement that could be arrived at would be for us to sleep on a camp bed in a dormitory.

I refused point blank. The vouchers said clearly that both of us were to have single rooms. We demanded to see the Commandant. She turned out to be the other woman behind the desk, and she backed up the receptionist. In the end I said I was going to leave, but only on receipt of a letter to my Moscow Partorg stating that our rooms had been allocated to someone else.

At this there was much demurring and a whispered consultation, and we were then told we could have the receptionist's own room— for one night only. She and the Commandant would share.

At six o'clock on the following morning, we were shattered into wakefulness by the sound of a booming gong being hammered loudly somewhere in the hallway. There were sounds of people moving about. But we were tired and went back to sleep, and did not turn up for breakfast until 10 a.m. We didn't get any. We were, they said, over two hours late—serving stopped at 7.45 a.m.

'Haven't you read the rules that are posted all over the place?' the Commandant asked.

The answer was No, we hadn't. She produced a copy there and then, and we saw from it that all day every day was organised like a soldier's, from 6 a.m. through to 11.45 p.m. at which time everyone was supposed to be in bed! I'm afraid I spoke my mind, which angered the Commandant.

'They are not silly rules, comrade,' she snapped. 'They are the rules of this recreation home and everyone has to obey them to the letter.'

'And what happens if one doesn't obey them?' I asked.

'In such a case a report goes to the organisation which sent the rebel.'

'As far as I am concerned, I will not obey them,' Abram said. 'I have come here to have a *holiday*.'

He tore the printed regulations from the wall and folded the sheet up, slipping it into his pocket. 'You are welcome to expel me and to report to my organisation. We will see what they have to say when they hear my side of the story and study your regulations.'

'Nobody has ever complained of our rules before,' the Commandant replied. 'The only person who can make exceptions, is our Chief Medical Officer. But you can't see him now as he is busy.'

When we knocked on his door, he bade us come in. He was a jovial looking fellow of about sixty with a bald head, unshaven face and brown eyes. He was sitting at a table, smoking a hand-rolled cigarette. 'What can I do for you?' he greeted us.

We made it clear that we had not come to be bullied. He told us candidly that the rules were the work of the District Partorg who firmly believed that every single minute of a Soviet citizen's holiday ought to be organised for him. He agreed to exempt us, but said that we must keep to the times of the meals. In his report to the Commandant he stated that 'after a thorough medical examination' he had come to the conclusion that we were not suited to taking part in the usual routine of the recreation home.

The receptionist told us that our rooms were now available. We were given pleasant rooms on the ground floor, the windows of which afforded a view over the sea. Our joy was short lived, however. When we came, dead on time, to the dining room, we were to find long wooden tables at which the inhabitants sat on both sides on wooden benches. The food served matched the whole atmosphere—it was worse than the Luks canteen food.

'I am not going to stay here,' I told Abram.

'Let's find a restaurant somewhere,' he agreed.

We found one, only a few streets away, and ate some good appetizing food.

Abram persuaded me not to tell the Commandant that we would be leaving, but to see whether the dinner at the recreation home would be better. It was not. We left the table in the middle of the meal.

'What is the idea of expecting people to eat such poor food?' I challenged the Commandant.

'I don't understand what you mean, comrade,' she answered. 'The food is not bad. I eat it myself. You are not prisoners. Go if you want to, we can do quite well without grumblers.'

We realised that, if we wanted to avoid trouble, we must make arrangements with our Editor and Partorg and get their consent to leave. Abram talked the Partorg round, and once he had achieved this, the Editor did not raise any objections. When he heard that we were in no particular hurry to return to Moscow he asked us whether we would be willing to represent *Mossoviet Publications Combinat* at the Red Army manoeuvres in Rostov and at some affairs in Kharkov and other places in the Ukraine. We agreed and so found the ideal way out.

The next morning a telegram from *Vecherniaya Moskva* arrived, addressed to the Commandant of the recreation home. This requested her to inform us that we had to break short our holiday, as we were urgently needed for work. When she told us this, there was an unmistakable glint of happiness in her eyes—she was no doubt pleased to be rid of us. But not half as pleased as we were to shake the dust of that place from our feet.

CHAPTER TWENTY-FOUR

Liquidation of the Kulaks

ABRAM suggested we should go to see one of his friends who lived on the collective farm of Nizhniye Syelo, some thirty miles from Rostov. I was glad to agree, because though I had read much about the collective farms, I had never actually visited one. And I knew from various whisperings that the actuality was far different from the newspaper reports.

We managed to get a lift in a Russian army lorry. We squeezed ourselves in amongst the soldiers, who were mostly in their teens and from all parts of Russia. While the convoy bumped over the dusty road, we sang melodious Russian songs, accompanied by mouth-organs and accordions.

The journey lasted just over three hours—in the Soviet Union this was quite a fair time for a distance of under thirty miles. They dropped us in the square in the middle of Nizhniye Syelo and waved us goodbye.

We had no difficulty in finding Abram's friend, Natan Moisevich Zuckerman. A likeable fellow of Abram's age with a weather-beaten face, he was genuinely pleased to see Abram whom he had not met for many years. He persuaded us to stay the night.

Nizhniye Syelo was a collective farm of medium size, and prided itself on having sixty-one houses. It was a typical Ukrainian village. The houses were in good repair, and the walls, painted snow-white, were immaculately clean. There were only a few people to be seen. The rest were all working on the land, and only in the dusty square in front of the Soviet building were some children playing—wild games of Cossacks and White Guards.

M

Natan Moisevich had a nice house in the centre of the main street. This he occupied with his wife, their four children and his own and his wife's parents. Though the house was quite roomy it was not big enough for ten people, but the whole family insisted on our staying with them, and made immediate arrangements to move two of their children and prepare their room for us. Our protests were in vain.

During the afternoon Natan Moisevich invited us to accompany him on his round of the farm. He held the title of Agronom and was a sort of leader, which did not, however, excuse him from having to work on the land like the others.

Nizhniye Syelo was part of the 'Golden Granary of the Soviet Union.' On the vast tracts of land they grew grain, and bred cows, pigs, geese, ducks and chickens. Work was at its height as the peasants prepared for the harvest.

Though we were guests of a 'prosperous' collective farm in the richest part of the Soviet Union, the dinner which we had in Natan Moisevich's house was quite plain—Ukrainian *borshch*,* very little meat, potatoes and home-made bread.

'You see how we live in luxury and comfort,' Natan Moisevich said cynically. 'For the first time in years we have something decent to eat before the harvest.'

'Was it as bad as that?' I asked.

'Even worse,' our host's father answered, chewing his bread. 'Last year all the newspapers lied and said that there was no longer any hunger in the country. Instead of writing your stupid articles, you newspapermen should have come to the collective farms and seen for yourselves how things were.'

'Don't attack our friends, *papochka*. They weren't the ones who wrote those lies,' said his son.

'I know, I know,' the old man replied. 'But it doesn't alter the facts. Last year we had only enough potatoes for three days of the week, and no meat at all, and the rest of the time we had to make *borshch* from grass and plants which even the cows wouldn't touch. But the Press said "there is no food shortage anywhere," and "the famine is a thing of the past." '

*Cabbage soup.

'I know, grandpa,' Abram agreed with the old man, 'I have been around a bit too. I know what it is to be hungry.'

'You are a good fellow, I can see that,' the old man cheered up. Though he was in his seventies he was still vigorous in body and mind. He went to the cupboard behind him and produced a large bottle of home-made vodka. 'Let's drink, friends. Let's forget our miserable lives. Let's be happy.'

'My friends will think they've come to a real anti-Soviet house, *papochka*!' his son chided.

'The devil take the Soviets,' said his father. 'If they are some of Stalin's *Katsaps* then let them go back to the Kremlin. If they are our friends then they will understand what a Ukrainian peasant thinks. And I know they understand me.' He filled the glasses and shouted: 'Let's drink to a better future. Let's drink to a life that's worth living.'

'To your health, grandpa,' I said and raised my glass. I liked the old man. He was an honest peasant who looked at life as he saw it. 'To a happy future, to a life that's worth living.'

'You see, Natan, your friend understands me,' the old man exclaimed happily and refilled our glasses. 'He is not going to the Cheka or whatever those devils are called to denounce us. He's one of us. Let's drink, friends.'

It was not long before the bottle of strong vodka was emptied and another brought.

When the children were in bed, and the women had departed for some committee meeting, we made ourselves comfortable, and the room was soon filled with the smoke of our papirosys. Natan Moisevich tried from time to time to calm the two old men down but made no impression; the old peasants felt the urge to talk and nobody would stop them.

'I am an old man and I have nothing to lose,' Kuzmyn Markovich, Natan's father-in-law, said. 'Whether I live a few years more or less is all the same to me, but so long as I live I will say what I like, whether the Cheka devils like it or not. They are all a bunch of gangsters, from the lowest, right up to the Georgian poisoner in the Kremlin. They hold power with their Mausers.'

Kuzmyn Markovich was a real Ukrainian peasant. Born seventy-three years before in the village, he had lived there ever since, leading a hard peasant life. He told us that in Tsarist times his father had owned a house and a few acres of land. He admitted that peasant life had always been hard, but added that his father had been able to bring up a family of seven and that not only did they always have plenty to eat and were properly clothed, but they were able to save some money.

'Don't think that my father was what they call a *Kulak*,' the old man went on. 'My father worked the land with his two brothers. The land gave him more grain, vegetables and potatoes than he needed and he sold it on the market and got good money for it. He had some cattle too, and pigs and poultry, and he was able to sell milk, butter, eggs, meat and poultry. They speak a lot now about the terrible life the people had in the old times, but I tell you all the talk about the *Okhrana* and Cossack terror is nonsense. I have a memory. I know what I am talking about.'

'But life was not all that good in Tsarist Russia . . .,' Natan Moisevich tried to soften his father-in-law's words.

'It was as Kuzmyn Markovich says,' his father interrupted. 'What do you youngsters know? Only what *Pravda* and *Kommunist* tell you. What they say is a lot of rubbish and propaganda. I always say: what has the Soviet régime brought us to? Misery and slavery. We peasants in the richest part of the whole country have nothing but hard work and for this we are rewarded with hunger and the fear that one day the Cheka will come and shoot us like mad dogs.'

'Listen to me, friends,' Kuzmyn Markovich took up the thread of the conversation, and filled the glasses again. 'When those maniacs in the Kremlin decided they would liquidate the *Kulaks* as a class, and draft all the peasants into collective farms, they sent a gang of Party Commissars and Chekists to our village. True, we had landowners who owned plenty, but there were only three of them. What did those bastards from Moscow do? They not only took the *Kulaks* to the square, but they also took anyone who had a better house and a little more land than the rest, and then mowed them down with their bloody Maksims in front of us all. They left our family in peace, but my brother Lev, who was always quick-tempered, started to shout that Russian bastards were murdering innocent Ukrainian peasants. Before anybody realised what was happening, a Russian Chekist shot Lev dead. For as long as I live, I will never forgive the swine for that.'

The old man then told us that every year commissions came to the collective farms and removed everything down to the last pint of grain, and the last pound of potatoes.

'They treat us like enemies,' Natan Moisevich's father went on. 'They come during the harvest and watch every villager. We have to surrender all the produce above the small individual allocation. They pay us for what we surrender, of course. But what is the good of a few dirty roubles? For a year's hard work one can hardly buy a *chuba** and a pair of boots. And then, a few months after the harvest, another commission comes and demands further produce. We tell them that our allocation, to which we are entitled by law, is not enough to last till the next harvest. They don't believe us and accuse us of being liars. They beat us and threaten to shoot us or send us to prison or labour camps as saboteurs. They look everywhere but there is nothing hidden and all they see is our allocation, so they take that away from us. All the begging and crying of the women and children doesn't help.'

'Nizhniye Syelo was once quite an important place with over two thousand souls,' Kuzmyn Markovich went on. 'The war and the civil war cost the village only four lives. Look at it now. The Cheka and the great famine reduced us to just over four hundred people, out of which two thirds are children of various ages. You will never be able to imagine what went on. One needs to live through such a thing to know about it. No words can describe what those poor children, those little wretches, looked like before they died of starvation. Skin and bone, getting thinner and thinner, weaker and weaker before they died. And we were helpless because there was no food. We ate up all the cats and dogs, we ate the horse manure for the grain it contained. Some even ate the flesh of people who had

*Sheepskin coat.

died.' He refilled the glasses. 'Let's drink, friends. Today we live, tomorrow we die. Let's drink while we can.'

There was a terrible silence after what the old man had told us. How could you ever again see Russia or the Russians in the same light as those innocent days in Czechoslovakia? When I left that farm, it was with an awful knowledge inside me.

CHAPTER TWENTY-FIVE

Tanks and Child Bandits

'I DON'T want a *katsap* in my house! To hell with all *katsaps*!'
This remark was addressed to me, and the woman, who was barring the door, meant it. I was embarrassed, but Abram, who had brought me here, eased the situation.

'*Babushka*, my friend is not a *katsap*, he is a foreigner living in Moscow.'

The change in the woman was instantaneous. She stepped aside, stuck out a welcoming hand, and said: 'Then come in, come in my poor friend, and may I say how it grieves me that you should have come to live in this unfortunate *paradise* of ours.'

The way she said 'paradise' left no doubt of her real meaning. She was a Ukrainian, and Abram and I were in the Ukraine. The woman was grandmother of a friend of Abram whose house on the outskirts of the old Ukrainian capital, Kharkov, we had come to visit. And in its way, the incident typified the attitude of most Ukrainians towards the Kremlin's people.

The Ukraine had its own language and its own customs. But it also had a massive dislike of the Russians. Dislike is probably too timid a word. Hatred would be more accurate. These people detested having Russian forced upon them as an official language. They squirmed under Russian Commissars, smouldered under the indignity of having Russians manipulated into the top jobs, and in general looked towards Moscow with all the resentment of an oppressed people.

The next day we went to Khateze. This was a huge complex of factories, employing over thirty thousand people and was operating on a twenty-four hour schedule.

Though all the entrances were closely guarded we were allowed in without difficulty as soon as we produced our Press cards, and we were directed to the office of the director, where presently the Partorg joined us.

'You have come to the most efficient and modern tractor factory in the world,' the Partorg boasted. 'We have designed models unequalled anywhere. We could export thousands of tractors every month and could earn masses of foreign currency. But why should we help capitalist tractor kings such as Ferguson and Ford to copy our machines? Besides this, our vast country is, as Comrade Stalin said at the Seventeenth Party Congress, becoming highly organised and hundreds of thousands of tractors are required to mechanise our agriculture. So we keep every single machine we produce, and send them all over the Soviet Union.'

'What are your production figures?' I enquired.

'This, comrade, I must not tell you,' said the Partorg. 'We have strict instructions from the Peoples' Commissariat in Moscow to keep our production figures secret. But I can tell you that in one single week we produce more than the biggest and most efficient tractor factory in the United States of America could produce in a month.'

'Are tractors the only things you produce?' I asked.

'Mainly,' he answered.

'Then why is Khateze so closely guarded by armed sentries?'

'Well, we also produce other machines,' the director said vaguely.

'There are two reasons why our factory is closely guarded,' the Partorg said quickly. 'One reason is that capitalist spies and saboteurs might try to get in . . .'

'Sergo Ordzhonikidze told me, when we last had a drink together, that Khateze now produces the new heavy tank and other similar machines,' I cut in, bluffing.

It worked. 'If Comrade Ordzhonikidze told you that, then there is no point in my denying it,' the Partorg said apologetically.

I could see by Abram's expression that he was enjoying this, and before I could say anything else, he suggested we be taken on a tour of the site.

My casual reference to Ordzhonikidze had clearly impressed

because minutes later we were led into a huge hangar-like shed where hundreds of workers—men and women—were working at conveyor belts. In another part of the hall we saw the finished product—huge steel monsters which looked frightening, and which six years later proved to be the most efficient type of tank then produced. In another part of Khateze we saw heavy armoured cars being mass produced. Was it any wonder armed sentries guarded the gates?

The Partorg had not, however, exaggerated in telling us that huge numbers of tractors were turned out. At the railway siding we saw hundreds of them ready for despatch. Much the same applied to another huge part of Khateze where lorries from three to ten tons, with and without trailers, were being turned out. And let it be said that although the products may not have been as modern as those produced outside the U.S.S.R., they were, nevertheless, sturdy and reliable, and well suited for the tasks for which they were manufactured.

'What is your verdict on our factory?' asked the Partorg, turning to me. 'Since you are a foreign comrade, you should be in a position to compare this industrial giant with similar works in the capitalist world.'

'Unfortunately I am not a technical man,' I answered. 'I have never been to a factory of this kind outside the Soviet Union. But Khateze certainly is impressive.'

* * *

During our stay in Kharkov we went to see the Commune of Feliks Edmundovich Dzhierzhinsky—the famous training centre for child bandits. Such a lot had been written about this 'jewel of Soviet educational methods' that we felt impelled to see for ourselves.

It was a huge old dilapidated house which once may have been impressive, but now looked just like a tenement standing alone in spacious grounds. Unlike most official buildings in Russia, this one had no sentries or guards outside.

'I am pleased to meet you, comrades,' the House-father greeted us when we entered and introduced ourselves. He was a man in his early forties, with a thin face and kind-looking blue eyes. His hair was shaved off in the Soviet manner and gave him the appearance of being completely bald. His clothes were shabby and on his feet he wore a kind of slipper worn by peasants.

'I'm Maksim Simonovich Dervenko and I am glad you have come to see us,' he said.

Abram shook hands with the House-father and said: 'We have heard so much about your successes that we had to visit you.'

'The credit for the success of this collective is not entirely mine,' Dervenko said modestly. 'Success was possible only because the boys collaborated with me. You see, we are like a big family here.'

Dervenko was House-father, Commandant, Partorg and security officer all in one. He was the first Soviet Partorg I met in the U.S.S.R. who was not a disagreeable type. He was likeable, sensible and understanding. He did not rule by force or terror, but applied tact and psychology and had thus been able to win over toughs and shape them into useful and honest citizens.

The War, the Revolution, and the civil war had orphaned hundreds of thousands of children, most of them aged between five and fourteen. They roamed in bands, hungry and desperate. They scavenged for as long as they could, or for as long as they were inclined, but there were too many of them, and food and money were not easily come by. So gradually they turned to other methods. They began to steal. They attacked in numbers. They looted. Sometimes they even killed, and quite suddenly the threat of the child bandits was a real menace. Tragic victims of circumstance, the children had become dangerous.

In 1930, when the menace of these children took on such dimensions that life in Moscow became unsafe even in broad daylight, the authorities decided to strike drastically. Dozens of G.P.U. and Militia lorries brought fully armed detachments to the Arbat district and surrounded this part of the Red Capital. They combed streets and houses thoroughly, caught the child bandits and took them to the large Central Market Hall at Arbat Square. Over fifteen hundred of them were rounded up and the G.P.U. Commandant who was in charge of 'cleaning operation Arbat' commanded his men to line up in front of the children, machine guns loaded and ready. The pitiful pleadings, the frightened cries, the unrepeatable curses of the children counted for nothing. Without trial or pretence, they were mowed down where they stood and cowered. The bodies were thrown into lorries, taken to a deserted field outside Moscow, soaked in petrol and set alight. I was told by eye-witnesses that the smell of burning flesh filled the air for many days.

Nor was this an isolated instance. Exact figures could never be ascertained, but it was generally thought that between 1921 and 1930 fifteen to twenty thousand children were shot by Cheka and G.P.U. men. However, the greater part were caught and taken to special homes, like the Commune of Feliks Edmundovich Dzierzhinsky which we were just visiting.

'It was not easy to convert the young offenders when they came here,' Dervenko told us while sitting in his office. 'They were used to stealing and looting, which was the only way they knew of getting food and clothing. They distrusted everybody, especially those put in charge of them.'

It was not easy to see how Dervenko had won them over. True he was sympathetic and quiet-voiced, but the children had long forgotten kindness and its kindred attributes. It was a measure of the man's remarkable ability and patience that these unattached little rebels had indeed reformed, by starting at the bottom and learning again the ways of normal existence.

More the pity then that when we saw some of them working in the optical factory, it was to see them working on a camera ('an F.E.D. comrade, the finest in the world') which was a copy of an already outdated German Leica.

At dinner that evening, Abram and I spoke with many of them—some had been robbers, others had committed crimes of violence, one was reputed to have been a killer—and found them charming and perfectly normal. And without exception they spoke of their past lives as being horrible and wasted.

But it didn't prevent one of them exercising his skill as a pickpocket, for an entertainment. As we were about to leave, he came to me and handed me back my wristwatch, wallet and cigarette lighter!

'Just a joke, you understand,' he said with a grin. 'I don't do it professionally any more!'

He didn't either. But there were still those on the loose who did, and only weeks after my return to Moscow, a friend of mine, Mark Rokosov, one of the editors of *Literaturnaya Gazeta*, was attacked, beaten up, stripped naked, robbed, and left bleeding one night in Moscow. He was lucky not to have died. The child bandits were never caught.

CHAPTER TWENTY-SIX

The Man Stakhanov

IT was in September 1935 that an obscure Russian miner, by his deeds and by virtue of his name, added a new word to the English language. Of course when he first came into prominence, nobody had any idea that his fame would spread outside the Soviet Union.

I well remember the morning editorial conference at which we first discussed doing a story on him. News had come in that *one hundred and two* tons of coal had been mined by one man in a single shift. It was an incredible claim, and at first there was general disbelief that anyone could have dug that amount of coal from the coal-face in the course of only one working period. Especially as there had just been a spate of bad publicity and complaints about poor production figures in the mines.

The Editor made two phone calls to higher sources to determine whether the claim was based on fact, or was merely a morale-booster. He was assured that the story was true and decided we should do a spread on it.

'But I want a personal piece,' he said. 'I want one of you to go to the mine, see this man at work, and write a colour piece. If it's true that he turned out that tonnage on his own, we could have something sensational.'

First choice to write the story was Abram, but Abram didn't want to leave his family again so soon after returning from our 'holiday,' and he put up some impressive-sounding excuse which convinced the Editor. Voroniezhsky, whose turn it was to go on one of these 'away' jobs, also excused himself by saying he had an interview lined up with a *Politburo* member in connection with a proposed new series. I was just as glad, because I was eager to see one of these Russian coal mines, and I accepted straight away when the story was assigned to me.

The plane I set off in was a very old wires-and-string contraption which looked as if it would disintegrate at any time, and when I was later told I would have to wear a parachute during the flight, any confidence I had left ebbed away.

Every time we hit an air-pocket on that flight—and we flew into any amount of them—I fully expected to see one of the wings snapping off and twirling away downwards on its own while we began a death dive. Mercifully it didn't happen, and, after stops for refuelling at Orel and Kharkov, we came down on a bumpy field at the edge of which a car was parked, waiting.

We were driven to the coal mine, and almost as soon as we had arrived, an embarrassed-looking young man was ushered into my company.

'This is Comrade Aleksei Stakhanov,' the Partorg said, introducing him.

Stakhanov shook hands with me, still looking messy.

'A fine example of Soviet modesty, eh comrade?' the Partorg said, clapping Stakhanov's shoulder. 'One hundred and two tons on one shift—a new world record,' the Partorg went on. 'And Comrade Stakhanov will *beat* that record himself. He will show the whole world, won't you comrade?'

Stakhanov smiled and nodded.

I looked at him and wondered how one ordinary man like this could have mined over a hundred tons on his own. It would have been an extraordinary output for fifteen men, let alone one.

'Could you, do you think, repeat the feat?' I asked him, 'or was it just a lucky combination of circumstances?'

'If I am not let down, it should be possible to do it regularly,' Stakhanov answered. 'I'm determined to try to do even better during my shift tomorrow.'

'I am sure you will,' said the Partorg. 'We will all give you every possible support. You will be an example to all the miners of the Soviet Union.'

The next morning at six o'clock I went with Stakhanov and his gang into the open lift cage. The Partorg who had the previous night spoken of the support he would give, remained on the surface.

The cage went down at an appalling speed through the dusty darkness, and at one stage I found myself wondering whether the wires had perhaps broken. But we came to a gentle enough stop.

It was then I saw how Stakhanov worked; or, to be more accurate, how Stakhanov *and his gang* worked, for I found that, in a way, I was disappointed to discover that the phenomenal 102 tons hadn't after all been mined by one man, but by a gang of men co-operating and forming a team to support a leader—in this case, Aleksei Stakhanov.

To be sure, he had worked out a new system, and like great ones, it was a basically simple one. Stakhanov had proposed that while he worked non-stop on the coal-face with his drill, the rest of his gang should follow close behind, clearing away the coal as he tore it from the seam, and reinforcing the tunnel. In this way, he personally was able to work unhindered. But the production figures attributed to him alone should really have been credited to the whole team. This apart, the *modus operandi* was a brand new one; it revolutionised theories of coal-mining, and the Stakhanovite system was on its way to becoming world famous and world-adopted.

And on the day that I went down the pit with Aleksei Stakhanov, I saw the record being pushed up from 102 to 104½ tons. It had been a six hour slog for the team with a bare ten minutes snatched for a meal break.

Back on the surface, the Partorg table-pounded and bellowed all the old hackneyed phrases and slogans; but I was impressed enough in my own right. I telephoned Moscow and spoke to the Editor.

'Stay there another day,' he said. 'The story sounds good, but it might still be only a flash-in-the-pan effort.'

On the next day, the Stakhanov shift produced a fantastic 111 tons; but an unforeseen snag hit them. The mine's clearance equipment wasn't up to the task of getting quantities as large as this to the surface, and as a result, the men following Stakhanov's shift were unable to commence on time.

The Partorg blustered his way through his excuses, and was embarrassed to be caught in the midst of them by the unexpected arrival of a bunch of Moscow journalists. It was only then I realised that, despite telling me to stay on for one more day, my Editor had run my story, and we, the non-Party paper had scooped *Pravda*, *Komsomolskaya Pravda*, *Kommunist*, and *Deutsche Zentral Zeitung* (the organ of the Volga-German Soviet Republic.) I took a good deal of ribbing that night in the Miners Club from the correspondents of these papers and many others.

Aleksei Stakhanov of course became a hero. His picture appeared on hoardings, in shop windows, on calendars and in magazines. He became the symbol of 'the perfect Soviet worker,' and, true to pattern, they brought him before the powerful leaders and pinned a medal on him.

Stakhanovism became the craze. They decided to apply it all over industry—in factories, on the railways, in offices, anywhere and everywhere; but its introduction had a new significance which the propaganda machine conveniently glossed over.

Up till this time, the policy of the *Comintern* regarding piecework was aptly summed up in their slogan 'Piecework means the murder of the workers.' Communist parties all over the world were continually encouraged to ruthlessly fight the concept of piecework which, as was said so often, 'was invented to squeeze the last drop of blood out of the workers.'

But now the wild enthusiasm over Stakhanovism meant a quick about-face, for it involved the wholesale adoption of piecework. In an industrially backward country as Russia then undoubtedly was, piecework inflicted terrible hardship on the workers. Earnings now depended on productivity; production was frequently held up because of power failures, or the shortage of raw materials; so, workers were thrown back on their extremely low basic wages which, in the main, were insufficient to keep the people much above a bare subsistence level.

There was no answer to it. The Party said Stakhanovism was 'in the interest of every single individual.' The purges were increasing in severity. To object meant death. The people starved in silence.

CHAPTER TWENTY-SEVEN

Even the Old

ON my return to Moscow, I received a shock. Not only was the flat in Trubnaya Ulitsa empty, but the doors of the room the Rissings had occupied, the kitchen, bathroom, W.C., had big red N.K.V.D. seals on them. I felt alarmed, realising that my aged landlords had been arrested. The papers in my desk and particularly all my personal things were in disorder.

For a while I was at a loss as to what steps to take. I knew I couldn't risk telephoning Abram or anyone else, because the telephone might be tapped. But what could be the reason for the Rissings arrest? And what had happened to Niura?

Since the door of my room was free from the N.K.V.D. seal, and since I was by decree, half owner of the offices of the flat, I decided to try to trace the Rissings. 'What do you want?' the Duty Officer asked when I telephoned Lubyanka. I gave him my name and address. He repeated: 'What do you want?'

'I want to know what I am to do to get your seals removed from the doors in my flat.'

'They can't be removed by anyone without our authority,' he shouted. 'Do you think you can waste our time with silly telephone calls?'

'Will you please listen to me,' I shouted. 'I am trying to tell you that the kitchen, the bathroom, and lavatory are sealed and I want to know if I can remove your seals as I have to use this part of the flat.'

'I've already told you that you are not allowed to remove any seals,' he repeated.

The argument went on for some time, but at last he said that he would send someone along. He was as good as his word. Shortly afterwards there was a loud stamping of nailed boots on the stairs and four N.K.V.D. officers, led by a captain, came and stood in front of me.

'How dare you remove the seal to this flat?' the captain began.

'I have not removed anything,' I told him. 'I rang your head-quarters and they sent you to remove the seals.'

'On my paper here it says that the flat is sealed.' He held an impressive looking document under my nose. 'See for yourself.'

'It says here that *four* doors have been sealed,' I replied when I read the document. 'The four seals are untouched.'

'There must have been a seal on the front door,' he declared.

He was very young and I was not keen on another set-to with the N.K.V.D. The experience at Sebastopol had been enough. I decided to try another method, and offered the four of them some vodka which they gladly accepted. When they were in a more mellow mood, I quietly pointed out the facts again to the captain.

'All right then,' he agreed. 'It says nothing about the front door being sealed and I'll accept your word for it.' He held his empty glass out and when I refilled it, added: 'I will remove the seals except the one to the room of those spies.'

'The Rissings?' I said. 'What have they done?'

'What have they done?' he repeated, and emptied his glass. 'Sabotage, of course, spying for the Gestapo. What else do you expect from Tsarist engineers?'

Engineer Rissing had been pensioned for years and had had no contact with the outside world. How on earth could he have spied?

'It is never an advantage to live in the same flat with enemies of the State,' the captain said. 'Not only did these Gestapo spies commit their criminal sabotage but they availed themselves of the services of that *kulak* woman who was their contact with the Fascists.'

'Amazing how you manage to find out things,' I tried to make this remark sound admiring.

'We have our methods,' he said proudly. 'Nothing escapes the N.K.V.D.' Then as he and his men started to remove the three red seals from the doors, he added: 'If you want to get in touch with the District Housing Committee about the other room you can do so. They might let you have it if you already hold a decree for part of the flat.'

I thanked him for his advice and gave him and his men another glass of vodka. During their short stay they had managed to empty three large bottles. They walked out as if they had taken nothing stronger than water.

I was extremely upset at what I had heard, and tried to think of something that might help the Rissings, whose only fault was that they had been born during the Tsarist régime. I discussed the matter with Abram, who promised to speak to an N.K.V.D. friend of his about the Rissings and their maid. Two days later the N.K.V.D. man told Abram what had happened. The Rissings had been 'tried,' found guilty, and executed. Niura had been luckier. She had been sentenced to five years slave labour. Nothing could be done for her.

I was heartbroken at what had happened. I had grown very fond of the Rissings, and their deaths touched me deeply. That two elderly innocent people could be wiped out, just like that, was in its own way as terrible as the mass murder of the children.

In a state of depression and anger I went to the Head of the District Housing Committee, and by bluffing and trickery (I used my position as a journalist to flatter him, letting him think I was preparing a eulogising portrait of him) I managed to get the whole of the Rissings flat allocated to myself. It was as well that I did go, because I nipped in the bud the plan to allocate part of the accommodation to an N.K.V.D. major. Fancy having to share a flat with a Secret Police officer!

However, there were many nights when I sat alone (the Rissings furniture was taken away, part of it stolen, and the remainder put into storage as having belonged to an 'enemy of the State') in the flat, and in the quietness I fancied I could hear the voices of the two old people in the next room. It didn't ease the situation one whit to know I'd never really hear their voices again.

CHAPTER TWENTY-EIGHT

Cold Hard Facts in Siberia

SIBERIA had always had, for me at any rate, the ring of remoteness about it. Even while living in Moscow I could never feel about Siberia other than that it was a far-distant, hard and possibly barren land, the very existence of which somewhat constituted a threat. I had not real knowledge of what it was like. Impressions had been garnered from a few photographs, and some extremely sketchy readings. But now, here was my chance to go there. And I wasn't exactly bubbling over with enthusiasm. There was still this idea of menace attached to the very word—Siberia. However, there was no way out. I was being sent.

Much propaganda about a new Siberian town called Komsomolsk was being churned out by the Press Department, and it grew to such proportions that an organised visit by writers and journalists was arranged. I was delegated to go by my editor.

Ten of us assembled in the hall of Moscow Aerodrome. With the exception of two famous Soviet writers, the rest of us represented the leading papers and periodicals of the U.S.S.R. We were provided with heavy fur coats, fur hats (which could be closed so that only the eyes and part of the nose were exposed), fur boots reaching high above the knees, and thick fur mittens. We looked more like explorers than a group of publicists, but we had to be equipped for the icy climate.

The aircraft which was to take us to Komsomolsk was an A.N.T. machine of the same type as the one in which I had travelled to Leningrad. The only difference was that instead of seats there were sleepers. A five thousand mile trip was a long one, no matter how you looked at it. The crew consisted only of the pilot and co-pilot, both youngsters hardly more than twenty years old. When I asked why no navigator or radio operator were on board, the pilot gave me an odd look and explained this would be a waste of manpower.

It was an uneventful journey during which we flew during the daylight hours, and slept on two successive nights at refuelling points. Two hours later than our scheduled arrival time at Komsomolsk (this was on the afternoon of the third day) the plane banked and began her descent for a landing. We could see no signs of runways or anything that resembled airport buildings. But vision was extremely restricted anyway as the plane's windows were almost entirely iced over. The aircraft didn't so much touch down as came to earth in a series of alarming hops before trundling along over a ridged and pitted field.

When we had eventually stopped and the roar of the engines died away, the pilot came back, smiling blandly.

'There you are, comrades,' he said, 'we have made excellent time.'

There was no mention of the lost two hours.

When the door of the plane was opened, a blast of searingly-cold wind tore into the cabin. Standing shivering alongside the aircraft, we looked in vain for any sign of life or habitation. There was none. It was bleak, wind-swept, and snow-covered. But no—there was *one* thing, a notice-board which was partly obliterated by packed snow. We went closer and made out the words 'WELCOME TO ——' A white crusting blotted out the name. We could be anywhere.

The correspondent of *Trud* (the trade union paper) went to the signpost and started clipping the concealing snow with a pen-knife. One by one he revealed the letters. Yes, we were in Komsomolsk all right. I could see no sign of the town, though, and wished it was a bit more impressive than its airport.

We stood shivering by the plane for a few minutes, dejection settling heavily on the group. Just as we decided to climb back into the plane to wait, four lorries in noisy convoy appeared in the distance and came towards us. The leading vehicle had two loudspeakers fixed to its cab roof, and no sooner had the truck stopped than the *Internationale* began to blare at us. But the twenty or so young men and women who bundled out of the trucks ignored the song, and crowded around us bellowing their welcomes, and apologising for being late.

The young Partorg, once the music ended, started to make a speech, but we were so cold and so obviously ill-prepared to listen, that he abandoned it and bade us all to climb into the lorries. During the ride into Komsomolsk, we gathered that it was not much of a place—yet. Most of its buildings were just wooden huts in which the workers, the builders of this new industrial town, ate and slept. Darkness was coming down blackly over the place as we slowed down, and it was just possible to make out two steel frameworks silhouetted against the sky.

We had arrived at a large wooden hut decorated with red flags and placards. It was the town's Soviet. The large assembly room was crowded with those who had come to greet 'the important publicists from Moscow,' and we had barely time to take off our coats and caps, when the Partorg began again to address us.

'It is a great honour for all of us that our government, under the leadership of our wise and beloved Josif Vissarionovich Stalin, has sent our country's best publicists here, so that the heroic story of the building of this town from nothing, can be told,' he began.

'As soon as Josif Vissarionovich disclosed his plan of incredible genius to build this town,' the Partorg went on, 'tens of thousands of Komsomols of both sexes, all over the country, went at once to see their organisers and begged to be allowed to go to Siberia to take part in the building of this new town which one day will be one of the most important in the whole of the U.S.S.R.'

Before I left Moscow, I had studied all the available material regarding Komsomolsk, and I knew that the Partorg was exaggerating grossly. Only a couple of hundred Komsomols had volunteered to go to Siberia. All the others had been *directed* to go, by their various organisations.

'Because this important town is being built by members of the Komsomol,' the Partorg went on, 'our beloved Josif Vissarionovich has, in his great understanding, allowed this place to be named Komsomolsk, for it is the town of the youth. It will become a symbol of Komsomol initiative and self-sacrifice. Generations to come will be reminded of what we have achieved, and the town will remain an everlasting monument to the heroic work of Soviet Komsomols.'

He went on and on, and in the end was cheered and clapped.

Together with some fifty specially selected workers he led the way to the adjoining room, where long tables and wooden benches were ready for us. In between more speeches, we ate a simple but good dinner followed by plenty of vodka.

When all the eating and drinking had stopped, the workers gone home, and the Partorg seemed settled down for another couple of hours of speeches or lectures, I suggested on behalf of all of us that we should be making tracks for our hotel.

The Partorg laughed out loud.

'Hotel comrade?' he said. 'What hotel do you expect to find here?'

'Well, where are we staying?' I asked.

'Here,' the Partorg answered. 'In the assembly room.'

'And the beds,' I said, 'where are the beds?'

'Oh, we have no beds,' he said. 'We don't use them. We sleep on the floor.'

The silence in the group was uncanny. We had come five thousand miles, and now we were being told there were no beds, and that we'd have to sleep on the floor! But worse was to come.

'What about blankets?' I said quietly.

'Oh yes, we've got those,' he said. 'Six.'

'Six blankets for ten of us!' I shouted. 'Comrade, you must be out of your mind.'

'Why?' he said. 'Some of you can share one between you.'

I was cold with fury now, and, ignoring him, turned to the others and suggested we go back and sleep on the plane. At least we would have some proper place to lie down. Seeing that he was out-numbered now, ten to one, the Partorg lost some of his insolence and indeed himself offered to drive us to the aircraft. He left, warning us that he would fetch us at seven in the morning.

With engines off, the inside of the plane was nearly as cold as the outside, and most of us lay in shivering misery before getting off to sleep.

The next day when we went round Komsomolsk I felt ashamed of my selfishness. In the biting Siberian wind, the builders of Komsomolsk were erecting huge steel constructions. The men were poorly clothed, many of them without gloves, others even minus coats. But they worked with an enthusiasm and stubbornness which was really remarkable. Many of them were from the warm south, and even those who came from other parts of the U.S.S.R. had never experienced anything like this icy climate.

Later, when we were shown round the huts in which the builders of the new town lived, I saw that the Partorg had not exaggerated. They really slept on the floors and, in order to be more comfortable, covered these parts of the floor where they slept with straw and paper. What I thought about the Soviet régime was one thing; but I could not help admiring these people who, under the most difficult conditions, half hungry and inadequately clad, were building an important industrial town from nothing. And it was not fear that made them do it; at least it didn't seem to be; they had an idealism and a deep desire for a better life. I like to think that these were the things that motivated their work in the frozen wastes that one day would be called the town of Komsomolsk.

CHAPTER TWENTY-NINE

The Searching Jews

WHEN we left Komsomolsk, the rest of the party headed for Khabarovsk, a town about two hundred miles further on and quite close to the Manchurian border. The U.S.S.R., I had long since found out, was a great place for anniversaries. Anniversaries were great excuses for speeches. They were celebrating some obscure anniversary at Khabarovsk. I'd had my fill of speeches, so I decided to give the place a miss and carry on instead to the Jewish Autonomous Region of Birobidzhan.

The setting up of this place had been one of the Kremlin brainwaves. On the surface, all seemed innocent and based on goodwill. But of course there were snags; like almost everything the Communist rulers did, this too had its political ulterior motive.

Bolshevik doctrine and propaganda maintained that *all* Soviet citizens were equal—regardless of their national origins. Now the Kremlin was not blind to attractiveness of this proposition to Jewish people, and centres were set up in various foreign countries with express purpose of attracting attention to a new scheme—the setting up of the new Jewish Autonomous Region of Birobidzhan where Jews would be welcomed and where they could live freely and devoid of prejudice or persecution. They would be coming to a region which yielded two harvests a year, and the Kremlin (so they were told) would undertake to supply them with all the necessary machinery, materials and seeds.

I had heard conflicting reports about the scheme, and by visiting the region, I knew I'd find out the truth.

The station turned out to be little more than a halt. Though it was not quite as cold as it had been in Komsomolsk, it was snowing furiously in small dense flakes.

'How far is it to the town?' I asked the railway official who was station master and porter in one.

'Not far,' he replied. 'But it's difficult to get there in this snow.'

'Would you telephone for some transport?' I asked.

'My telephone is out of order. For over a month they have been promising to repair it but I'm still waiting,' he said.

'How do you communicate with other stations without the telephone?' I asked.

'Ah,' he said with a grin. 'I have the telegraph. But there isn't much communication anyway, nothing much happens on this line.'

When the locomotive had taken on its water and coal supply and the train rolled slowly out of the station, the station master asked me to climb in next to him on the sledge.

'Where do you want me to take you?' he enquired. 'To the town Soviet?'

'First take me to a hotel, please.'

'Hotel?' he laughed. 'There's no such thing in Birobidzhan.'

'Where can I stay, then?'

'You must arrange that with the town Soviet,' he replied. 'They'll fix something up for you.'

I did not see a single motor car or lorry; the only vehicles we met were horse-drawn sledges.

'Here we are,' said my companion stopping in front of a building decorated with the normal red flags and placards. 'Good luck to you.'

'What do I owe you?' I enquired.

'You don't owe me anything,' he answered. 'I gave you a lift, that's all, and good luck to you.'

I did not insist on paying him, as many people in the Soviet Union considered it an insult if one tried to tip them or pay them for services rendered. I thanked him and went into the Soviet.

After having looked into various empty rooms, I at last found a middle-aged woman sitting at a table, writing. She asked me whether she could be of any help so I told her that I had come to

Birobidzhan to write about the Jewish Autonomous Region. She shook hands with me and told me that she was Deputy Mayor and at the moment was in charge of the Soviet. The Mayor, it appeared, was away.

I thanked the woman and asked where I could find a room in Birobidzhan. She said that the *gostinitsa*★ had rooms available. Lifting the telephone receiver she spoke to someone in Yiddish, then turned to me with a smile, saying she had arranged for a nice room to be prepared for me.

'Is it very far to the *gostinitsa*?' I enquired.

'No, it's just round the corner. I'll come with you and show you the way. I couldn't let you go alone. You are a stranger here and might lose your way. That wouldn't be hospitable. Here we know how to look after our guests.'

I was given a clean comfortable room, and while I was putting my clothes and other belongings away, the Deputy Mayor ordered a meal. I had to persuade her to join me.

During the meal I learned that her name was Rakhel Weingarten. She had come from Saratov two years previously with her husband and three children, and said she was glad they had come. She asked me to come and visit her home whenever it suited me, so that I could see how she and her family lived.

Although Rakhel Weingarten was a sincere woman, she was not typical of the population. She and her husband had been members of the Communist party for many years and they were accustomed to seeing things through party eyes. Besides this, she had always lived in the Soviet Union and was used to country life, which was probably the reason why she was so pleased with her new home.

It did not take me long to find out what conditions in the Jewish Autonomous Region were like. Rakhel took me to a club and introduced me to some of those present. When she left after a while (she said she had a report to finish) the conversation became easier.

'It is much better now,' a sympathetic looking fellow of some thirty years or so told me as I sat down at his table and asked him

★Inn.

how he liked life in this part of Siberia. 'It has greatly improved since I came here over three years ago.'

'Where do you come from?' I asked him. With a name like Jack Miller, and an American accent, he stood out as someone to talk to.

'From Brooklyn,' he said. 'I fell for the propaganda I read about Birobidzhan.'

It sounded as if his words had an undertone of regret. 'Are you sorry that you left the United States and came here?' I asked.

'Yes and no,' he replied candidly. 'As you probably know, conditions in America aren't ideal and it is not always easy to get work. I was a lorry driver over there but I was often out of work, which might or might not have been because I was known to have sympathies for Soviet Russia. To cut a long story short, when I was told that in Birobidzhan I would have a secure future, I made up my mind to chuck everything back home, and come here.'

Jack Miller was only one of fifty other adults (many of whom had their families with them) who left America. When they arrived in Russia, they were housed in a large reception camp at which other contingents arrived daily from different parts of the world. During their stay (they were informed that they were waiting for the numbers to reach the six hundred mark) they were given various lectures on the political thought of their new country, and glowing pictures were painted of the life that lay ahead.

Then came the day when they all boarded a special train for the long journey to Siberia.

'It was an odd feeling arriving here,' Miller told me. 'I mean you wouldn't exactly call Birobidzhan a metropolis, would you! But it was heaven compared to the joint they took us to in army trucks the next day. Right out in the middle of a forest they dumped us, and told us "go ahead with it." Babies and all went! All they left us was food, fuel for the bulldozers and tractors, and their promise to bring more food in a fortnight.'

He must have thought from my expression that I doubted his words for he called a young woman to join us. He did not tell her what he had said to me but invited her to describe the day the Red Army transported them from Birobidzhan.

'Why, that's no secret, everybody knows it,' Ruth Klimsa (who had come from Slovakia with her parents) said. 'You should have seen the disappointment, especially of the mothers of small children, and of the old. They implored the Red Army men to take them back.'

'We were not the only ones to whom this happened,' Miller went on. 'And this was probably the reason why fewer and fewer foreign Jews arrived here. People wrote home, and relatives who had stayed behind decided not to come after they had heard what the conditions were like.'

Ruth and Jack then told me that, not having any other alternative, they got on with the job, first erecting some temporary wooden houses. This had not been an easy task because most of the immigrants were not familiar with this type of work—many had worked in offices, as sales people in shops and stores. But they managed, somehow.

'With a lot of sweat, will-power and hard work, we gradually cleared a fair-sized territory from the forest,' Jack Miller went on. 'The next difficulty was to level the new land and plough it. This we managed too, and got it ready for cultivation. The Red Army convoys, however, did not keep their promises. They brought some food sure enough, but no seeds, and we had to wait a full year to reap the benefit of all that hard work. What a winter that was! If it hadn't been for the animals which we shot, we would have died of starvation.'

'A lot of hard work still has to be done before our region can be called a prosperous one,' Ruth Klimsa added. 'Now we are at least allowed to keep a fair share of what we wrest from the soil and it is sufficient to keep us going and provide a surplus so that we can buy clothing. But our first two harvests the year after we came, were a terrible disappointment. Not because the harvests were poor, but because the grain commissions took virtually everything from us.'

During the few days I stayed at Birobidzhan I spoke to dozens of people, not only in the town but also in the surrounding settlements, and got ample confirmation that it was just as Ruth Klimsa and Jack Miller had told me. I also tackled Rakhel Weingarten, the

Deputy Mayor, who did not attempt to deny the fact and, explaining matters in the proper *bolshevik* ideology, said that this had been a kind of teething trouble which was only to be expected.

There was another grievance which the people of the Jewish Autonomous Region bore in their hearts. The propaganda centres had promised the immigrants-to-be that the Soviet government would give the new settlers every assistance and would let them have all the necessary machinery and supplies to enable them to build up their country speedily and efficiently They *were* given some bulldozers and tractors—though not in sufficient numbers— but these were not provided free by the government as promised. The immigrants had to pay high prices for the machines, seeds and everything else. And the only relief the Soviets granted them was that they were allowed to pay in regular instalments spread over ten years.

'I must say they got us here under false pretences,' said Vaclav Kunz—a typical Jewish peasant who had come with his family some three and a half years earlier from Moravia. 'Had I known I would never have sold my small-holding back home and brought my wife and kids here. A lot of hard work in a rough climate and not much for it. What grieves me most is that by coming here I have deprived young Esterka and Yankele of a better life. But one has to accept things as they come.'

Scores of people in Birobidzhan, most of whom had come from foreign countries, talked in a similar way. They did not try to convince me that life in the Soviet Union was the best and most free in the world, as everybody tried to assure me in other parts of the U.S.S.R.

Moscow never sincerely meant to provide a home for Jewish people where they would be free from racial persecution. The idea suited the Kremlin's purpose and it was a powerful move in the propaganda campaigns against the 'reactionary' Zionist movement in Palestine. Under the pretence of giving the Jews racial freedom and independence by allotting them a vast territory of good land, they made it possible to get considerable numbers of people into this part of the country, which was quite frequently the scene of armed attacks by Manchurian military units. A buffer state which provided the country with additional grain and other agricultural produce, was created. And it had its own military values. The strong frontier garrisons of the Far Eastern Command of the Red Army, consisting of both men and women, fraternized strongly with the Jewish people of Birobidzhan. During harvest time they came in considerable numbers with lorries and other equipment, and helped the settlers in the fields. In cases of illness they sent medical officers or transported people to the nearest hospitals, and many of them spent their leaves in the town. At first there was a slow trickle of marriages, and in time more and more Jews and Gentiles were wed. The population rose and the number of mixed marriages increased. When, in 1938, I revisited Birobidzhan, the town and surrounding villages were growing, and the national and religious character of the Jewish people was diminishing.

I was glad that I had left the delegation of publicists and had gone to Birobidzhan. It was one of the most interesting experiences I had during my stay in the U.S.S.R. and I left the Jewish State with a great sympathy for its people who had been tricked by the cunning of Stalin.

★   ★   ★

I was fortunate enough to get a lift in a military plane as far as Krasnoyarsk, and from there I took the Trans-Siberian Express to Moscow. I had a compartment to myself; the food in the dining car was good and the personnel on the train pleasant. There was also a carriage on the train used as a kind of dance hall in which loud-speakers reproduced gay music.

When I entered the dining car for the first time, I was pleased to see Lyubov Abelovna Yenukidze, the instructor at the *Workers' Aviation Club*. When she saw me, she invited me to her table and we had an enjoyable evening together. During my visits to the aviation club I had never been able to get better acquainted with her, as she was always very busy and had usually disappeared somewhere by the time I had finished jumping. Talking to her now I found that she was not only a beautiful girl but also most charming and intelligent.

As the days and nights went by, we saw more and more of each other. By the third day, I knew that this was much more than a warm friendship. This girl's looks, her manners, her personality, were all weaving a subtle spell around me, and by the time we said 'Adieu' at Moscow, I knew I was in love with her. I had never known a twelve-day period to slip away so fast.

CHAPTER THIRTY

Criticism from Within

BACK in Moscow, Lyubov and I continued to meet, and our love blossomed. She came often to my flat in the evenings, and even cooked some of my meals for me. When she asked me to meet her father for the first time and have supper with them, I invented all kinds of excuses because I feared that never ending political lectures would spoil the evening. However, as I did not want to upset the girl, I had to accept, and with mixed feelings went to her father's flat which was a stone's throw from the Kremlin.

'I am glad to meet you, Bernard Frederickovich,' Abel Yenukidze said greeting me like an old friend. 'I wanted to meet you because Lyubochka has told me such a lot about you.' Abel Yenukidze had been a famous Revolutionary, a close friend of Stalin's since boyhood. But I was not to know that he had steadfastly refused to become a party robot.

'Your daughter always talks about you, Comrade Yenukidze,' I began.

'Don't call me "Comrade Yenukidze," simply call me Abel,' he interrupted. 'Lyubochka's friends are my friends, so don't let's be formal.'

He was a man of medium build with a slightly flabby face and whitish hair. I couldn't help liking him, right from the start. He made no propaganda speeches nor did he attempt to justify the policy of the *Politburo*, or find excuses for the appalling conditions in the U.S.S.R. On the contrary, he liked to criticise. He sincerely believed that sound criticism led to improvement. He saw things as they actually were, and not in the light his comrades in the Kremlin wanted them to appear.

o

After my first meeting with him I was constantly in and out of his flat and he used to come quite frequently to mine in Trubnaya Ulitsa, to sample what Lyubov and I had prepared for supper.

One evening I spoke to him of my disappointment about the low earnings of skilled Soviet workers who, since the introduction of the Stakhanovite piecework policy, were worse off than they had been before. 'Of course,' I added, 'they probably are better off than they were before the Revolution but . . .'

'How do you reach that conclusion?' Abel interrupted me. 'The average earnings of a locksmith are now some two hundred roubles a month, whilst before the Revolution a man in that trade earned about fifty roubles. A skilled roller gets four hundred roubles now, where he only made up to eighty-five roubles in old times. Turners, smelters and such like go home with some two hundred and fifty roubles while, under the Tsar, they used to earn only fifty-five roubles. If you go by figures they get much more now than they ever earned before. *But*, what is a Soviet rouble? Only a dirty piece of paper. Before the Revolution, a rouble was a lot of money.'

I had heard Abel Yenukidze criticise conditions before but was surprised to hear him speak like this.

'Before the Revolution, one paid from fifteen to twenty roubles for a bespoke suit from one of the best tailors, and it wore for ever,' he went on. 'Now, if you are lucky enough to get a suit at all, you have to pay up to a thousand roubles for some ready-made rubbish which has no shape, does not fit properly and becomes threadbare in no time. That is fifty times as much as it was during the times of *batiushka* Tsar. And yet people now earn only four to six times as much as they used to in the old days. A pound of ill-tasting bread costs fifty-five to ninety kopyeks, but excellent bread only used to cost about two kopyeks. For a pound of low-quality meat we now pay about six roubles but the best cuts never used to cost more than eight to nine kopyeks.'

'How was it with unemployment?' I asked.

'There was some, of course, but it was not grave,' he replied. 'Of course, if you read our propaganda books it would appear that half of Russia was out of work. You see, "paper is patient" as we say in Russian. But I tell you conditions in Tsarist times were by no means as bad as our propaganda makes them out to have been. I don't mean to say that everything was wonderful, because if that had been the case we would not have risked our liberty preparing for the Revolution. But we all thought things would turn out differently.'

'Things would doubtless be different if the capitalist world did not prepare a bloody war against the Soviet Union,' said his daughter repeating what she'd read in *Komsomolskaya Pravda*. 'If we did not have to put all our efforts into armaments and fortifications, we would probably be the most prosperous country in the world by now.'

'Lyubochka, you are a good listener and retailer of official propaganda,' her father replied in a friendly voice. 'What else can you say? How can you know? You are too young; you don't know what life was like before. Our people swallow even the most outrageous propaganda these days. You youngsters believe all this nonsense about life being much better for the working people than it ever was before and that it will gradually get better and better.'

'But what can be done, *papochka*?' his daughter asked. 'Overthrow Stalin and the *Politburo*?'

'Not at all,' the *Old Bolshevik* said earnestly, 'but conditions ought to be improved. This is not merely my own opinion, most of who fought against the Tsar and assisted Lenin to establish the Soviet Union think so. Why people cannot be paid higher wages so that they can live like human beings is beyond me. If you are content, if you have enough to eat, if you are adequately clad, if you have a room to live in, you are bound to work more enthusiastically and don't need to be forced.'

'Why don't you try to convince Stalin?' I asked.

'My dear boy,' he said with a laugh, 'to persuade Stalin that something he proposed, sanctioned or even tolerated should be changed would be utterly impossible. I was his friend when he was still Sosso, Koba, the Abrek and all that. Haven't I tried many times? And not only I, but also Sergo Ordzhonikidze, Misha Kalinin, and many others. We could not change his mind in much less important things, let alone a major issue like this. He wouldn't even listen.'

Reading this, anyone who did not know Abel Yenukidze might jump to the conclusion that he was an Oppositionist who disagreed with Stalin and his *Politburo*, and who would support any movement whose aim it was to overthrow the Kremlin dictator and his braves. That was not so. Abel Yenukidze would always stick up for his friend and would be the first to stand by Stalin if any danger threatened him. But this did not prevent him from calling a spade a spade and criticising most strongly anything that deserved criticism, if he was certain that his remarks would not inflict any harm on the leader of the Soviet Union.

'You may perhaps have heard that some years ago many of us, including Sergo Ordzhonikidze, Misha Kalinin, Valerian Kuibyshev and Sosso's wife Nadiezhda tried to stop Stalin from sanctioning the campaign to propagate free love. In our opinion family life is the soundest backbone of any country. Stalin just laughed, called us old-fashioned *muzhiks* and said: "Sooner or later the capitalist world will stage a war against our country. We need an increase of our population and plenty of it. We will build crèches and fill them with the new Soviet generation." The free love campaign was launched, and statistics soon proved that the population was increasing by three million a year.'

'If Stalin's motive was to increase the population, I don't understand why those women who don't want children can have an abortion in any hospital, on demand,' I said.

'If Stalin could, he would prohibit abortion too,' Abel explained. 'But, you see, our propaganda always stated that your body belongs to you and no state has the right to force you to have children against your will. This is why Stalin does not infringe on the rights of Soviet women in this respect. But you must know that all over the Soviet Union great propaganda is made to persuade pregnant women not to undergo abortion but to bear their children. There are rumours in the Kremlin that in order to encourage women to have more children, premiums will be paid for each birth.'

In fact, a decree to this end was issued by the Soviet government. But abortions still went on, and on an enormous scale.

'Whatever your opinions on the subject of family life or free love,' Abel said, 'we must admit that Stalin keeps his eye on improvements in child-care and education. It is really extraordinary how wonderfully the crèches are and what care the children receive. And our educational system—isn't it unique? In what other country has everybody, and I repeat everybody, the right and possibility of going to a university and of becoming a scientist, engineer, doctor or whatever he is suited to be. In what other country does a student receive all his education absolutely free and, on top of that, gets a monthly grant from the government equal to the salary of a skilled worker? If Stalin had not achieved anything else, for this alone he would deserve to be head of the U.S.S.R.'

What Lyubov's father said was only partially true. What he did not say was that the education the Soviet students received at their universities was sub-standard. But this I would not say, though I did not have to guard my words when talking to him. He knew it as well as I did.

CHAPTER THIRTY-ONE

Stalin's Marionette Show

DURING the early months of 1936 I began to hear rumours of quickening activity in the business of rounding up and imprisoning *Old Bolsheviks*. It was Abram who first told me, and as time went by I began to notice for myself that in many of the places I had to visit during the course of my newspaper work, older men were being replaced by fanatical younger men. Abram told me that his N.K.V.D. contacts informed him that it was all being done on Stalin's direct orders.

And then one day at Madame Lunacharsky's, Yevgenia Pyatakova confirmed it.

'Yes,' she said, 'everything points to the fact that a mass trial is being prepared, and I'm being told it is to take place in public with Zinovyev and Kameniev as the key figures.'

This indeed was astonishing news, but much worse was still to come. Inside information had it that the scientists, again working to Stalin's directives, had perfected the Scopolamine-like drug. They had carried out numerous tests on the wretched inmates of the *Politburo Prison Lefortovo* and even in the Kremlin Hospital, and had succeeded in breaking down many of these human guinea pigs. In their state of total submission these people, it was found, would confess to almost anything.

But Stalin wanted to go even further. He wanted unequivocal verbal confessions, IN PUBLIC SESSION; and he wanted this done by big name figures who would testify to having plotted, with Trotsky, the downfall of the whole Party, and of Stalin in particular. Stalin therefore consulted with Yezhov, and between them they chose as the leading figures Valentine Olberg, a secret agent of the N.K.V.D.; Isaak Reingold, a friend of Kameniev; and Richard Pickel, a former Secretary of Zinovyev's Secretariat.

Yezhov was to be the supervisor with Yagoda seeing to it that the various stipulations from above were carried out to the letter.

Olberg, the first of the trio already named, had at one stage been sent to Berlin to spy on the Trotskyites with the express purpose of trying to infiltrate their ranks. He had in fact at one point tried to have himself appointed Trotsky's secretary, and very nearly succeeded. After a spell back in Russia as a teacher in Stalinabad, he was then despatched to Czechoslovakia (Hitler had come into power in Germany) to spy on the German émigré parties. By 1935 he was back in Moscow, and was appointed to a teaching post at the Marx-Lenin School in Gorky. His job was to keep an eye on any Trotskyist activities among the students. There was none.

This then was the man picked by Stalin and Yezhov to give testimony at the coming public trial. It was explained to him that because of his excellent work against the Trotskyites he had been chosen to help the Party and N.K.V.D. to unmask Trotsky as the organiser of a conspiracy against Stalin and the Soviet Government. Needless to say, he was assured that he need not worry about any verdict of the court, as this would be only a matter of tactics and that, in fact, he would be promoted for his exclusive services to the Party and N.K.V.D. and would be given a good position afterwards.

Olberg believed his overlords and Yezhov was able to supply his friend and master Stalin with a signed deposition in which Olberg stated that Sedov had sent him, on Trotsky's instructions, to the U.S.S.R. so that he could organise terrorist acts against Stalin! Olberg also stated that after his arrival in the U.S.S.R. he managed to get a job as a teacher at the Marx-Lenin School in Gorky so that he could get in touch with other Trotskyites there. He even stated that he had endeavoured to recruit students to carry out an assassination plot on Stalin at the May Day Parade in Moscow. In the same deposition Olberg also testified that with Trotsky's knowledge, he had been an agent of the Gestapo.

When Stalin saw this deposition he was pleased but demanded

further 'confessions' so that a wider scope could be lent to the Trotsky conspiracy. Olberg was requested to accuse his closest friends from Latvia and Germany, who, in 1933 had escaped from Hitler's persecution and found asylum in the U.S.S.R. Olberg refused. He was willing to take an active part in the prosecution of Trotsky, Zinovyev, Kameniev and other prominent anti-Stalinists, but he was not willing to do this last thing. He was told that it was not his job to criticise, and that if he refused to obey N.K.V.D. orders he would be transferred from the status of a fictitious defendant to that of a real one. He signed the N.K.V.D. documents.

Stalin was satisfied and told Yezhov that these depositions would be one of the nails in the defendants' coffins.

The second N.K.V.D. tool was Isaak Reingold. He did not have such an exciting history as Olberg, and had been chosen merely because, as a member of the Collegium of the People's Commissariat for Finance, he had met Kameniev in Sokolnikov's country house. He was a hard working bureaucrat and had climbed to the important post of Chairman of the Cotton Syndicate.

But Reingold was not such easy game for the Stalin-Yezhov plans as Olberg had been. He did not fall for the line that it was the duty of every good Soviet citizen to help the Party and the N.K.V.D. in whatever they asked. He never ceased denying vehemently that he had taken part in any conspiracy, and insisted the last time he had seen Kameniev was in 1929. When it became evident that this man's will could not be broken, it was decided to administer the new drug. Reingold became less difficult, and when Yezhov himself came to see him and told him, in the name of the Central Committee, that if he assisted the N.K.V.D. against Kameniev and Zinovyev, he would not only prove his devotion to the Party and his innocence, but would also be rewarded for his services with a leading position after the trial, the drugged victim gave in and signed what the N.K.V.D. had prepared for him.

Isaak Reingold's deposition stated that he had been a member of the Trotsky-Zinovyev organisation; that he had taken part in preparing for the assassination of Stalin, and that he had done all this under the peronal supervision of Kameniev, Zinovyev and

Bakayev. His 'testimony' also mentioned the former head of the Soviet Government, Aleksei Rykov, and the former members of the *Politburo*, Nikolai Bukharin, Mikhail Tomsky, Smirnov, Sokolnikov, and others.

When Stalin studied Reingold's deposition he returned it and demanded that it should be changed. One of the additions he wanted was 'Zinovyev said: "It is not enough to fell the oak; all young oaks growing around it must be felled too." ' Another was 'Stalin's leadership is made up of a granite too hard to expect it to split by itself. Consequently, the leadership will have to be split.' Reingold signed.

Richard Pickel, the third tool, was a member of the Union of Soviet Writers and I knew him quite well. He was the director of the Moscow *Kamernyi Teatre*, and had no interest in politics. He devoted himself only to the theatre, his literary work and to his affaires with pretty actresses.

Pickel had it impressed upon him that there was no real threat to him contained in his arrest. He was, they said, merely a useful figure for publicity purposes, particularly as he had at one period been Secretary to Zinovyev, and would therefore be a great aid to the N.K.V.D. in their efforts to get a conviction. Zinovyev, they told Pickel repeatedly, was a sly enemy of Stalin and an accomplice of Trotsky.

But Pickel was hesitant about signing the document they put before him. The hesitancy was born out of fear—fear that the court would sentence him. However, some of his 'friends' in the N.K.V.D. hastened to reassure him. No matter what the court's findings, they said, Richard Pickel would never go to prison. Indeed the reverse would be the case; he would end up in a remunerative and influential position, they said. To add authenticity to these promises, Yagoda himself came to see Pickel, corroborating everything that had already been said. And when even Reingold (who had been friendly with Pickel for many years) smilingly admitted that he too had signed the 'confessions' on the basis of the same bargaining, Pickel gave in.

In his deposition Richard Pickel stated that, together with

Reingold and Bakayev, and acting on Zinovyev's instructions, he had plotted Stalin's assassination. He also corroborated Reingold's statement that the former Trotskyist, Dreitzer, had organised the attempted assassination of Klim Voroshilov.

Stalin's satisfaction with Pickel's deposition was reflected in the fact that he passed it at once without any instructions for changes or amendments.

The scene was now almost set, and Stalin at last gave the go-ahead when Yezhov provided him with a 'confession' from the N.K.V.D. agent Holtzmann. Holtzmann was another who had become a willing pawn in this elaborate death-game.

The gist of his document was that in 1932 he had met Trotsky's son, Sedov, at the Hotel Bristol in Copenhagen, and from there had gone with Sedov to see Trotsky from whom he'd received detailed instructions for Stalin's assassination.

This was all Stalin required. He summoned Yezhov and told him that final arrangements could now be made for the trial which would not only be held in public, but broadcast. Further, he informed Yezhov that he had no objection to *any* means of interrogation which the occasion might call for, and that Yagoda should be told this.

Because of this diabolical freedom, 'confessions' were obtained from every one of those who had been arrested with the exception of Zinovyev and Kameniev. And the latters' confessions were the ones Stalin wanted most of all.

The two ex-Soviet leaders were doughty characters who refused to be taken in by the golden promises of future freedom and power. At this point, a peculiar state of affairs arose involving the N.K.V.D. interrogators. These found themselves unable to conquer the respect they had built up for Zinovyev and Kameniev. A number of them had indeed heard and applauded speeches made by the two ex-leaders under the presidium of Lenin. To have to break such men down now by drugs was unthinkable. They couldn't do it.

So it was that Yagoda, Mironov (who was in charge of the Kameniev investigation) and other senior N.K.V.D. officers reported to Stalin at the Kremlin and admitted their failure.

Stalin was livid and delivered a lecture to the effect that no man should be able to withstand pressure if the full weight of it was applied. He told them to go away and try again. But Mironov still could not make any headway, so Yezhov took over. He played sadistically on Kameniev's love for his children and threatened to put Kameniev's son on trial if his father refused to comply. Then he showed him the depositions recently obtained from Reingold. Kameniev accused Yezhov of being a grave-digger, a careerist who had wormed his way into the Party, a cynical monster. Yezhov did not reply and left Kameniev to Mironov.

Now Mironov was no soft-hearted interrogator. He was fully aware that Kameniev was to be considered 'an enemy of the State,' but there was something within himself which held him back from administering the drug to the old leader. But in the light of the persistent failures, Yagoda stepped in and made the decision.

The interrogation of Zinovyev was taking a parallel course. He was just as obstinate. In a sense his resistance was even more heroic than Kameniev's because he was suffering from asthma, and on occasions Dr. Kushner had to be called in to apply all his skill to prevent him from dying before the trial.

At last, after he too had been given a shot of the drug, Zinovyev asked to be allowed to have a talk with Kameniev, indicating that a meeting with his old comrade-in-arms might result in their both agreeing to stand trial in the way Stalin demanded.

Yagoda was of the opinion that this was a good idea, because the N.K.V.D. might learn something about the 'plotters' plans. The chief of the technical department satisfied himself that the microphones hidden in the cell were in good working order.

Kameniev tried to convince his friend that Stalin's promises were worthless. He added that he would only feel safe if such an important promise was made to them by Stalin in front of the *Politburo*. Kameniev informed Yagoda in both their names that they were prepared to testify at the trial only if their condition was accepted.

Incredibly, Kameniev and Zinovyev were taken to Stalin's office in the Kremlin, where besides Stalin, Voroshilov and Yezhov were present. Stalin confirmed that none of the *Old Bolsheviks* would be executed, that the families of the accused would not be prosecuted, and that in future the death sentence would not be applied to any former member of the opposition.

The physical sufferings came to an end, and the tough prison became, as far as Zinovyev and Kameniev were concerned, more a kind of sanatorium. They were given special food, proper beds, could take a bath or shower whenever they wished, were allowed to read books; doctors came to look after their health (not forgetting of course to give them small shots of the new drug to keep their will-power weak). Mironov and the other investigators were thus able to prepare the depositions for the coming public trial.

★   ★   ★

While the preparations for this marionette show were proceeding very satisfactorily, Stalin decided he would explode some more sensations, to give the show a still more genuine and convincing character in the U.S.S.R. and abroad. He made up his mind to approach the famous writer Maxim Gorky, who in Russia enjoyed the reputation of a defender of the down-trodden and who was regarded as a humanist, not afraid to stick up for his beliefs and ideals.

Stalin's idea was that Gorky should lend his name to the 'trial'; such a course of action would add seeming authenticity and integrity. Stalin communicated his brainwave to Yezhov.

'The old fellow will never do it,' Yezhov opined.

'Nonsense,' replied Stalin. 'I know Gorky. If he is approached in the right way he will do it. Every man has his price and I'm willing to pay high.'

Stalin ought to have remembered that Gorky had turned down the offer to write Stalin's biography, and had also refused to contribute articles to *Pravda*, and other Soviet papers, glorifying the 'Great Leader, the Sun of Socialism, Josif Vissarionovich Stalin.'

Stalin now sent for Gorky and put his proposition.

'How dare you ask me to put my name to your plans!' Gorky replied. 'I condemn not only individual terror but also state terror. I condemn the way our people are forced to lead a life worse than slavery, worse than ever they had under the blackest reign of Tsarism. It is my sacred duty to raise my voice to inform the world of what is going on in our poor, unhappy Russia.'

Nobody could speak to Stalin like that and expect to live. Gorky was dismissed from Stalin's presence.

'The old fool has gone mad and in his madness he might become a serious danger,' Stalin said when the old writer had gone. The words were tantamount to a death sentence.

Stalin was determined to make the death of Maxim Gorky look natural. Gorky had been suffering from tuberculosis, a fact known all over the world, so it was not unexpected that Gorky should suddenly fall ill. The Soviet Press wrote about the grave illness of this beloved and famous writer. The medical bulletins revealed that Gorky's health was deteriorating rapidly, and on the 18th of June it was suddenly announced that Maxim Gorky had died of heart-failure. For on the 14th of June 1936, Maxim Gorky had died, poisoned on Stalin's instructions. The poison itself had been given by Stalin to Yagoda. And just to ensure that no embarrassing revelations would emerge, Gorky's son Peshkov was also killed.

Maxim Gorky was mourned by the Soviet people and by admirers all over the world. He was given a State funeral with all the trappings.

It was an elaborate mockery of a great and proud man who refused to stoop to the dictates of the world's greatest murderer.

★   ★   ★

In the mean time the public trial of Zinovyev, Kameniev, Smirnov and others was being prepared at high speed. The day came when all depositions were ready and the public prosecutor Vyshinsky was ready to go ahead.

But Stalin was in a ferment lest the trial, by any remote chance, turn into a replica of Hitler's *Reichstag Trial* which had taken place three years previously. So, like a great theatrical venture, Stalin's trial was rehearsed and rehearsed and rehearsed until all knew their lines perfectly.

On the 19th of August, the first public trial of the sixteen opened

at the Trade Union Building in Moscow—Vasiliy Ulrikh was the
Presiding Judge, and Andrei Vyshinsky the Public Prosecutor. The
hall was full of people from factories, offices and institutions;
journalists—I was among them—sat next to foreign diplomats.

The microphones which were placed everywhere and which gave
the impression that the trial was being broadcast live, were connected with recording machines, and only when the censors had
carefully vetted everything that had been said, were they released
for transmission.

Although Stalin was fully aware that everything had been rehearsed for weeks on end, he was not going to take any chance
that one or other of the defendants would blurt out something that
he (Stalin) would not like the outside world to know.

However, the 'trial' of Zinovyev, Kameniev and the fourteen
others went as per script. With exception, that is, for Smirnov's
testimony. This was delivered in a manner so loaded with irony
that Vyshinsky became increasingly uneasy. He smarted visibly
under the sarcasm, and when it came to his closing speech, he made
pointed reference to Smirnov's sarcastic attitude.

Then came the last pleas of the defendants. All eyes and ears
were turned to Kameniev and Zinovyev. Kameniev spoke first.

He confirmed in full detail his earlier confession, said he was
guilty of everything of which he had been accused, and instead of
pleading anything even remotely resembling extenuating circumstances, seemed to be trying to prove that he did not deserve a
shred of mercy.

He had just sat down at the end of his speech when, dramatically,
he jumped up to his feet once more and said: 'I should just like to
add a few words—some things I want to say to my two children.
One is a pilot, the other a Pioneer. Standing here now as I do, with
one foot in the grave, I want to tell them: no matter what my
sentence may be, I consider it just. Don't look back. Go forward.
Together with the Soviet people follow Stalin!'

Everyone in the court room was shaken by this outburst. I myself
felt a surge of twin emotions—pity for the man, and a feeling of
murderous hate for Stalin. When I looked round I could read

sympathy for the unfortunate victims in the eyes of the assembled. Even the faces of the judges, for a moment, seemed to soften.

Then Zinovyev rose. Breathing with difficulty he began to speak without emotion—there was nothing left of the brilliant orator who in former times had been one of the most dynamic speakers of the *Comintern*. After the first muttered words, he managed to control himself and spoke in the same way as his comrade-in-arms Kameniev had done. He said:

'My defective *Bolshevism* became transformed into anti-*Bolshevism*, and through Trotskyism I arrived at Fascism. Trotskyism is a variety of Fascism and Zinovyevism is a variety of Trotskyism.'

Those who knew Zinovyev's style of speech had no difficulty in knowing that these words did not originate from him, but that they resembled the clumsy style of Stalin.

At 7.30 on the evening of the 23rd of August, the 'trial' came to an end and the court withdrew.

Although the verdicts and sentences had already been decided by Stalin, they stayed out seven hours, coming back at 2.30 a.m. on the 24th of August 1936.

In dead silence, Ulrikh began to read, and spoke for fifteen minutes. When he arrived at the part which dealt with the sentences, nervous coughing broke the silence of the court room. Ulrikh paused. When the noise ceased, he began to name the defendants one by one, and announced that each of them had been sentenced to death by shooting.

For a moment everyone present in the court room watched in silence as Ulrikh put down the paper from which he had just read the verdict. Then the silence was broken by a piercing shriek. It was one of the sentenced, the little man Laurye, who shouted hysterically:

'Long live the cause of Marx, Engels, Lenin and Stalin!'

The defendants were led out of the Trade Union Building by their N.K.V.D. escorts and taken direct to the cellar prison of Lubyanka and were put in holes similar to those in which they had been kept before they had made their bargains with Stalin.

On the part of the accused, there was still a lingering, desperate belief that Stalin would keep his promises that the sentences would not be final. But the sentences were confirmed when the Supreme Council of the U.S.S.R., in which Stalin was a deputy, rejected their appeals.

Kameniev, Zinovyev, Smirnov and Ter-Vaganian demanded to see Stalin; he visited Kameniev only. What was said between the two is not known, because the conversation was *à deux*. The only certain thing known about this secret conversation between Stalin and Kameniev in a cell at Lubyanka is that it lasted a very long time.

The sixteen duped men were shot, and the newspapers of the 25th of August 1936 carried the fact that sentences on all the convicted had been carried out.

*   *   *

The trial reverberated through the Soviet Union like a cannon-shot. In Moscow and other large cities people formed spontaneous demonstrations to show that they stood behind Stalin against the opposition. They had fallen for the propaganda completely, and believed that the opposition leaders had been responsible for every-thing which spelled hardship. When they found that the mass arrests still went on, that prices still remained high and wages low, and that everything was as bad as before, reaction set in throughout the country and was directed against Stalin.

Six days after the sixteen accused had been shot, the official Danish Government paper *Socialdemokraten* published a sensational story revealing that the Hotel Bristol in Copenhagen had been demolished in 1917. Holtzmann could not have met Trotsky's son Sedov there in Copenhagen in 1932.

As a further proof it was also pointed out that Sedov was not even in Denmark at the time his father was there. Examination papers and other records from the *Technische Hochschule* in Berlin, where Sedov took his examinations on the crucial days, confirmed this.

It was also proved by correspondence between Sedov and his father. Clearly Sedov had not met Holtzmann at all.

When Stalin learned what had been discovered abroad, he ordered an immediate enquiry into the circumstances.

The enquiry revealed that the blunder had been caused by Stalin's friend and confederate Nikolai Yezhov. He it was who had thought the best place for a secret meeting would be a hotel. Molchanov, the chief of the Secret Political Department, who handled the technical side of the preparation of the trial, was then instructed by Yagoda to obtain the name of a suitable hotel in Copenhagen. However, Molchanov, being cautious, ordered his secretary to ask the Foreign Department to recommend a number of hotels in *Oslo* and in Copenhagen. Molchanov's secretary took down the information over the telephone and prepared a typewritten memorandum which he handed to Molchanov. Unfortunately for Molchanov, however, the Oslo hotels were mistakenly listed as being in Copenhagen, and vice-versa. Molchanov chose the Hotel Bristol, believing it to be in Copenhagen, and so it turned out at the trial that the Hotel Bristol was transplanted from Oslo to Copenhagen.

Stalin now had a good excuse to depose Yagoda. He had not forgotten how Yagoda had double-crossed him in December 1934 by flying to Leningrad to see Nikolayev before Stalin's arrival in connection with the Kirov murder. So Yagoda was dismissed without explanation in September 1936. Since, however, it would not be good tactics to let the Head of the N.K.V.D. disappear without a trace, Stalin made him Commissar for Postal and Telegraph Communications. Nikolai Yezhov became the new Chief of the N.K.V.D.

The new Chief of the Secret Police installed himself in Lubyanka with three hundred specially picked and trusted henchmen. His first act was to list those suspects who were to be purged. The purge began in the N.K.V.D. itself, to root out Yagoda's people. Men, who a short while before had executed innocent people were themselves shot in the cellars of Lubyanka.

Yenukidze, Ordzhonikidze, Kalinin, Petrovsky, Chubar, Kaganovich, Beria, Mikoyan and other members of the *Politburo* and Central Committee did what they could to prevent the killings, but Stalin brushed them aside.

There was no stopping the impetus now.

P

CHAPTER THIRTY-TWO

A Strange Fight

In the late summer of 1936, our editor at the Moscow evening newspaper *Vecherniaya Moskva* decided that my colleague and friend Abram Abramovich Kraskyn and I should represent the paper as Special Correspondents at the autumn manoeuvres of the Red Army in the Ukraine. Consequently, Abram and I reported at Moscow Red Army H.Q. for our credentials and were issued with officers' uniforms. It was the custom in the U.S.S.R. that newspapermen must wear Red Army officers' uniforms while attached to any unit.

The next morning we were flown by military aircraft to Rostov-on-Don, from where a Red Army staff car took us to the nearby Divisional H.Q. from whence the manoeuvres in this part of the Soviet Union were directed. The army-games had just begun and Abram and I were told by the C.O. that they were to be a true to life enactment. I had not taken part in any manoeuvres previously and was therefore quite impressed with the continuous movements of our division, especially as we moved about in a staff car and felt quite comfortable.

On the third afternoon, we arrived at the Ukrainian Collective Farm village Krasnoye Znamya, where we were to spend the night. The N.C.O.'s and troops put up tents in the fields outside the village —despite the angry protests of farmers who insisted that their harvest would be spoilt. The officers decided that they, as well as Abram and I, would sleep under a firm roof. There was, however, only one spacious building in Krasnoye Znamya—an imposing house with whitewashed walls. Although this was the house of the mayor and his large family, the C.O. did not abandon his plan and ordered the mayor to vacate the ground floor of the house to make room for us.

'I would not advise you to stay at this house,' the mayor told the C.O. on hearing his command, and there was a strange look in his eyes.

'I did not ask you for your advice, comrade mayor,' the C.O. raged. 'I want accommodation for the twenty-two of us and that's a military order!'

'If you insist, comrade commander, I won't stay in your way. I'll clear out the ground floor immediately but, unfortunately, I cannot provide beds or blankets because we just haven't any.'

'That's all right,' the C.O. nodded.

The officers helped the mayor and his sons to clear out the ground floor which consisted of only one large room. It was big enough to accommodate all of us on the floor boards. The officers' cook prepared quite a good meal in the kitchen of the house and afterwards the usual considerable quantities of vodka were consumed.

We were to leave the village at dawn because 'a surprise attack on enemy forces' was planned, so we retired to our floor boards early to get as much sleep as possible.

In the middle of the night we were awakened by loud shouts outside and, for a moment I thought the 'enemy forces' had surrounded the village and were intending to take us prisoner. My theory was strengthened when, a moment later, the door was thrust open and fierce looking soldiers tore into the room. But, instead of complying with the rules of military manoeuvres, they started to smash the butts of their rifles on to the heads of the surprised Red Army officers.

Within seconds, a real battle was under way. The officers who were not yet wounded took their pistols and fired at the fierce attackers. But, although their bullets struck the attacking soldiers at point-blank range, they seemed bullet-proof and continued smashing at the officers with their rifle butts. For some inexplicable reason, neither Abram nor I was hit, even though we both wore the Red Army officers' uniforms.

Then, when the attackers thought they had finished their gruesome task, they left the room through the open door, shouting and

swearing in Ukrainian. Around us was a horrible mess. Some of
the officers were dead, others were unconscious, and still others were
groaning with pain. The C.O. lay on the floor in a pool of blood,
his head split open . . .

The fierce shouting and firing of pistol shots in the house brought
several N.C.O.'s and Red Army men from outside Krasnoye
Znamya to the scene. When they saw what had happened, they
immediately informed Rostov-on-Don Red Army H.Q. by radio,
and a couple of hours later, doctors and ambulances, together with
high-ranking Red Army and Secret Police officers, arrived.

While the dead and injured were taken away, Abram and I—
—the only ones to remain unharmed—were interrogated. We told
the Army and Secret Police investigators everything we had seen,
but when I mentioned that the attackers wore different uniforms
from those I had seen anywhere in the U.S.S.R. during my stay
there, a Secret Police colonel shouted at me that "only one type of
uniform exists in the Soviet Union as you ought to know!' so I
did not bother to add that the attackers' uniforms looked like those
of Red Guards, pictured in the countless publications about the
Civil War.

Next to be interrogated was the Mayor of Krasnoye Znamya.
Neither the Red Army top-ranking officers nor the Secret Police
interrogators seemed to mind that Abram and I remained present.

'What do you want me to tell you, comrade colonel?' the mayor
said when the Secret Police interrogator asked him what he knew
about the murderous attack. 'If I tell you the truth you won't
believe me,' he explained, 'so it's better you tell me what you wish
to hear and I'll say it.'

'I want to know from you what you know about this massacre!'
the colonel thundered. 'I want the truth, do you understand? The
truth!'

'Well, comrade colonel,' the mayor said uneasily, 'the Ukrainian
Red Guards attacked the comrade officers because they were
Russians . . .'

'What drivel are you talking, you idiot?' the Secret Police in-
vestigator yelled threateningly. 'Don't you know that there have

been no Red Guards since the Civil War ended?'

'I said you wouldn't believe me, comrade colonel . . .'

'You really insist that the attackers were Red Guards?'

'Yes, comrade colonel,' the mayor nodded. 'Everybody here will confirm it. Ever since these guards were shot here by a White Russian firing squad in 1918, they come back. They are Ukrainians and they hate the Russians. That's probably why they attacked the comrade Red Army officers . . .'

The Secret Police colonel did not believe the mayor. Neither did the Red Army officers. They all accused him of being somehow involved in the attack for, as a Ukrainian, he must have hated Russians. And so he was arrested. They also arrested Abram and me—despite our protests. And, in the same 'Black Raven,' as they called the Secret Police prisoner-vans in Russia, we were joined by the entire male population of the village.

They took us to Rostov-on-Don Secret Police Headquarters.

For two full days and nights we were interrogated almost non-stop by uniformed Secret Police investigators who did their best to bully us into signing confessions that we had taken part in the murder of eleven Red Army officers and that we had also participated in injuring the rest of them. No one yielded to this concentrated pressure. They then threatened to keep us in custody until we would change our minds and sign the required confessions.

On the third morning of the ordeal we were suddenly released. At first Abram and I thought that we had received help from Moscow, but when the collective farmers were also released, we gathered that something else must have persuaded the Secret Police overlords to change their minds and not carry out their threats.

It was decided that Abram and I should return to the Red Army division which was now continuing the Autumn manoeuvres some five miles from Krasnoye Znamya. As our journey took us through that village, the Secret Police provided a large open lorry on which all who had been arrested that fateful night were to travel.

I managed to place myself next to the mayor. Fortunately I had a fair knowledge of Ukrainian and was able to speak freely with the man. He turned out to be a most friendly, jovial type.

'You said the soldiers who killed and injured the Red Army officers were Ukrainian Red Guards,' I said after we had talked a little about trivial things.

'They didn't believe me, did they?' he replied gruffly.

'Well, they didn't believe me or anyone else either,' I retorted.

'Do you believe me?' he asked and looked searchingly into my eyes.

'Why shouldn't I? That's why I'd like to know more about it.'

'I don't mind telling you,' he said obligingly. He accepted the cigarette which I offered him and, inhaling the smoke deeply, continued to speak: 'During the Civil War after the October Revolution, our district frequently changed hands. One day we were under the Red Guards, the next under the Red Army. Another time, the Whites took over and so on. I was then twelve years old and remember those terrible days very clearly.'

He spoke in great detail about the merciless Civil War and eventually came to the night when the Ukrainian Red Guards were shot in the house that he now occupied in his capacity of mayor of the collective farm village.

'The Russian Whites silently surrounded our village and created the impression that the territory was no-man's-land in order to lure the Red Guards into the trap. The Ukrainian Guards fell for it and occupied my present house. The Russian Whites then quietly surrounded the building, overpowered the sentries outside, and afterwards mowed down the surprised Red Guards in the house with their machine guns. Every single one was killed. Later they were burned in the village square . . .'

'And you think that they came back as ghosts while we were there, and attacked the Red Army officers?' I cut in.

'I know it was them,' he insisted. 'I have seen them come to my house often enough. I know what Red Guards' uniforms look like, I have seen them all the time during the Civil War.'

'You just said that the ghosts of those killed Red Guards came to your house often,' I tried to clarify the position. 'Have they ever attacked anyone else?'

'Why should they?' the mayor asked, surprised. 'They don't

harm Ukrainians, they only attack Russians because they hate Russians.'

'But the Russian officers who they attacked and killed were not their White Russian enemies . . .'

'Reds or Whites doesn't make any difference,' he explained. 'They were Russians and that's sufficient for Ukrainian nationalists to kill them.' He looked at me and added: 'Don't you remember that I tried to warn the C.O. not to stay the night in my house? You and your other newspaper friend stood next to him and heard what I said. I feared the Red Guards might come, but he cut me short. If these officers hadn't been in my house, nothing would have happened to them.'

'What I can't grasp is why they didn't attack my friend and me?'

'You are a foreigner and he's not a Russian,' the mayor explained. 'They only attack Russians.'

'How could they have known that we were not Russians?' I persisted.

'They just know. I told you that they come often enough to my house and they never harm anyone. Sometimes, when they came, we had a party going on downstairs and many people were there, but they never hurt anyone. Ask whom you want in the village, they all know that what I'm telling you is the truth.'

'It's as Nikolai says,' commented an old villager who sat on the other side of the mayor and who had listened to every word we had spoken. 'I myself saw them often . . . they are good men.'

'If you don't believe them to be ghosts, how do you explain that none of them was hurt or killed by the bullets which the Red Army officers fired at them during the attack?' the mayor demanded in an effort to convince me that the story he told me was correct. 'You were in the room. You must know that at least some of the attackers would have been wounded or killed at such short distance if they were real people. But you can't wound or kill ghosts. Perhaps this convinces you that I'm not talking a lot of drivel.'

'I am not doubting what you say,' I assured him. 'I only wanted to get from you as many details as possible.'

Later, when Abram and I rejoined the Red Army division, we

learned by chance that our sudden release from Rostov-on-Don Secret Police Headquarters was due to a report by Soviet ballistic experts who confirmed that quite a few of the attacked Red Army officers *had fired* their Mausers. When it was established that the bullets from their pistols had hit the walls, and the door and window frames, they were forced to accept the conception about ghosts having been responsible for the strange raid. Even they had to acknowledge that, had the attackers been human beings, at least some of them would have been struck down by the concentrated fire from expert shots at close range. But these reasons were naturally never officially disclosed. Soviet ideology did not accept the existence of a spirit world or any other super-normal phenomena, so it was more advantageous for the N.K.V.D. to declare the case closed.

There had been, however, a serious leak. The newspapers *Krasnaya Zvyezda, Kolkhoznaya Gazeta, Kommunist, D.D.Z.*, and others *had* already published reports about the 'Strange Fight' and disclosed the names of killed and wounded Red Army officers *before* the N.K.V.D.'s secrecy clamp down. The only recourse for the Secret Police was to swear all editorial staff to future secrecy and recall all published copies of the report. But by then many people had learned what happened in the Ukrainian *kolkhoz* village on that fatal night in 1936. Years later, I met many people who gave me a true account of that 'Strange Fight' which Abram and I had witnessed.

CHAPTER THIRTY-THREE

The Second Trial

ONE morning when I went to my office I found Abram sitting on my desk, swinging his legs to and fro, and wearing a triumphant smirk on his face.

I had hardly said 'Good morning' when he held up a sheaf of papers and slapped them with the back of his hand. 'Here it is,' he said, 'your let-out.'

I didn't know what he was talking about, and I told him.

'This rule,' he said, 'I've been studying it, and if you go about things in the right way, you'll be able to sever your connection with the Party.'

I was still puzzled, so Abram sat down with me and went through the latest decree about Party membership. In essence it said that foreigners residing in Russia would no longer be allowed to be full members of the Soviet Communist Party. They were required to become Sympathisers.

This was an insult to communists who had been members of their own national parties for years before coming to Russia, but it came about because of the deep-rooted distrust of all foreigners which the *Politburo* entertained.

Abram went into the advantages of breaking my ties with the *Comintern*.

'Provided you convince them that you are still what they term "an honourable member of the community",' he said, 'in other words, avoid being expelled or resigning, you will be free of Party commands, you'll no longer be expected to be a Party robot. And you'll get respect for being a non-Party *Bolshevik*.'

He advised me then on the precise line of argument to take (it involved quoting Stalin at great length on the benefits of building up a strong cadre of non-Party *Bolsheviks*); after some sticky minutes in the presence of the Partorg, things finally turned my way, and I was given my freedom from the Party. I was required neither to be a Sympathiser nor a Probationer.

I lived with anxiety for a few days, but nothing happened to indicate that I would be victimised. In fact within a matter of weeks I was amazed to be presented with a car (a new 'M. I.') 'for excellent work and staunch devotion as a non-Party *Bolshevik*.'

I had much to be grateful to Abram for. I felt as close to being happy as I had for a long time.

But one could never stay happy for very long in Moscow. Misery and fear were ever-present. Arrests and beatings were the mildest activities of the N.K.V.D. Stalin's whip had long since become a pistol—and it was a pistol aimed indiscriminately at friends and enemies, young and old.

I was aware that a second trial was in the course of preparation; the knowledge was rendered more painful because a man I had known well—Karl Radek—was to be one of the new puppets.

Poor Radek, who had personally done so much to glorify Stalin, nearly lost his reason when they took him in for interrogation. He begged and pleaded to be allowed to see Stalin, but he was refused; his letters were confiscated, and one night he was confronted by no less a person than the Chief Interrogator, Molchanov.

Molchanov drove Radek almost to breaking point. Mironov, another of the top organisers of the second trial, later revealed that Radek suddenly, at the end of an attack from Molchanov, shouted: 'All right! All right! I'll sign everything now. I'll admit anything you want me to—that I wanted to murder the whole *Politburo*, that I wanted to make Hitler the head of the Kremlin. But one name I will add to the accomplices you have written down—that of you, Molchanov!'

Mironov said there was a stunned silence for some seconds, then Radek screamed the name over and over again, 'Molchanov! Molchanov! Molchanov!'

When he quietened down, Radek said sarcastically: 'If you believe, as you try to convince me, Molchanov, that one should sacrifice oneself for the good of the Party, then let us both sacrifice ourselves, shall we? And do you know something, comrade— Yezhov would jump at the proposition. In order to have one Radek confess, Yezhov would throw a dozen Molchanovs to the wolves.'

★　　★　　★

The second public trial—The Trial of the Seventeen—opened on the 23rd of January 1937. History has recorded what the results were—thirteen of the accused were sentenced to death; four were given prison sentences. One of the four was Karl Radek.

Radek's behind-the-scenes help had won him a reprieve from the death sentence, but though great pains had been taken to ensure that no mistakes like the *Hotel Bristol* effort of the first trial would mar the occasion, nevertheless there was a sensation. And only Stalin was to blame this time.

Part of the fabricated evidence the Great and Wise insisted on being in had to do with an alleged meeting between Pyatakov and Trotsky in Oslo in mid-December 1935.

However, on the 25th of January 1937 (i.e. two days after the trial opened) the Norwegian newspaper *Aftenposten* exploded this lie. According to Pyatakov's evidence, he had arrived by aeroplane at the Oslo airfield. But *Aftenposten* was able to reveal that *no* civil aeroplane had landed at Kjeller airport *during the whole of December.* The airport records themselves confirmed this to be true.

Prosecutor Vyshinksy was hard put to bluster his way through this, but his troubles had only begun, for Trotsky himself, through the foreign Press, threw down the gauntlet.

First he demanded details of Pyatakov's flight arrangements, visa, etc. As Trotsky declared: 'If it should be proved that Pyatakov actually visited me, my position would be hopelessly compromised. If on the contrary I can prove that the story of the visit is false . . . *the entire system of so called voluntary confessions will be shown up for what it is—lies.*'

He even challenged them to have him extradited from Norway.

It was a brave challenge. It was in vain.

But not one hundred-per-cent, because despite the heavily organised 'spontaneous' demonstrations of faith in Stalin when the trial ended, three inscriptions were daubed on two factory walls (Elektrozavod and the bearing factory Sharikopodshipnik) which read:

'DOWN WITH THE MURDERER OF THE LEADERS OF THE OCTOBER REVOLUTION', 'DEATH TO THE POISONER OF OUR GREAT MAXIM GORKY' and 'KILL THE GEORGIAN REPTILE'.

So not all of Russia was blind.

CHAPTER THIRTY-FOUR

Ordzhonikidze's Death

THE official announcement of the sudden death of Sergo Ordzhonikidze reached us in Pyatigorsk, where Abram and I had just arrived
for the Congress of Caucasian Publicists.

The announcement said:

TRAGIC DEATH OF OUR SERGO ORDZHONIKIDZE
Kyslovodsk, 18 February 1937.

The Central Committee of the Soviet Communist Party
announces with deep sorrow that our beloved Sergo Ordzhonikidze has died tragically.

Comrade Ordzhonikidze was travelling by car to Moscow.
The car crashed a few kilometres outside Kyslovodsk. Doctors
at the hospital to which he was taken said Comrade Ordzhonikidze was killed instantly.

As Sergo had been our friend, we telephoned our Editor and
obtained permission to go to Kyslovodsk and get the story of
Ordzhonikidze's death.

When we arrived at the hospital and asked to be taken to the
doctor who issued Ordzhonikidze's death certificate, the receptionist
seemed to be at a loss. 'No casualty case has been brought to us,'
she said.

We made her look up her ledger but according to this no patient
had been admitted for the last four days.

'There must be a mistake somewhere,' the hospital Commandant
told us when we went to see him. 'No one has died in this hospital
for over a year and we have not had any casualties here for the last
six weeks.'

221

'Is there any other hospital in the neighbourhood?' Abram asked.

'No,' the Commandant said. 'But it is just possible that Comrade Ordzhonikidze might have been taken to the surgery of the *Militia Kommandatura*. Have you tried there?'

We drove straight to the Militia where we were able to see the Chief without difficulty. Comrade Ordzhonikidze's body had not been brought to his surgery.

'Could you perhaps tell us where Comrade Ordzhonikidze's body has been taken?' I enquired.

'That's difficult to say,' he replied. 'You see, there are so many sanatoriums in the neighbourhood. Maybe he was taken to one of them.'

'Could we see the smashed car?' Abram asked.

'I don't know anything about a smashed car. It has not been brought here.'

This was strange. The Militia held the function of police in the U.S.S.R. and it was their job to deal with any accidents. 'Where could the car have been taken to?' I asked.

'*Nieznayu*,' he replied. 'Perhaps the N.K.V.D. took charge of it. The best thing is to go and ask them.'

On our way to the N.K.V.D. Headquarters we passed Ordzhonikidze's villa, so we stopped to have a word with his secretary or member of the household. When we entered, an N.K.V.D. captain asked us what we wanted. We had to establish our identity, and after he had studied our Press cards very carefully he told us he could give us no information, and if we wanted to know any more, we should go to headquarters.

It was, however, impossible to see the Kyslovodsk N.K.V.D. Chief. The duty officer did his best to persuade us to write in, and when he saw we were not prepared to accept his suggestion, he tried to persuade us to see a minor officer. Eventually, we managed to see an N.K.V.D. major, a man of about fifty, with rows of decorations on his tunic.

'Perhaps you can tell us where Comrade Ordzhonikidze's body has been taken to?' Abram addressed the major.

'Why, he is in his villa,' the officer answered without hesitation. 'Haven't you been to his villa?'

'We went there on our way here, but one of your people refused to let us in,' I said.

'We want to try to find out where the body had been taken to, and where his car has disappeared to,' Abram added.

'The car hasn't disappeared at all,' the major replied. 'It is in the garage. Why should it disappear?'

It was all too clear that there was something fishy about Sergo Ordzhonikidze's death. 'Is the car badly smashed?' I asked.

'Why should it have been smashed up?' the major replied. 'It hasn't been out of the garage for several days.'

'Where is the car which crashed then?' I went on. Ordzhonikidze might have been travelling in a Government car.

'I don't know what you are talking about,' the major said. 'No car crashed. It is really amazing what fairy-tales you newspaper people invent.'

We pointed out to him what the official announcement stated— that Comrade Ordzhonikidze had been killed in a road accident.

'How such an announcement came to be made is beyond me,' he replied. 'Comrade Ordzhonikidze was, as you probably know, a very sick man, and he died suddenly in his villa. There is nothing accidental or mysterious about it. He died from natural causes.'

'Would it be possible for us to see the body?' Abram asked.

'Why?' the major snapped.

At this moment another officer entered. He wore the flashes of a colonel. 'Are these the two who are making trouble?' he said in an unfriendly tone.

'We aren't making any trouble,' Abram replied in an icy voice. 'We have been sent by our paper to write the story of Comrade Ordzhonikidze's death. That is why we have come to Kyslovodsk.'

'Do you mean to tell me that your editor instructed you to check on what the N.K.V.D. is doing?' the colonel hissed.

There was little doubt that a slip had occurred similar to that in the case of the murder of Kirov in December 1934. At the time we were in Kyslovodsk N.K.V.D. Headquarters we did not know what had happened between Stalin and Ordzhonikidze, but we had no doubt that Ordzhonikidze had been murdered.

'If you will take my advice,' the colonel continued, 'you'll go straight back and forget what you originally came here for. We are acting on orders from the highest quarters. That is all I can tell you.'

He walked with us to our car, and stood there until we drove off.

Our editor was not surprised when we telephoned him and told him what had happened.

When, a week later, we returned to Moscow, we learned that the man who had been in charge of the Press Department when the first announcement was made, had been arrested and shot. Somebody had to pay for the Kremlin's blunder.

Some time later, a new version of the death of Sergo Ordzhonikidze was released. This one just said he had died 'of natural causes.' There was no explanation of the previous story.

Some time after the funeral, Abram managed to get hold of the report which Ordzhonikidze had made in his own handwriting immediately after Stalin left on the 17th of February 1937 after visiting Ordzhonikidze in the latter's villa at Kyslovodsk. During this meeting Ordzhonikidze insisted that Stalin should revise his plans, and give instructions to Yezhov to stop the mass murder of the Soviet people. He also insisted on an extraordinary meeting of the *Politburo* being called at once, to arrange for economic conditions to be improved. Stalin answered in an offensive way, and the meeting became more and more stormy, finally ending with Ordzhonikidze saying in a threatening manner:

'. . . and don't think that you will be able to shut me up this time!'

Stalin realised that Sergo Ordzhonikidze meant what he said and promised he would call an extraordinary meeting of the *Politburo*, so that Sergo could present his case.

The next day Sergo Ordzhonikidze's *sudden* death was announced.

The conclusions are obvious.

CHAPTER THIRTY-FIVE

The Trial That Never Was

HAVING executed every Chekist who might betray the secrets of the N.K.V.D. and nearly everyone who at one time or another had any connection with the opposition, 'Our Beloved and Wise Leader' decided to 'clean up' the Red Army. He knew that many high ranking officers were far from being his most devoted followers and, fearing that those who held the weapons might one day use them against him and his *Politburo*, he decided to act. The only persons who had any knowledge of his actions were his most devoted assistant Molotov, who nodded obediently to everything the master said; and Yezhov, who was to be the man in charge of the operation.

On the 11th of June 1937, the Government announced officially that Marshal Tukhachevsky and seven other leading commanders of the Red Army—the Generals Eideman, Feldman, Kork, Prymakov, Putna, Uberovich and Yakyr—had been arrested. The communiqué stated that the generals had been plotting the defeat of the Red Army, and they would be charged with high treason.

Abram had known Tukhachevsky, Kork and Yakyr fairly well, and I had met Tukhachevsky, first during the manoeuvres in the Ukraine, and several times after. We discussed the sensational news, and were convinced that none of the accused was guilty. Only a few days before this announcement they had been openly praised in various newspapers and periodicals as 'the pride of the Red Army' and 'the best military strategists of the U.S.S.R.'

The same evening we met several of our well-informed friends at Rosa's Salon, though the circle had shrunk considerably—Yevgeniya

Pyatakova had been sent to a slave-labour camp because she was the sister of Yuriy Pyatakov; Karl Radek had been sentenced to ten years imprisonment; and several others had either disappeared without trace or were in the clutches of the inquisitors of Lubyanka.

'Today I heard from Vyacheslav (Molotov) that Tukhachevsky and other generals had planned a *putsch*,' Chernov told us. 'It was ingeniously planned. The Kremlin garrison was to shoot the leaders, capture the less important ones and proclaim a military dictatorship with Tukhachevsky at the head, and Yakyr as his deputy. As soon as this was done and the military government proclaimed, the Nazi army was to help establish order, for which Hitler was promised some territorial concessions. They had planned their coup for a long time and had supplied the German generals with information about our fortifications, defence plans in case of war, strength of the Army, Navy and Air Force, armament-production, and so on.'

The accusation was too ridiculous for words. The mere fact that there were three Jews among the accused generals ruled out the suggestion that they were Hitler's spies. The remaining five Red Army commanders were hard-bitten German-haters.

'What Molotov told you is fantastic,' I said to Chernov. 'It is very hard to believe that Tukhachevsky and the others could be mercenaries of those Germans whom they hate like poison . . .'

'I don't know what to believe myself,' Chernov replied. 'One cannot, of course, be certain that Vyacheslav is not telling the truth, and that Tukhachevsky and the others plotted to overthrow the government and to install themselves.'

'This sounds preposterous, especially if one takes into consideration the fact that neither Tukhachevsky nor the other arrested commanders had any political ambitions but regarded themselves merely as militarists,' Abram said. 'Neither Tukhachevsky nor the others would ever wish to be rulers of the country.'

'It looks to me as though a third show trial is being prepared,' I spoke my thoughts aloud. 'Had it only been Tukhachevsky and one or two of the other military leaders, I might have been inclined to give the prosecutors the benefit of the doubt, but as all the commanders have been arrested and the Red Army is left virtually without military leaders I cannot help feeling this is another move to liquidate the whole existing apparatus, and to replace it with new people, especially chosen.'

The next day, the 12th of June 1937, an official announcement stated that the trial of Marshal Tukhachevsky, and the generals Yakyr, Uberovich, Putna, Kork, Prymakov, Feldman and Eideman had taken place *in camera*, and that the judges consisting of seven high Soviet Army commanders, had found the accused guilty, and sentenced them to death by shooting, and that all had been executed.

Very shortly afterwards an officer of the N.K.V.D. who had been closely connected with the 'Tukhachevsky affair'—as they called it at Lubyanka—told Abram:

'Immediately *after* the execution of Tukhachevsky and the other generals, Yezhov summoned the Marshals Budienny and Blucher, and the Generals Alknis, Lybenko, Byelov, Kashiryn and Shapozhnikov, gave them a prepared 'court verdict' to sign, and informed them it would be announced that they had been the judges. Each of them signed the 'verdict' without hesitation, because they realised that refusal would mean arrest and a charge of being an accomplice of Tukhachevsky.'

We also learned from Red Army, N.K.V.D. and other well-informed sources, that after the murder of Tukhachevsky and his colleagues, mass arrests took place amongst other officers of the Red Army. Anyone who had had any close contact with the executed generals automatically became a suspect. The fact that Tukhachevsky had been the head of the Soviet armed forces for a great many years is alone sufficient to indicate the enormous numbers reached by these mass arrests and liquidations. Hundreds of Red Army officers disappeared every day, all over the Soviet Union, and their relatives—even distant ones—were sent to prisons or slave-labour camps. New officers, hand-picked by Yezhov's men, filled the vacancies. But even they sometimes shared the fate of their predecessors, because it was discovered they were either relatives or friends of one of those arrested.

Needless to say the constant arrests and changes of commanding officers greatly undermined authority, and discipline declined rapidly. This reached such proportions that it is no exaggeration to say that the Red Army became extremely demoralised. But Stalin, who was kept informed of this critical state of affairs, was determined to show his iron fist and to put matters right, and appointed Political Commissars; these were devoted members of the Soviet Communist Party—people whom he could trust completely.

'Stalin has now restored political commissars to the Army,' said Abel Yenukidze, the day the official announcement about this had been made. 'During the civil war the Party attached political commissars to the military commanders because many of them were ex-Tsarist officers and the Party could not trust them fully. But this was abolished by Lenin at the end of the civil war. And now Vissarionovich reintroduces the same system. He obviously regards the Red Army commanders as his enemies. This is a very bad policy and can easily turn the whole army against our Party and government. One day, they might even try to do what Tukhachevsky never even dreamed of doing.'

Though Yenukidze was no longer in Stalin's good books, he nevertheless did his utmost to influence his old-time friend. But Stalin ignored him and said something about some *Old Bolsheviks* suffering from softness of the brain. The arrests and executions went on.

'When Stalin murdered the leaders of the October Revolution, the Soviet people knew why he did it,' Bukharin said one evening when we met at our weekly tea party. 'But nobody can understand why he had to annihilate his most outstanding military commanders whom he himself selected and appointed. He is destroying his own military machine which was the bulwark of his personal power. The most serious thing of all is what is happening to the temper of the people. They are furious at these new massacres which to them are inexplicable.'

At that time Bukharin was still close to the *Politburo* and he was continuously being consulted about various matters. He too tried to speak to Stalin, as Yenukidze and many other Soviet executives had done, but to no good effort.

One of Stalin's most despicable acts was his method of appointing the 'judges' of the 'secret trial' of Marshal Tukhachevsky and the other seven military commanders. The authoritative names of the 'judges' had served his purpose, and the question now was how far each of them could be trusted to keep the matter secret. Stalin and Yezhov went into this question very thoroughly, because it was of the utmost importance that these men (who had unwittingly become witnesses of the grave crime) should keep their mouths shut. They decided that only Marshal Budyenny and General Shapozhnikov could be fully trusted. The others were reclassified 'not reliable' and Stalin instructed Yezhov to make arrangements for their liquidation. Yezhov's instructions were to get rid of them quietly. He did so. Within a year all were dead.

As to the two surviving 'judges,' Budyenny and Shapozhnikov, 'The Wise Man in the Kremlin' had been right in one case only. This was in regard to the ex-Tsarist Colonel Shapozhnikov who, during the Revolution, had witnessed the liquidation of a great many of his colleagues and had always kept this a secret. When Stalin noticed him and took him under his wing, he became his devoted follower and supporter.

Budyenny, once a sergeant in a Tsarist Cossack regiment, who had become a legendary Red Army leader during the days of the civil war, had only two aims in life—drinking and seducing his secretaries. When drunk (and this was often) his tongue loosened alarmingly and he had a tendency to reveal all sorts of secrets. Inevitably, in one drunken bout, he talked about having been a 'judge' at 'the trial that never was.' Encouraged, he told the whole story. And the story got back to Stalin's ears; Budyenny paid dearly for his stupidity.

CHAPTER THIRTY-SIX

Cain and Abel

WHEN Lyubov's father, Abel Yenukidze, was sent away from Moscow on an inspection tour, Lyubov was concerned over the fact that no letters arrived from him. I tried to reassure her that he was all right, but she was still worried because she said it was unlike him not to keep in constant touch. However, we saw a lot of each other during these weeks, and the period together gave us both the opportunity to confirm our love for each other. She was everything I had ever hoped to find in a woman. And her declarations of love for me were touchingly simple and so obviously sincere.

We were sitting in my flat one evening listening to ballet music on the radio when there was a knock on the door. I opened it to find Abel standing there. I was shocked at his appearance. He looked suddenly old and ill. Lyubov, who had followed me to the door, pushed past me and took hold of her father's arm.

'Don't you feel well, *papochka?*' she said in a worried voice.

'It's nothing. I'm all right,' her father assured her. 'Don't worry, Lyubochka.'

Though he hadn't eaten the whole day, he would not have supper with us, saying that he did not feel like food. All he wanted was vodka.

'Has anything happened to you, Abel?' I asked. 'Is there anything I can do for you?'

He sat staring uneasily past me. I asked him again, and leaned forward and touched his shoulder.

'No, no, nothing—I'm all right,' he answered, 'I'm only tired . . .'

Gradually Lyubov and I succeeded in drawing him out of his depressed mood.

'I may as well tell you,' he said at last. 'I have, as you know, been on a confidential tour with other members of E.K.K.I. and the Central Committee, to various parts of the country. It was part of our task to visit "Forced Labour Camps." I have seen things I would never have thought possible. Had anyone told me even *part* of what I have seen with my own eyes, I would not have believed him. I would have dismissed it as subversive propaganda . . . I still feel sick when I think of it . . .'

He paused as if wondering whether he should continue or not. Then he began to talk again.

'You and I, all of us, know from official reports that big and important projects have been built by forced labour,' he said. 'When we read that the White Sea Canal, the Moscow-Volga Canal, the irrigation of Kolkhida, the important dams, railway tracks, roads and so on have been built by forced labour, we accepted this. We rarely, any of us, thought beyond it. It was sufficient to know that our country was taking huge strides forward. We knew, of course, that the builders came from various forced-labour camps, but most of us, I dare say, thought that they received fair working and living conditions. *Our* prisons and labour camps were not institutions where prisoners were punished, but where they were to become good and useful Soviet citizens. What blind fools we were! Not even the worst *katorga* in the blackest reigns of the Tsars was anything like our forced-labour camps. I know. In my time I have watched the Cossack guards in the *katorgas* and seen how they treated prisoners. But I can tell you, those conditions were a paradise compared with what is going on in our Soviet forced-labour camps today.'

Abel described how the inmates of the forced-labour camps all over the country were squeezed into ramshackle wooden huts, where virtually they had to sleep on top of each other. No beds, not even wooden planks were allowed; the prisoners were forbidden to put straw or paper on the floors; they had to sleep on the bare earth. Blankets didn't exist for them.

There was no form of wearing apparel provided. The slaves had to wear what they arrived in, no matter how ragged or inadequate. A lot of these unfortunate people had been taken from the warm

South and were transported to the Arctic Circle. They died of exposure if nothing else.

They were required to pay for what passed as food, but the quantity they could buy was limited to the money they could earn; and this in turn was curtailed by a totally unrealistic system of fixed working norms. The norms were calculated on the output of people in full health who had, prior to arrest, been working full time on work of an identical nature.

Consequently, only those who fulfilled the norm received the full pittance, and this was just enough to pay for a plate of tasteless watery soup, a couple of pounds of sour black bread, a few potatoes, and 'accommodation.' If anyone, by a great stroke of luck, managed to work more than the stipulated norm, he or she was paid an extra 'wage' and could buy another slice of bread or scrap of stale margarine. Since a great number of those who found their way to the camps were either office workers, or others physically unsuited to heavy manual labour, they just could not even get near the norm. They were paid on a proportional basis. This meant that they were unable to buy the amount of food their bodies needed to keep fit. They had to decide whether they would scrap the soup, the bread or the potatoes. The fact that they had not been able to get enough food the previous day resulted next day in their being weaker and producing even *less*. If they were too weak to work, or collapsed from exhaustion and fell ill, no wages at all were paid. No food was given to them either. The slave-drivers pitilessly applied the Soviet motto 'he who does not work need not eat.' The sick and the weak were put out of their huts and left to die.

'Dozens of people die every day in each camp,' Abel said. 'They burn them and send the bones to collecting stations. From there they are sent on to centres where they are ground down and made into fertilizer. What does it matter if thousands of innocent people die! Stalin and Yezhov merely ensure that plenty more are arrested. And if too many people are arrested, why the N.K.V.D. just open new camps to take the surplus. No one is safe in our country any longer. Let's be frank, those people who have been arrested by the thousand could never have all been oppositionists or saboteurs. Many must be honest, hard-working people who only want to be allowed to *live* and work.'

Neither Lyubov nor I said anything. We knew that Abel was speaking the truth. We let him carry on.

'Look what Stalin did to his friends and devoted supporters—he killed them because they knew too much,' he went on. 'Look what he did to Sergo—Sergo who had been his friend since we were boys—Sergo who more than once risked his life to save Stalin. He poisoned Sergo. I suppose I am next on the list—I am the second of Stalin's real boyhood friends.'

He stopped and looked at us both, and he was biting hard on his lip. He looked away for a moment, then turned back and said:

'You two should get married as soon as possible. Please do as I ask. You could both get out of here and save your lives . . .'

'And what about you, *papochka*?' his daughter said in a frightened voice.

'I will use all my influence to make the Passport Office issue an Exit Visa,' Abel said unselfishly.

'I wouldn't leave you behind,' Lyubov said determinedly, tears filling her eyes. 'Either all of us go, or I shall stay.'

Her father said in a quiet voice: 'I am old, I have lived my life . . . And what is worse, I have come to the sad conclusion that I have believed all my life in something that does not exist.'

I couldn't bear to hear him talking like this. I said: 'There is plenty to live for. I too have realised that I believed in something that does not exist. It was a very hard blow to me when I discovered it, but it is not the end of the world. One goes on living——'

'When one is young, everything is easier,' Abel cut in. 'Don't bother about me, children. Do what I ask, try to get out of here before it is too late.'

'We will, Abel,' I promised, 'but only on one condition: that you make the necessary arrangements for getting an immediate temporary assignment for yourself somewhere abroad. Then you need never return. You could stay with us.'

'It is not easy for a Soviet citizen to . . .'

'You are still powerful enough to be allowed to go abroad on official business, if you suggest it,' I interrupted him.

Until late into the night we talked about our future plans, and when, in the small hours, Abel finally left us to return to his flat, both Lyubov and I were feeling much easier in our minds. We'd convinced Abel of the soundness of my suggestion. He agreed with the plan and said he would start straight away to fix up a foreign trip for himself.

★   ★   ★

Though we had promised Abel to get married without delay we could not do so the next day, because Lyubov had to fly to Odessa where she was to do some special parachute jumping before a commission of experts. I had done my best to try to dissuade her from going. Often in recent times I had begged her to give up her dangerous profession if she really loved me. But there was an unconquerable gaiety in the way she insisted that she *did* love me, and that parachute-jumping was no more dangerous than walking. This time, however, she did promise me to give it up—once the Odessa assignment was over.

As luck would have it, I too was going to Odessa to cover the display of air strength for the paper; so at least Lyubov and I would be together on the trip there and back. I was now at the stage when I could hardly bear to let this lovely creature out of my sight. And yet—and yet there was something nagging at me all the way to the airport next morning.

I turned to Lyubov and said: 'Look, *please* don't go. Go back to the flat. I'll telephone them for you and say you've been taken ill. You can wait there for me, and as soon as I get back from Odessa we'll be married. *Please?*'

'I have to go, darling,' she replied. 'I promise you that it will be my last jump. I'll keep my word.'

However much I tried, I could not persuade her to change her mind. She insisted that she could not let the display down. Experts from all over the Soviet Union were coming to it. I realised it was useless to make any further attempt to persuade this determined and conscientious girl. I tried to convince myself that my sudden fears for her safety were the outcome of the depressing story which Abel had told us.

The display was due to commence on the day after Lyubov and I arrived at Odessa, but there was a temporary postponement due to the non-arrival of a number of the services' chiefs. Not that Lyubov and I minded. The weather was marvellous, and Lyubov adored the sun.

Even the refusal of the registrar to marry us (because we were not residents of Odessa) failed to dampen our spirits. Those days before the display began were easily the happiest of all the time I spent in the Soviet Union. On the last night, we sat together going over the plans for our wedding which would take place when we got back to Moscow.

On the following morning, I kissed Lyubov goodbye and made my way to the Press box. I had no sooner sat down than a distant humming sound began to grow into the great loud roar of many aircraft approaching in formation. We looked up to see them coming in over the dropping zone, big bulky transports packed with parachutists and equipment. And then we saw them, little dots in the sky, as the parachutists jumped and fell and then slowed down as the white 'chutes billowed open above them. It was a tremendous sight.

The highlight of the day, of course, was to be the delayed-action jump of Lyubov. She was to jump from fifteen thousand feet over the Black Sea, and would come down in a long free fall before opening her parachute. Waiting speed boats would rush to pick her out of the sea.

I sat with my heart in my mouth as her plane climbed into the cloudless sky. Then it levelled off, and I sat terrified with binoculars hard against my eyes. I saw the figure detach itself and fall spiralling through space. I could see Lyubov's arms flung wide as she hustled downwards, downwards towards the sea.

Surely it was time now to pull the rip-cord. But no. She plummetted down and down. I snatched the binoculars away from my eyes for a moment to see how much further she had to go. Good God! What was happening? She was rushing towards the sea. She'd be killed.

'Open your parachute, *open it!*' The words burst from my lips. '*Open it!*'

I tore the glasses away and watched horrified as my Lyubov fell at appalling speed—and then, O God, she hit the sea, and the water rose in a great glistening white cloud, and Lyubov had gone.

I ran, falling and tripping, sobbing all the way, and jumped from the pier into the last of the speedboats which was just moving off. Some of the other boats were already circling the area where Lyubov had gone into the sea, and I could make out sailors standing up with boathooks at the ready while heads bobbing in the water showed where divers had gone overboard to recover her.

Just as the boat in which I was travelling reached the area, I saw them lifting something aboard one of them. We got close enough for me to see that it was Lyubov. She was lifeless, her eyes staring into the blinding sun—the sun she loved so much and would never again enjoy.

During the eternity it took us to reach the shore again, I kept hearing her voice over and over again. 'I promise you it will be my last jump,' she had said. 'I'll keep my word.'

And now she was dead. She had kept her word all right. But surely that wasn't the way she had meant to keep it? Surely she hadn't been talking about suicide. Surely she hadn't meant *that*.

I found out the answer. She hadn't committed suicide. Both the ripcords—both of her ordinary parachute and the emergency one—had been pulled, but the 'chutes had failed to open.

So the bastards had got her too!

*   *   *

As soon as I got back to Moscow I went straight to Abel's flat. I had to see him, to talk to him, to seek and try to *give* consolation. He had lost a daughter, I the girl who was to have been my wife.

But when I got to the flat, I was to be confronted by the big red seal of the N.K.V.D. Abel as well! I didn't know what to do. I sat on the stairs, stunned, and then cried as I had cried few times in my life.

At last I stood up and went slowly down the stairs and out into the street.

With Abram's help I tried to find out as much as possible about Abel Yenukidze, whom I was sure I would never see again, because there could be no doubt that Stalin had put an end to the legendary 'Georgian Trio of the Kremlin' which had consisted of Sosso, Sergo and Abel, and which originated from the days of their youth.

And it was then I learned a remarkable thing about Abel Yenukidze—something which even Lyubov had never known. It was this: Abel was not Lyubov's father at all.

Abel in fact had never married, but as a young man he had, one day in Tiflis, come across a derelict house from inside of which he could hear a baby crying. Going in to investigate, he found the mother dead, shot through the head. Alongside the corpse was the crying baby. He picked up the baby and took it outside and made enquiries in the neighbourhood as to the identity of the dead woman. Nobody knew.

Moved by a surge of compassion for the orphaned mite, Abel took the little girl to some friends and made arrangements for her to be looked after.

'But the child must have a name,' they told him. 'What shall we call her?'

Abel Yenukidze had looked at the baby, and without looking at the faces of his friends said: 'Call her Lyubov.' The word meant, simply, beloved.

In time Abel adopted Lyubov. To the day of her death she had never known.

Abram found out from Stalin's bodyguard, whom he knew fairly well, that a few days after his return to Moscow from his inspection tour Abel went to the Kremlin. Stalin told him he had decided to put him on trial as an important move to popularise the Party. A heated argument followed during which Abel, who could not believe that his old-time friend really meant what he had said, refused to oblige.

When Abel returned to his flat, N.K.V.D. officers were there waiting for him and arrested him on a charge of espionage and high treason.

'Abel Yenukidze is not being treated in the usual way,' Abram said to me one day, repeating what he had been told by one of the interrogators dealing with the Yenukidze case. 'It is extremely difficult to pin anything on him. He had never taken part in any opposition and has, until the hour of his arrest, belonged to the small and intimate circle of the Kremlin. The N.K.V.D. does not exclude the possibility that the two old friends might be reconciled and they fear that, if that happened, Yenukidze might strike back at those who had ill-treated him.'

From then on no more news trickled through. I began to hope that the fears of the N.K.V.D. officers might be right and that the two survivors of 'The Georgian Trio' might be reconciled.

It came as a terrible shock to me when, on the 19th of December 1937, a short government communiqué announced that a secret military court had sentenced Abel Yenukidze, his friend Lev Karakhan, and five others to death for espionage and terrorist activities, and that the sentences had been carried out.

Abel Yenukidze's death not only shocked his friends and all those who had ever met him, it also shocked his political enemies, for it was an accepted fact that the Georgian *Bolshevik* had always remained an honest and upright human-being who would never turn spy or be an accessory to terrorist activities.

When Lev Trotsky heard about it, he protested very strongly at Stalin's crime, though he had always regarded Abel Yenukidze as his political enemy. In one of his articles he wrote:

'Cain, what hast though done to thy brother Abel? After this hateful murder, Cain Dzugashvili shall be thy name in Russian history.'

CHAPTER THIRTY-SEVEN

Race Against Time

MY disillusionment had reached its summit. Russia, far from being a 'Worker's Paradise,' was a hell upon earth. To watch one's fellow human beings go through the whole gamut of degradation was in itself a searing experience. But to know that the currency of human life had been cheapened beyond belief (and at the dictates of a warped egomaniac) was much more than I could stand.

Textbook Communism went out of the window. Ideals were exploded into smithereens. Unhappiness and fear, and an over-burdening desire to get free, to be clean of, to forget the nightmare were the emotions that ruled my existence.

From all the evidence, Stalin was a deranged and dehumanised man whose evil was untouched by any hint of regret or understanding. Russia, his own land, was bleeding from millions of wounds—almost all of them inflicted by the tainted hands inside the Kremlin. By early 1938 it was estimated that between *eight hundred thousand and one million* people had been *liquidated* since Kirov's murder in December 1934! All these people divested of life at the collective whims of a single individual.

And March 1938 saw another 'public trial'—the third charade. Amongst the accused this time was Yagoda, now fallen far from grace. He would be sentenced to death. Three famous Soviet doctors also stood indicted. They were: Professor Pletniev, Dr. Levin and Dr. Kazakov. Their 'confessions' were tailored by Stalin; elaborate admissions to having murdered Gorky, Kuibyshev and Menzhinsky.

I knew the whole ghoulish routine by heart almost, but was

surprised when Krestinsky blazed in anger when asked if he pleaded guilty.

'I plead not guilty,' he shouted. 'I am not a Trotskyist. I was never a member of the bloc of Rights and Trotskyists, of whose existence I was not aware. Nor have I commited any of the crimes which I am charged with. I plead, in particular, not guilty to the charge of having had connections with German espionage.'

Krestinsky's action was so unexpected that everyone in court was stunned. His was the first case in the Moscow trials of a defendant daring to use the court as a speaker's platform. Many of us listening in the courtroom hoped that here at last was a man who had mustered enough courage to expose to the world the dreadful secrets of Stalin's trials. But our hopes were in vain; Krestinsky was not allowed to say another word. As soon as he was taken back to his cell at Lubyanka, the new drug was given him in generous quantities.

The next day, Krestinsky was brought back to court along with the rest of the accused, and sat, docile and bemused-looking. He sat like that throughout the day, and then during the evening sitting he suddenly got up and repeated the following words: 'Yesterday, under the influence of a momentary feeling of false shame, evoked by the atmosphere of the court, and the painful impression created by the public reading of the indictment, and aggravated by my poor health, I could not bring myself to say that I was guilty.'

The President of the Court then asked him whether his declaration amounted to a plea of guilty. Krestinsky confirmed that he pleaded guilty to all charges. The pattern had been re-established.

On the 13th of March 1938, eighteen of the accused were sentenced to death, three got prison sentences. Eighteen more bodies were added to the massive total.

★　★　★

Over five million people were working and dying in the slave-labour camps. Amongst them were people I had met—the young American girl Susan Goldberg; the architect Messin and his wife Mono; Abram's secretary Anyuta; the cheerful waiter in the restaurant of the House of the Press, Nikita; my compatriot who had been at the *Lenin School*, Bremer and his fiancée Vera; and many, many others. There were times when I would have almost welcomed death.

My periods of depression and desolation of spirit were becoming ever more frequent, and it was Abram who bore the brunt, listened so sympathetically, tried so hard to cheer me up. Then one evening when we were leaving *Vecherniaya Moskva* he took my elbow and, when we were safely out on the pavement, said: 'Bernard Frederikovich, I want you to come home to my flat, there is something urgent I must tell you.'

'Tell me here,' I said. 'We're safe enough in the open.'

He didn't reply. He merely jerked his head and tugged me to follow.

Now Abram was a trusted man, and as such did not have his apartment wired with concealed microphones. Even so, he made frequent checks, and knowing the techniques, he was able to ensure that his rooms were not, as the Americans say, 'bugged.'

As soon as we had taken our coats off and had glasses of vodka in our hands, Abram walked away a little from me, then turned and faced me squarely.

'I asked you to come here, because what I have to say is very serious,' he said.

'Well hurry, Abram, and say it!' I snapped. 'Don't make a drama of it.'

'It is dramatic enough in itself,' he replied. 'The N.K.V.D. are after you.'

I felt my mouth drop open. I was unable to talk. I gulped back a mouthful of vodka and got a violent coughing attack which made my eyes stream. When I had composed myself again, Abram said: 'Mironov came to see me this afternoon. For a while I thought it was just an ordinary business-with-pleasure visit, but when he asked me to show him the machine floor where the presses are, I knew there was something on his mind. Down there, with the roar of the machines, no-one can listen in to your conversation. It was then he told me.'

'But what did he tell you? What *could* he tell you?' I asked.

'That your name was given in a deposition an arrested victim made to him this morning.'

'Couldn't this be a bluff?' I said.

'It's no bluff. Mironov took quite a risk if you want to know. He still likes you, considers you a friend, and he tipped me off so that I could tell you how things are.'

'You're a fool Abram,' I said. 'I'm probably being watched already, and they'll link your name with mine, and——'

'Don't panic,' he said quietly. 'With a bit of luck you might just get out of here. When Mironov warned me he promised that he would do his best to hold this information back from his superiors for a few days. Of course, one cannot be sure whether he'll succeed or not, but it's worth trying to get you away.'

'But how?' I said. 'If I apply for an exit permit they will suspect that I want to get out. In all probability, they'll refuse to issue it.'

He suggested that I should make capital of the Munich crisis by trying to persuade our Editor to send me to Czechoslovakia as special correspondent. That very same day news had reached Moscow that the Nazis were concentrating troops on the Czechoslovak frontier. It looked as if they would try to attack the Sudetenland.

'You know how difficult it is to get consent from the Passport Office to go abroad,' I said.

'Fortunately you are not a Soviet citizen and you have a valid foreign passport,' Abram said. 'If we can convince our Editor that it would be of vital importance to have a special correspondent at the scene of the trouble, I think you might just manage to slip through. Now as I see it, the only way to push the old man on this, is to let him get the impression that several other editors are after your services.'

'But how do we get that impression across?' I asked. 'Not even *one* editor has approached me.'

Abram was picking up the phone as I spoke. He didn't reply to me but asked instead for a Leningrad number. When the call came through I realised what he was up to. He spoke to the editor of a

Leningrad paper and did a wonderful job of persuading the man that his paper needed me to cover the situation in Czechoslovakia.

In the end he elicited a promise from his friend in Leningrad to wire our editor on *Vecherniaya Moskva* asking for my services as Special Correspondent.

Then Abram phoned the periodicals *Za Rubezhom*, *Krasnyi Sport*, and *Literaturnaya Gazeta*, and sold each of them on the same idea. All promised to wire our editor immediately. Although it seemed a clever enough device of Abram's, I was full of pessimism.

If the N.K.V.D. were out to get me, surely they'd succeed. It was only a matter of time; and the little bit of time available to me was entirely dependent upon how long Mironov could, or would hold back the incriminating deposition.

I went back to my flat that night in a state of extreme nervous tension. I was unable to sleep. Every car or lorry that passed outside in the night had me sitting up in bed, sweating. I kept waiting to hear the clump of boots on the stairs, the banging on my door, the rough announcement to get up and dress and leave—and for what destination?—it could only be one—Lubyanka.

* * *

Unable to snatch anything more than a few minutes sleep, I got up at half-past five, and was at the office before anyone else arrived.

When Abram eventually came in (I had my back to the door at the time) the noise caused my heart to race and I spun around to face the door, fearing the very worst. Before I had a chance to talk, he put a finger to his mouth to hush me, then pointed to an ear to indicate that we were being overheard. I nodded. Then he started to talk in an almost exaggeratedly loud voice:

'There are some telegrams here for you Bernard Frederikovich.'

I said: 'Thank you' and took them.

Abram made a circle with the thumb and forefinger and then pointed to a ventilation grill high on the wall. I knew then what he was up to. He had discovered that they had decided to bug my office, so everything we said from now on would be recorded.

Abram winked. It said in effect that we'd have to play out a verbal charade of our own.

I opened the first of the telegrams. It was from the Leningrad paper. I read it silently. It said:

Propose you accept assignment as special correspondent in Czechoslovakia either for our paper alone or in conjunction with your Combinat Stop Please advise immediately when you can leave and state your conditions.

The other telegrams ran on similar lines.

'What is the news about the Munich crisis this morning?' I asked Abram loudly.

'It seems as if Hitler plans something drastic in the near future,' Abram replied. 'The trouble is that not sufficient information is available from the news agencies.'

'These telegrams are from various newspapers asking me to go as special correspondent to cover the situation for them,' I said. 'I don't know what to reply. To be frank, I'm not too keen on going.' I tried to make the lie sound convincing.

'A true Soviet journalist puts duty first.' Abram said in lecturing tones, playing his role very well. 'I know how you feel about Katya, you want to chase after her morning noon and night. But you must realise that the common cause comes first.'

Katya didn't exist, never had done until she was dramatically born in Abram's mind. I almost laughed, but managed to hold back just in time. Anyway, in reality there was nothing to laugh at in this life-and-death game we had embarked on.

I tried to make my voice as resigned as possible as I said: 'Yes, I suppose you're right. But if I have to go abroad at all, which I don't want to do, it would have to be for our own paper. I'm not particularly overjoyed at the prospect of working for someone else.'

'Well, that's for the editor to decide,' Abram said. 'He should be in by now. Let's go and see him.'

The editor was reading the telegrams addressed to him when we went into his office. He kept us standing there until he had finished, then he looked at me and said: 'If you're going abroad at all, you'll cover this story for our Combinat. I don't go pinching people from anywhere else. Let them find their own correspondents. In any event, I had already decided to send you.'

We both knew this to be nonsense. The thought had probably never entered his head until he received the telegrams. He at once telephoned the Commandant of *Mossoviet Publications Combinat*, submitting his suggestion and received consent straight away, subject to the approval of the Press Department. The Head of the Press Department did not oppose the plan; on the contrary he expressed his appreciation of the editor's initiative. However, his approval was subject to the consent of the *Comintern;* this was because I was a foreigner and was not under the actual jurisdiction of the Soviet Communist Party.

'Where does the *Comintern* come in?' I objected. 'You know I've not been a Party member since 1936. How can the *Comintern* decide this matter?'

'You are right,' replied the Editor, 'but the Press Department told me that they consent subject to the *Comintern* not objecting.'

I now began to feel that my luck was draining away. The *Comintern* would clearly have to be contacted, and I had no illusions about my former section leader, Birne, if he was drawn into it.

The editor phoned the Head of the *Comintern*, and had only begun to explain the situation when that worthy individual said it was no concern of his, it was a matter for the section leader to decide. So Birne *was* to be involved. As he tried to get through to Birne, the editor motioned me to pick up the phone extension.

As soon as the editor had put the facts before him, Birne said: 'I can't see what this has to do with us. We've had nothing to do with your employee since 1936. He's your responsibility.'

'Listen comrade,' the editor said patiently, 'the Press Department has sanctioned this man's trip, but said that the consent of the *Comintern* also must be obtained.'

Birne still wouldn't give in. He was as awkward as he knew how to be, and the editor's anger steadily rose. In the end he roared into the mouthpiece: 'Very well comrade, you play it that way and I shall play it mine. I will now, immediately, just as soon as I have finished telling you, put the facts before Comrade Stalin's Secretariat.'

Birne backed down and said there would be no need to do that. He would, he said, issue the necessary document.

The race against time was now definitely on.

During the morning our despatch rider collected the documents from the *Comintern* and the Press Department. With these and an official request from *Mossoviet Publications Combinat*, I applied at the passport office for permission to leave. Needless to say, I had to fill in a very long questionnaire before I was seen by the N.K.V.D. officer in charge.

'When do you want to leave?' he asked me when he had studied the forms.

'I don't want to leave,' I replied. 'My paper has ordered me to go.'

Watching the face of the officer, I noticed with joy that I had given the right answer. 'When does your paper want you to go?' he asked then.

'At once.'

'Do these scribblers think they can dictate to us? To issue an exit visa it usually takes a week or two.'

'That suits me admirably,' I said. 'In fact, if you could make it *two* weeks, I would be most obliged to you. My girl-friend is on leave and . . .' To make it sound more genuine, I added: 'But do me a favour please. Tell my Editor and the Press Department that it will take some time before permission can be granted so that they won't think that I myself am delaying my own departure.'

'What do you take the N.K.V.D. for?' the officer flared up. 'You don't seriously think we would cover up your skirt-chasing and delay your important departure?' He stamped my application forms and the accompanying documents, asked me to hand him my passport, and said: 'Come back tonight after six o'clock.'

'Will the exit permit be ready then?' I asked.

'Do you think I asked you to come because I want to see your face?' he snapped. 'You'd better forget your women, and tell the editor to make arrangements for your passage.'

Of course, it still did not follow that they would give me the exit permit. If incriminating details were passed on from Mironov's department, Lubyanka would be my destination.

I returned to my editor and told him what the officer had told me. I needed a Polish transit visa which I could not get without my passport, and I would not have this back until after six o'clock in the evening; the Polish Consulate would be closed by then. *Mossoviet Publications Combinat*, therefore, booked a sleeper for me on the train to Niegoreloye the next evening, and I was also given a contract to sign which bound me to work exclusively for *Mossoviet Publications Combinat* for $500 a week plus $250 per month unaccountable expenses. The Soviet State Bank sanctioned this and gave me my salary and expenses for six weeks in advance, in dollar notes.

When I arrived at the Passport Office shortly after six o'clock, my heart began to beat rapidly. I was asked to take a seat in the empty waiting-room, and the longer I waited the more nervous I became. I felt the urge to get up from my seat and pace the room, but I could not be sure that some hidden eyes were watching me, so I remained seated, smoking one cigarette after another.

At last—according to the clock on the wall it was ten minutes to nine—an officer in the uniform of an N.K.V.D. captain came in. He had a thick file under his arm.

'Are you waiting for an exit permit?' he said to me.

'Yes.'

'You want to leave the Soviet Union as soon as possible?'

'I don't,' I replied. 'If it was up to me I would prefer somebody else to go.'

'Why have they picked on you in particular?' he asked.

'You had better ask my Editor and the Press Department,' I said.

'Do you speak German?' he asked.

He must have spoken either to *Mossoviet Publications Combinat* or the Press Department, because one of the deciding factors for my appointment apart from my Czech nationality had been my knowledge of languages.

'*Natürlich*,' I replied in German, '*sprechen Sie auch deutsch?*'

'*Niepanimayu*,'* replied the captain. Then, out of the blue, he asked me: 'You intend to remain abroad for good?'

'No. I shall return as soon as my Combinat and the Press Department allow me to.'

'Why didn't you ask for a return visa?'

'I did. Look up my application forms and you will see that I did.'

He pretended to have forgotten it.

'You are right. Excuse me.' Putting the file back under his arm, he said: 'We issue return visas only for a period of three months, and it isn't likely that you would be back by that time.' He looked at me searchingly.

'I don't think I'll be abroad for more than six to eight weeks,' I answered. 'It might well be that I'll be back in a month.'

'That doesn't depend on you but on your Combinat and the Press Department,' he replied. 'Whether here or abroad, you are under their strict orders.'

I nodded. 'But in my opinion there will be no *need* for me to stay abroad for long.'

'Here is your exit permit and your re-entry visa, valid for three months,' he said. 'If your Combinat or the Press Department insist that you stay longer than this period you must apply to the Soviet Consul for an extension.'

I could hardly believe it was happening. I opened my passport and saw both the exit permit and the re-entry visa. 'Thank you,' I said.

'Tomorrow morning you are to go to the Polish Consulate for your transit visa,' the captain went on as he walked with me to the exit. 'Be there at ten o'clock sharp. We will make the necessary arrangements for you to enter and leave the Consulate unhindered.'

I thanked him again.

As I walked along Lubyanka Square I kept touching my breast pocket to make sure that I still had my passport.

Of course, there was still the possibility that I might be stopped in Niegoreloye. But that was in the future, and I could only afford to be concerned with the present.

*I don't understand.

I went to the House of the Press where I was due to meet Abram. He was at a table with two others. I was not going to take chances.

'My luck is out,' I said as I sat down. 'They have given me an exit permit. Now I'll *have* no excuse.'

'What a lucky dog you are being sent abroad,' said Grisha who was an editor of *Molodaya Gvardiya* and whom we all suspected of being an N.K.V.D. informer. 'There's nothing I wouldn't give for the chance of going abroad.'

'The trouble is that Bernard Frederikovich has found himself a very willing female,' said Abram. 'All he can think of at the moment is sowing his wild oats as often as possible!'

'I *still* say he's a lucky dog,' repeated Grisha.

All the others joined in then, all agog at the idea of someone going 'outside;' and all the time I had to play down my own inner delight at the prospect of getting away from the U.S.S.R. and leaving it behind for good.

At the end of the meal, I went back towards Abram's office with him. We talked of inconsequential things, putting off as long as possible the saying of goodbyes. And when they were said, it was with care and a forced frivolity that were engineered for any listening ears. But no hidden microphones could photograph our faces, and it was in these that the true say lay. We had been very close; Abram had been a marvellous friend in a nest of vipers.

*   *   *

With so much to do the following day, I found the hours slipping away very quickly. This was to be my last day in Russia, but for me the hours couldn't go too quickly. I bought some expensive presents and stowed them deep in my cases, but even so, I still had a considerable amount of money left over, and a car I'd never again use. So I sat down and wrote a letter to Abram telling him the car was now his, and the money too. And then there was just enough time left to go to the District Housing Committee and tell them I wanted some friends of mine to use my apartment in my absence. There were the usual obstreperous objections before they finally agreed that my friends could move in.

Just as I got back to my apartment, a big black Mossoviet car arrived to take me and my luggage to Byelorussky Station. I sat in the back and looked at the building I was leaving behind me for ever. A thousand different memories flitted through my brain, but always one in particular pushed its way to the foreground—a memory of a beautiful girl who had enchanted me, enriched my existence, and then been murdered before my eyes. It was only on Lyubov's behalf I shed tears as the car pulled away from the kerb and headed for the station. But I was not out of Russia yet; I still had to physically leave the place.

It was almost unbelievable to see Abram standing on the platform waiting for me.

'What are you doing here?' I said. 'I mean you know I'm delighted to see you, but how——'

'No more questions,' he said smilingly. 'Let us get aboard!'

In the compartment I just sat and looked at him. He represented so much of what I had found to be good in this alien land.

'Well,' I said at last, 'so we can say goodbye properly Abram Abramovich?'

'Yes,' he replied. 'But not yet.'

'Not yet?'

'No,' he said, 'that can wait until we arrive at Minsk.'

'Minsk?' I said, astonished.

'Yes,' Abram said, laughing. 'I've wangled a trip there on a story which I *hope* will come off.'

So typical of Abram!

We were in the middle of a meal in the dining car when he suddenly leaned towards me and said:

'How I wish I were going with you!'

There was so much longing in his voice that for a moment I hardly knew what to say.

'Try to follow,' I said. 'Try to get them to send you as a special correspondent.'

Abram laughed a small hopeless laugh. 'Oh I'll try all right,' he said. 'I'll *try*.'

After a while he said: 'Be sure to tell them the truth about Russia,

Bernard Frederikovich. Tell the whole world. Tell them what it's really like, how the people have suffered and are suffering. Make sure they know these things.'

Then he looked away and, still without looking at me, wiped his eyes with his handkerchief.

We didn't sleep that night. We went back over the years we'd known each other, relived our experiences. And then it was morning and we were pulling into Minsk. When Abram was ready to leave, he clasped my hands in his and looked at me, shaking his head from side to side in little movements as he bit on his lip to stop the quivering. The tears were running down his cheeks; then he turned abruptly and left me. But when the train pulled out and eventually turned a bend in the track, I saw that he was still there, a diminishing lonely figure standing, watching.

★   ★   ★

The short journey from Minsk to the frontier station of Niegoreloye seemed to last an eternity, and the nearer I got to the frontier, the more doubtful I became as to whether I would be in time to get out of the 'Workers' Paradise' before Lubyanka flashed through the message that I was wanted for questioning. I tried desperately hard to keep my nerves under control, and when at last I left the train and stepped into the customs hall I knew I looked calm.

It appeared that I was the only passenger leaving the Soviet Union, and this knowledge terrified me, because I felt I'd have a better chance of slipping through unnoticed if I were just one of a group. However, all of a sudden my nervousness vanished and I got the strange sensation that I was no more than a spectator of what was happening.

'For how long are you going abroad?' the officer-in-charge asked me.

'I can't tell you, it depends on how long *Mossoviet Publications Combinat* and the Press Department want me to stay abroad,' I replied. I was surprised that my voice sounded completely normal.

'Your re-entry visa is valid for three months,' the officer went on. 'Is it likely that you will be returning within this time?'

'Of course,' I said. 'In any event they told me at the passport office that if I had to stay longer, the Soviet Consul in Prague would extend the visa.'

'But you do expect to be back within three months?'

'Yes,' I said. 'I've already told you so.'

'Why do you need such a lot of clothes for a stay of only three months?' he asked.

'As I am representing a leading Soviet newspaper abroad, I *have* to be well dressed,' I replied. 'Or do you think a Soviet correspondent ought to look shabby, and give capitalist newspapers the opportunity of saying that people in the U.S.S.R. must have no proper clothes?'

He did not reply to this. 'Have you anything else to declare?' he asked.

I declared everything I had bought and said: 'These presents being of good quality, will serve as examples of the high quality of Soviet manufacture.'

He gave me a sceptical look, then said:

'Are you glad to be going abroad?'

'As a matter of fact, I am not,' I said, trying to make my reply sound as convincing as possible. 'Unfortunately, orders have to be obeyed.'

At this moment a young N.K.V.D. colonel walked across the hall and came straight to us.

'I hope you will be happy abroad,' he said casually to me.

'I would be happier to stay in Moscow,' I countered.

'But life abroad is quite gay, I'm told,' he continued. 'Plenty of things in their shops—everything one wants . . .'

'It depends on what one wants,' I said. 'Maybe *you* would like life in the capitalist world. I do not. I know it too well—after all I have come from there.'

'Very interesting, very interesting,' he replied. 'Come, let's have a drink.'

I remembered the first time I had received that innocent invitation —on my arrival at Niegoreloye, when was it, a hundred years ago? With horror the thought came to me that the have-a-drink invitation was now only the prelude to arrest and imprisonment. So the message from Lubyanka had beaten me? Well, I might as well play the game to its end.

I went with the colonel, and after he had handed me a vodka, he said:

'So you don't want to go abroad? Perhaps I can oblige you; perhaps I can find something wrong with your papers . . .'

'That would be nice,' I said and it took an awful effort of will to say the words. 'You see, my girl-friend is on holiday, and if you could delay my journey . . .'

'Is she pretty?' he asked, and something about the way he said it, and the look in his eyes, convinced me that the man was a lecher.

I began to describe the mythical girl Abram had invented. 'Very pretty,' I said. 'She's tall, with the longest legs you've ever seen; she has the grace and passion of an animal, and she's very . . . accommodating.'

For a moment the colonel in him was lost; then by a conscious effort he shook the image away from his eyes and his military authoritativeness reasserted itself and he snapped: 'I'm sorry comrade, I cannot be of help to you. The Press Department and your own organisation have given you their orders. You must obey them, girl friend or no girl friend.'

We finished our drinks quickly and he came with me and saw me on the train. I sat alone in the compartment after he'd gone and tried to will the train to move. Every second of delay meant a second nearer arrest. I began to sweat and gasp for breath. Would the damn train ever move?

And then I heard the clump of footsteps in the corridor. O God, had I got so far only to be hauled back? So far; so near to Poland, just down the tracks there a little; and now here they were coming for me. I sat back and closed my eyes and waited. The heavy steps came nearer, and I could feel a sob building up in my chest, and I was about to stand up and scream my futile, angry defiance when, miraculously, the steps passed right on! So it wasn't them. A train guard, nothing more.

And then the train was moving, and we were leaving the frontier station, and I sat there unable to move as the wheels clicked slowly, slowly over the points, and Poland came closer, foot by foot.

There was another stop which was measured, all through the ages of its length by my pounding pulse. They were changing crews. O hurry them, God, *hasten* them!

And finally, once more the train began to move onwards and onwards, and suddenly I was crying out loud and uncontrollably; I was free, and I cried for Lyubov and Abram and all the poor tortured people of the cursed country behind me.

Chance in a Million

VERY shortly after the end of World War Two, I had to fly from London to Prague, on official business.

During the short journey from Kbely Airport to the centre of Prague, I saw Red Army officers and men roaming about everywhere. The sight made me shudder. They were all heavily armed, many of them with sub-machine-guns in their hands. Armoured cars and light tanks with Soviet stars on them stood about everywhere. At many crossroads Russian women-soldiers helped to control the traffic.

Prague on this day reminded me of Moscow—Soviet flags and red posters all over the place. The city, which before the war had prided itself on its cleanliness, was filthy. The inhabitants were shabby and dispirited.

It was impossible to choose a hotel—rooms were allocated by the centre responsible. I was reminded of Soviet conditions. The distributing officer, a middle-aged Czech, told me that the only vacant room in the whole city was at the Hotel Axa, which was modern and in the centre of the capital. He told me that most of the occupants of the Hotel Axa were Russians but that this need not worry me, because they were well-behaved. Besides, Prague was under Czechoslovak rule and the Czechoslovak authorities ensured that law and order was maintained.

I did not then know that the Russians who, at the time of their entering Prague, had been cheered by the people as 'liberators from Nazi terror,' had become the most hated people. The word 'Russian' had come to have the same meaning as 'Robber' and 'one who rapes.' The people who had welcomed their 'Slav brothers' with open arms, now wished them a thousand miles away.

During my stay in Prague I found out, with disgust, that the victors behaved in a worse manner, if that was possible, than I had ever seen in their own country. They roamed in groups along the pavements and pushed the inhabitants of the city into the roads. They shot out the street lamps and robbed the scared people of their watches, which they then fastened one above another on their arms. I often wondered how they behaved when occupying Germany, the country which they hated so much. In Czechoslovakia they looted shops, stole and used violence if anyone tried to defend his property; they raped women and young girls.

The Czechoslovak police at the start were powerless, because the Soviet High Command had made it absolutely clear that any Soviet offender was to be dealt with by Army authorities and by them alone. In fairness to the Red Army Command, it must be said that some offenders who committed serious crimes, were very severely dealt with—much more harshly than if the Czechoslovak authorities had stepped in. A number of rapists were sentenced to death and shot.

In many streets and squares of the city's centre Soviet soldiers traded all kinds of things. In the course of their advance across the European Continent they had looted everything there was to loot. They all had watches, many had cameras and they bartered their loot for liquor—preferably vodka or brandy. I saw Russian soldiers giving as many as three gold watches for a bottle of home-made liquor. Cameras—Leicas, Contaxes, Rolleiflexes and similar valuable makes—went for two bottles of liquor. The sons of Central Russia and Soviet Mongolia did not care. They would have other chances of looting and, besides, the drink made them happy.

★   ★   ★

While returning one evening to the Hotel Axa I became aware that I was being followed. For some time, a Russian soldier had been trailing me. When I increased my pace, so did he. It was soon obvious that he was trying to catch-up with me. I knew that

Russians in Prague arrested civilians quite frequently, but I did not want to spend the night with my nose against the wall of the Russian Headquarters. I hurried on, but the soldier ran and caught up with me. 'Your documents!' he rapped as he drew level.

I could not see his face in the dark. 'What right have you to stop me?' I asked.

His face was in shadow, but as soon as I spoke he brought up his two hands, and I instinctively ducked to avoid the blow. But it was no blow—he merely put his hands on my shoulders and said: 'It *is*! It *is*! I knew it was you! Bernard Frederikovich, don't you recognise me?'

I looked at him in amazement. This 'soldier' was none other than my old friend Abram Abramovich!

He was laughing and hugging me, and then he pushed me back from him and manoeuvred under one of the few unbroken street lamps so that he could examine my face.

'I saw you crossing a road,' he said breathlessly, 'and my heart almost stopped. So I followed you, and now, oh . . .'

He embraced me suddenly and kissed me, saying with emotion: 'After all these years . . . after all that has happened.'

So often since my sudden departure from Soviet Russia, I had thought of Abram, Nina and little Demyan, and prayed that nothing might have happened to them. I had gone over in my mind exactly what I would say if I ever saw him again. Now, being with him, I could not find the right words and only managed to repeat how happy I was that we had found one-another again—I was overwhelmed.

'So I had to come all the twelve hundred miles from Stalingrad to Prague to find you,' he said. 'Never in my life would I have thought this possible.'

There was so much we had to tell each other. Seven long years had elapsed since we had said goodbye at the railway station in Minsk.

'The morning after you left, they came to Trubnaya Ulitsa and to *Vecherniaya Moskva* to arrest you,' Abram said. 'Thanks to Mironov they were too late. But you say you are staying at the

s

Hotel Axa—under the very noses of the N.K.V.D.! You obviously have more luck than sense, otherwise you would be already on your way to Lubyanka. Tonight you ought to be safe. I'll stay with you, but tomorrow morning you must leave that place. You are a wanted man—the N.K.V.D. has long arms.'

This was typical of Abram; he did not think of his own safety, he was merely concerned with mine. I learned *en passant* from him that the N.K.V.D. had arrested him on his return to Moscow from Minsk, because he had been my friend; only by the skin of his teeth had he managed to talk himself out of that very dangerous situation, and had been allowed to return to his job at *Mossoviet Publications Combinat.*

During the seven years which had elapsed since I had seen him, he had aged, and his black hair had become grey; his eyes remained as lively as ever.

'You helped me to get out to safety,' I said, 'now I will do for you what you did for me . . .'

'We will speak about that later,' he cut me short. 'But for pity's sake don't talk so loud, one never knows who might overhear us.'

From then we spoke in whispers.

'How are Nina and little Demyan?' I asked. 'The boy must be quite grown-up by now.'

Abram looked at his feet, then back at me. He had to make an effort to speak, and when he did talk, his voice had a strange strangling quality about it.

'They are no more . . .,' he said, then went on quickly: 'I have done everything I could. The last time I saw them was when I had to report to the barracks of the Moscow Garrison. I had to go to the front at once. They were in Moscow then. I managed to make use of the communication line from time to time, and did everything humanly possible to get news of them. Without any result. When we came to Berlin and the Nazis capitulated, I had many messages broadcast over the all-Soviet Radio Network, asking for any scrap of information. Again no result. When we came to Prague, I managed to fly to Moscow for five days. I went to see everyone who knew them and who might have seen them.

"*Nieznayu*"* was all I heard . . .' His eyes were quite dry, but there was a haunted look to them. 'All those people who must have known did not dare tell me the truth. It was easier to say that they didn't know . . .' He drew on his cigarette and added: 'They must have been killed during one of those attacks on Moscow . . .I don't know . . . All I know is that they are no more—otherwise I would have found something out . . .'

I squeezed his hand in sympathy. I knew how he had loved his little Demyan and Nina, and I said, against my conviction, that they might still turn up one day. 'They have probably been evacuated and may be living somewhere in Central Russia in safety——'

'No, no, Bernard,' said Abram, shaking his head. 'It's no use trying to kid oneself or shut one's eyes to the truth. Demyan and Nina are no more . . .' He lit another cigarette and inhaled the smoke, staring into the emptyness. Then, after he had pulled himself together, he said in his usual voice: 'Millions have been killed. Amongst them are many, many Demyans and Ninas. But life goes on . . . Let's look forward, towards the future. Let's try to help to ensure that no more wars are staged, so that people never again have to suffer what our generation has had to . . .'

*   *   *

In my room at the Hotel Axa we conversed in whispers in case the rooms had already been 'bugged.' Having been away from Russia for so long I found it a new experience again to have to watch every word. However, huddled close in the centre of the room, and whispering softly, we were pretty sure that listening devices (if there were any) would be foiled. Abram told me of his war experiences, and how Moscow and its people had suffered. It was already early morning when he brought up the possibility of his own escape.

'As you can imagine,' he said, 'I have often thought about it, and coming here to Prague made me more determined than ever to try to get away. I have explored all the possibilities, and the best one seems to be to try to get to Pilsen by train. Pilsen, you see, is in

*I don't know.

the American Zone. The difficulty is, however, that the Soviet guards at the check point on the demarcation line only let people through who have a special pass which allows them to go from one zone to the other. These passes are issued by the American, Czechoslovak and Soviet authorities. To attempt to get without a pass is tantamount to suicide.'

'If that is so, I'll get you a pass,' I said. I was determined to get the document at all costs. 'But before you risk your escape, I'll go to Pilsen myself to find out whatever there is to be found out.'

'Before you do anything for me, you've got to get out of this hotel,' he insisted. 'You'd better pack your suitcase now, so that we can leave before anything drastic happens.'

A quarter of an hour later we left the Hotel Axa—unhindered. Abram led me to the Hotel Paris, which he considered the safest of the lot, because of R.A.F. personnel being billeted there. I was extremely lucky. They had a room which was to become vacant the same day and I was given it.

*   *   *

I had no difficulty in obtaining two passes for the crossing from one zone into the other—they even suggested that I myself should fill in the particulars of the person travelling. I was just in time to catch the train to Pilsen.

It came as a surprise to me, to see how many people were travelling from one zone to the other—most of the seats in the four carriages were taken. The people in my carriage were typical Continentals who readily entered into conversation. They all confirmed the fact that there was hardly any trouble at the check point on the demarcation line and that the Russian guards took only such people off the trains, who did not produce some kind of document. They all agreed that the Russians appeared to be illiterates, accepting anything that looked like an official pass.

When we arrived at the demarcation line and several Russian officers came to our carriage, commanding: '*Dokumenty! Pokazhitie! Dokumenty!*'* I decided to find out for myself how much truth

*'Documents! Show them! Documents!'

there was in what my fellow-passengers had said. I had a pass to the Prague Swimming Baths, and I decided to hand this to the guards. The guard looked at it for a moment, was obviously satisfied when he saw the round rubber stamp, handed it back to me, saluted and let me continue on my journey. I now knew that it was not so difficult to get out of the Soviet zone of Czechoslovakia.

During my short stay in Pilsen, home of the well-known beer and Skoda Armament Works, I looked up some of my acquaintances who had been posted there. To those who could be of any help to Abram, I described him and his plans, and at the end, I left with assurances that he would not be returned to the Soviet authorities, but would be regarded as a political refugee.

On my journey back to Prague, I produced the proper pass for the Russians at the check point. The reaction was more or less the same as on my outgoing journey, and again they let me through without asking a single question.

★　★　★

Back in Prague, I met Abram as previously arranged, at a little café opposite the station. We had chosen it because it was not frequented by Russians, for no liquor, nor much food could be obtained there, and none, or very few women ever went there. This was no place for a Russian soldier who wanted to eat, drink, and pick-up a woman. The café was practically deserted and we were able to sit alone in a corner without fear that anyone could overhear our conversation.

'We can take the train for Pilsen which leaves in just over an hour's time,' I suggested when I had told Abram everything. 'Let's go to my hotel so that you can change into one of my suits.'

'I can't leave tonight,' he replied. 'I have to be on duty in half an hour and won't be free before six o'clock tomorrow morning. If I don't appear at the check desk they may get suspicious. It is better to go tomorrow. I can take the train which you took today.'

'All right then,' I agreed. 'Come straight from your duty to my hotel, we will have breakfast together and I will come with you to Pilsen so as to make sure that you get through all right ...'

Abram was full of excitement when, next morning, he came to my room. He was confident that it would be child's play to get through to Pilsen, with the pass I had got him.

'But what if any of the guards at the check point recognises you?' I said.

'That would be a chance in a million ...'

'It was a chance in a million that we two met here in Prague,' I interrupted him.

He said, with a smile: 'I am now the man whose name is on the pass. If anyone speaks to me in Russian, I will reply "*ich verstehe nicht*" and will talk in German which, fortunately, I speak well enough. If they don't like my German, I can talk in French which I know even better.' He looked at himself in the large mirror and was pleased to see how well my suit fitted him. He put on my hat and pulled it well down over his forehead. 'I would like to know who would recognise me in this outfit,' he said confidently. 'I bet that even you would find it difficult.'

Everything went according to plan. The train to Pilsen was again quite full, which meant that the Russian guards at the check point would not have much time to study every single traveller. We managed to find seats close to each other and we sat there, hoping for the best.

As on my previous journey, the Russians boarded the train at the demarcation line and demanded to be shown the documents. Again I showed them the pass to the Prague Swimming Baths, hoping that they would query it and that I would occupy them longer than necessary and thus not leave them much time for the other travellers. My trick did not work. The guards barely looked at my pass, saluted and went on. The same happened when they came to Abram. A little later they left the train and we steamed un-hindered towards Pilsen.

Abram, my dear friend who had done so much for me, was free.

But it was not until we had left the station in Pilsen and were safe in the American zone, that Abram said: 'At last!' He pressed my hand hard, trying to express his happiness. I knew exactly how he felt.

I had to return to Prague the same day. However, I boarded the train happy with the knowledge that Abram was safe. The next time we met would be in the free Western world.

Abram today lives and works on the American Continent.

Glossary

Agronom: Agricultural expert.

Bezbozhnik: The anti-religious journal.

Bolshevik: Member of the majority faction (*Bolshinstvo*) of the Russian Social Democratic Labour Party after the split at the Second Congress in Brussels and London in 1903.

Central Committee: The executive committee of the All-Union Communist Party, of which Stalin was the Secretary-General since 1922.

Cheka: Secret Police of the U.S.S.R. The name originated from the initial letters of *Cherezvychaynaya Kommissia* (Extraordinary Commission) for combating counter-revolutionary activities.

Comintern: Communist International.

Deutsche Zentral Zeitung (*D.D.Z.*): Organ of the Volga-German Soviet Republic.

E.K.K.I.: Executive Committee of the Communist International.

G.P.U.: Successor of the Cheka. The letters stand for Gosudarstvennoye Politicheskoye Upravleniya, meaning State Political Administration; Russia's Secret Police.

Iskra Revolucii: Spark of the Revolution; international languages printing works in Moscow.

Izvyestiya: Organ of the Soviet Government.

Katsap: Ukrainian swearword for Russians.

Kolkhoz: Collective farm.

Kommunist: Organ of the Ukrainian Communist Party.

Komsomol: Communist Youth League of the U.S.S.R.

Komsomolskaya Pravda: Organ of the Communist Youth League of the U.S.S.R.

Kulak: Rich landowner.

Kultorg: Cultural Organiser.

Literaturnaya Gazeta: Literary journal.

Lubyanka: Headquarters of the Secret Police in Moscow.

Mossoviet: Moscow Council.

Muzhik: Illiterate primitive peasant.

N.K.V.D.: Successor to the G.P.U. The letters stand for Narodnyi Kommissariat Vnutrennykh Dyel, meaning People's Commissariat of Internal Affairs; Russia's Secret Police.

Okhrana: Tsarist Secret Police. Short for Okhrannoye Otdyeleniye, meaning Department of Safety.

Oktiabriata: Communist Party organisation for pre-school age children in the U.S.S.R.

Partorg: Party Organiser. The backbone of the V.K.P.B.

Pioneer: Communist Party organisation for school children in the U.S.S.R.

Politburo: Executive Committee of the Central Committee of the V.K.P.B.

Pravda: Organ of the V.K.P.B.

Proforg: Trade Union Organiser. These are the same cadres in the trade unions as the Partorgs are in the Party.

Putyevka: Voucher.

Rabochaya Moskva: Daily newspaper of Mossoviet.

Shestidnievka: Six-day week.

TASS: Soviet News Agency.

Torgsin: Special stores where payment must be made in foreign currency, gold, etc.

Vecherniaya Moskva: Evening newspaper of Mossoviet.

V.K.P.B.: Communist Party of the U.S.S.R. The letters stand for Vsesoyuznaya Kommunisticheskaya Partiya, Bolsheviky, meaning All-Union Communist Party, Bolsheviks.

Zavdok: Works Doctor.

Index